IMAGES
of America

AROUND ST. CLAIR

I0809005

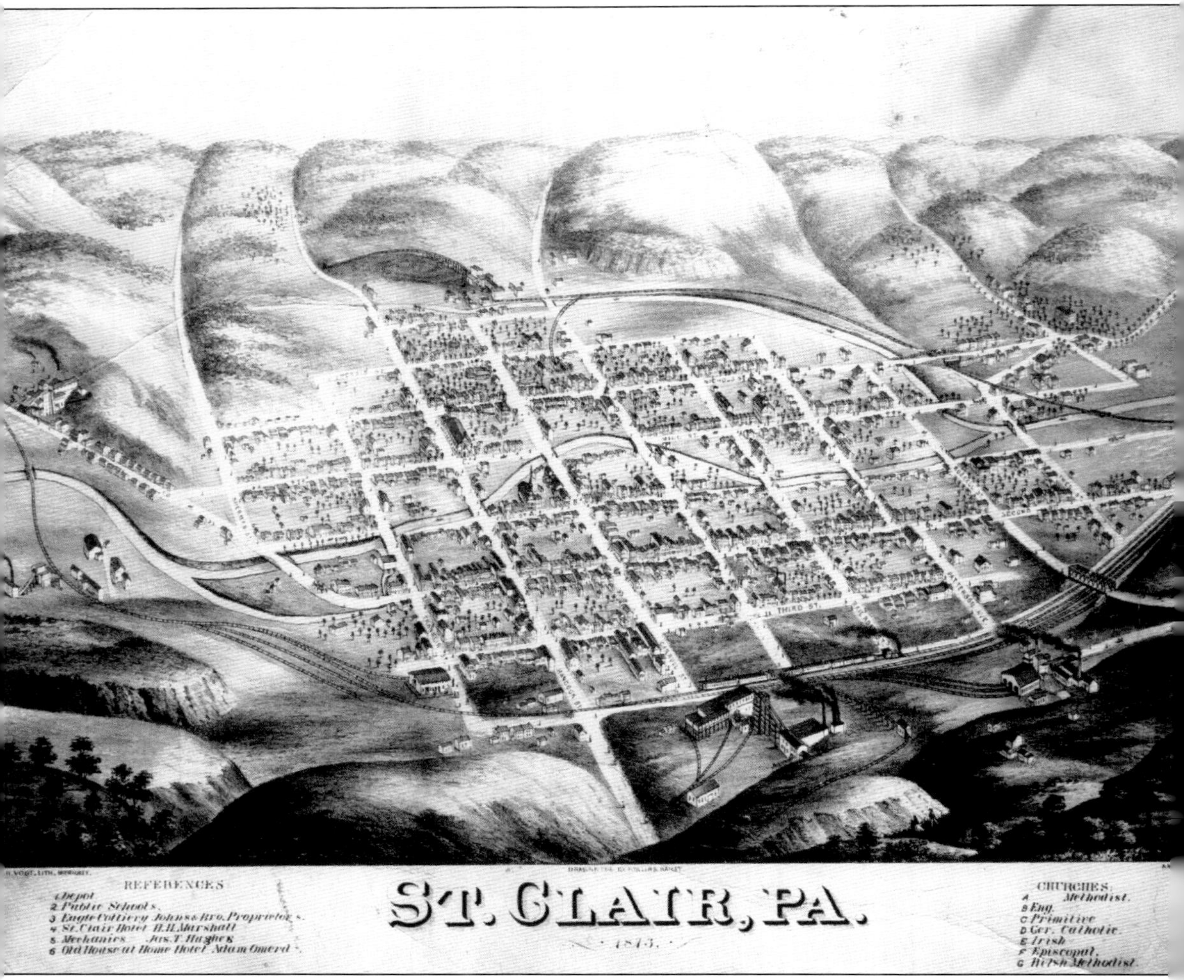

This early sketch from 1875 shows the town of St. Clair, incorporated in 1850. St. Clair lies in a valley with the Mill Creek running through the middle of town. The streets of St. Clair were laid out and given names around the mid-1830s by the Carey Group, which consisted of Philadelphia investors Henry C. Carey, Isaac Lee, and Abraham Hart. All streets were planned to run parallel or at right angels to Nichols Street. Nichols Street was named to honor Saint Clair Nichols, the farmer and landowner who sold the tract to the investors from Philadelphia.

On the cover: Please see page 20. (Courtesy of Edward and Carol Quirin.)

IMAGES
of America

AROUND ST. CLAIR

St. Clair Community and Historical Society

ARCADIA
PUBLISHING

ISBN 978-0-7385-6579-8

Published by Arcadia Publishing
Charleston, South Carolina

Printed in the United States of America

Library of Congress Control Number: 2009920851

For all general information contact Arcadia Publishing at:
Telephone 843-853-2070
Fax 843-853-0044
E-mail sales@arcadiapublishing.com
For customer service and orders:
Toll-Free 1-888-313-2665

Visit us on the Internet at www.arcadiapublishing.com

Contents

Acknowledgments		6
Introduction		7
1.	Making a Living	9
2.	Coming Together with Organizations	29
3.	The Railroads	41
4.	The Great Coal Era	49
5.	Education	75
6.	Sports	87
7.	Religious Diversity	95
8.	Native Sons	103
9.	Military	107
10.	Around the Town	117

ACKNOWLEDGMENTS

The members of the St. Clair Historical Society Committee have scoured archival files in search of photographs and images that portray the town as it appeared during the growth and height of the anthracite coal-mining boom. The society extends a special thank-you to the many residents and former residents of St. Clair and its environs who have provided photographs, images, and information for this book. Unless otherwise noted, all images appear courtesy of the St. Clair Community and Historical Society.

I want to express my gratitude for help with writing captions for many of the photographs to Val Davis, Jim Hess, and Bonnie Baker. Thanks go to William Van Stone and Robert Scherr who worked so hard helping me pull all this together. Thanks and appreciation to David Pukas for allowing us to use his sketch of the 17 churches of St. Clair that he drew at a time when all the churches were open with active congregations. Special thanks go to Robert Scherr, a longtime town historian, for sharing his extensive knowledge and photograph collection with the historical society for use in the publication of this book.

Finally I wish to thank our editor at Arcadia Publishing, Erin Vosgien, for providing the means, inspiration, and expert guidance on this project.

—Dawn Morris-Bicht
President, St. Clair Community and Historical Society

INTRODUCTION

Since its founding, one of St. Clair's chief assets has been its proximity to the southern anthracite coalfield of Pennsylvania. This location helped foster the town's ethnic diversity and rich history. The prospect of employment at one of the many coal mines, canals, or railroad businesses near the town made the area an attractive place for immigrants seeking a new life in America.

The earliest inhabitants, arriving in the 1830s, were mainly from England, Wales, Germany, and Ireland. Large numbers of emigrants from Poland, Ukraine, Lithuania, Hungry, Russia, and Czechoslovakia—and smaller numbers from other regions—followed the original wave of settlers. In search of steady employment and better wages, the Welsh and English emigrated from the industrial region of their homelands. Most of these transplanted workers were experienced miners or tradesmen whose skills were necessary to the operation of collieries, lumberyards, and ironworks. German arrivals typically were farmers, lumbermen, trained artisans, and shopkeepers. Land around St. Clair was plentiful and relatively cheap, and the dense forests of giant gum, spruce, and oak trees provided an abundance of raw material needed to support these trades. Ireland, at this time, was not an industrial country, and most Irish families lived on small farms, which some owned and others rented. Many of these families were forced to emigrate because of changes in the Irish farming industry. Landlords were turning their land into pastures for beef cattle. They made more space for animals by evicting human tenants. Irish farm owners also expelled families who had not paid their rent after the potato blight had robbed them of their only source of income. When they arrived, these impoverished Irish tenants often ended up in manual labor jobs mostly in the local mines. Meanwhile eastern Europeans also left their homelands to escape political and social turmoil and to seek higher paying jobs that could bring them an improved quality of life. They also secured positions that required hard manual labor mostly in the mines.

Each new ethnic group became a piece of the region's patchwork quilt. Just as each square in a quilt has its own color and texture, every cultural group operated with their own kinship system supported by distinctive languages, religious beliefs, and cultural practices. The thread holding these diverse groups together was their common need to earn a livelihood through work related to the coal industry. Men either worked directly in the mines or were employed by businesses that supplied the mine owners with necessary goods. An explosion, flood, strike, or equipment breakdown would close the mines. Any work stoppage would have a domino effect on all other businesses in the town since they all catered to the mine industry.

With the passage of time, the community was drawn together by many factors. As the use of the English language became more common, barriers between groups broke down. Eventually groups began to share customs and trade recipes. Marriages between members of distinct groups led to multi-faith unions and paved the way for families to move into different areas of the town where they could live apart from their own ethnic community.

St. Clair separated from New Castle Township and became an independent borough in April 1850. A visitor to St. Clair would be surprised by the many activities that bombarded their senses. The hills surrounding the town were covered with star-shaped flowers of mountain laurel and fragrant trailing arbutus. Steam rose from the engines huffing and puffing at the collieries that stood on all sides of town. The shrill sound of whistles called the miners to work in the morning and dismissed them in the evening. Wind blew clouds of coal dusts from the culm banks, and horses kicked up powdered clay from the unpaved streets. The buzz of saws rose from sawmills and carpenter's hammers pounded as new homes and buildings were being constructed. Sounds from the blacksmith's shops filled the air, as iron was being forged and shaped into horseshoes for the mules in the mines and balusters for wrought-iron fences. In the center of town, the streets were wide and lined with rows of neatly whitewashed new houses. Homes of artisans with their attached shops advertised services and products of carpenters, tailors, butchers, bakers, and shoemakers of the town. Men, tired, weary, and covered in the black of coal dust from a long day's work in the dangerous mines, were seen entering the taverns. Many of the miners coughed from the dreaded and expected miners' asthma, a disease also known as black lung. Taverns in town not only had bars and tables for drinkers but also a dining room and sometimes meeting rooms, some of which were large enough to be called a "hall." They also served as hotels with accommodations for visitors and permanent residents. On Sundays, men, women, and children in their Sunday best clothing hurried as the church bells rang out, summoning them to one of the three services being held.

As railroads supplanted the stagecoach and canals as a means of transportation across the country, St. Clair became the home of the largest classified coal yards of the world. In 1913, the St. Clair coal yards were built on the site of a large swamp at the southern end of town. It was a sight to behold with a complete circular engine house, called the roundhouse, large enough to house 52 modern sized locomotives. Empty train cars were made up and dispatched to the northern collieries, and all loaded cars were assembled and sent to southern markets. Many people visited this site often to witness the variety of interesting activities that took place here daily.

As well as being industrious and hardworking, the men of this mining area were very patriotic and answered the call to the defense of their country. St. Clair had the greatest percentage of men from the entire county of Schuylkill in the Civil War. Schuylkill County furnished the largest average of Pennsylvanians. Pennsylvania furnished the largest quota of all the states. Following the Civil War, groups such as the Patriotic Sons of America and the Grand Army of the Republic were formed to honor these comrades. From then on, men and women have proudly fought to preserve our freedom in every major war. St. Clair has always respected and honored the bravery of the men and women who have served in the armed forces by holding patriotic parades, erecting monuments, and forming veterans' organizations.

The images in this book were selected as representative of the way the people of the area lived and overcame and rose above the hardships of the harsh life in a mining town.

One

Making a Living

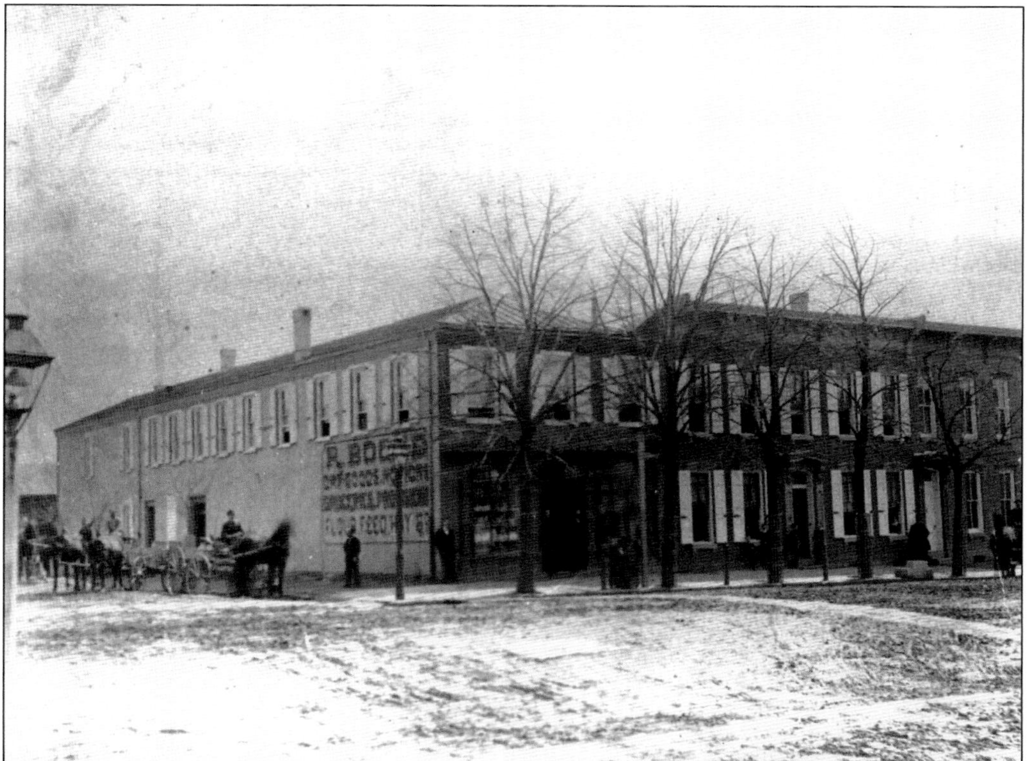

The Boone building, a general store, on the corner of North Second and Franklin Streets was owned by Ransole Boone and his wife. The business was later carried on by his sons. Children on the block remembered the cases always full of penny candy. The Boones were also the parents of Adm. Joel T. Boone.

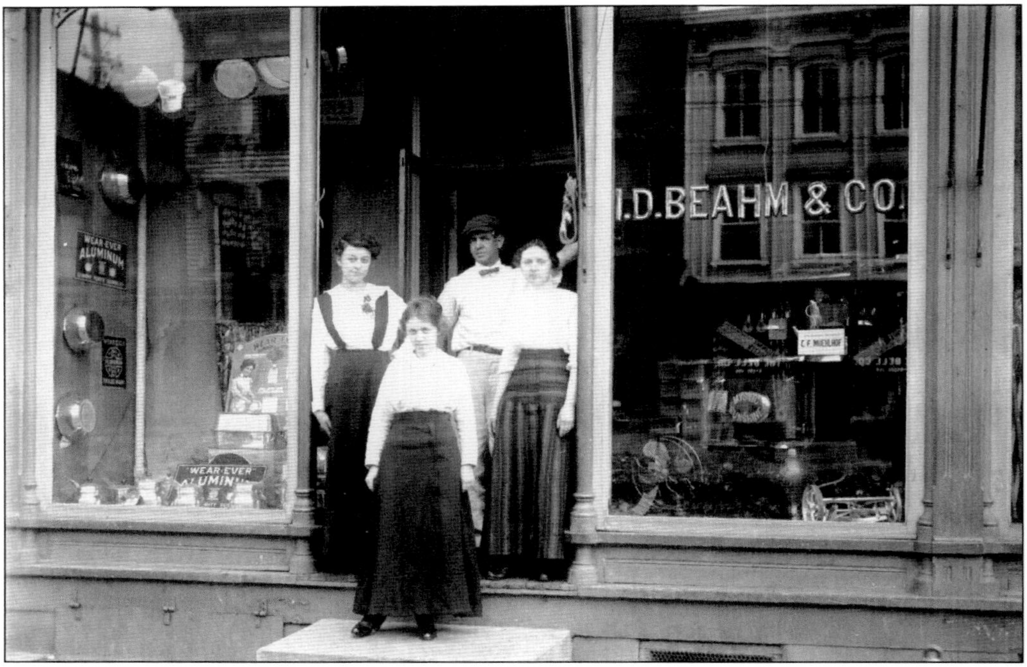

This popular general merchandise store was located next to the Citizens Bank on North Second Street. On the window is I. D. Beahm and Company, named for a well-known Pottsville businessman and investor in the Mount Hope and Hooker Collieries. The window at this time contains early electric appliances and Wear-Ever aluminum merchandise.

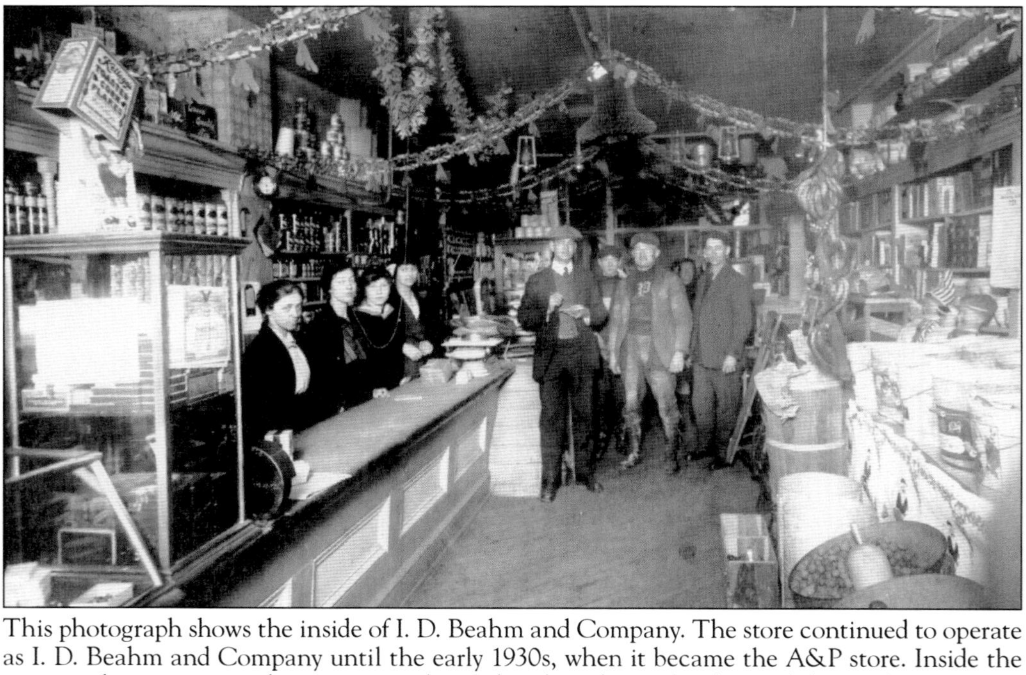

This photograph shows the inside of I. D. Beahm and Company. The store continued to operate as I. D. Beahm and Company until the early 1930s, when it became the A&P store. Inside the store apples, onions, and potatoes are located in barrels on the floor, while overhead mining supplies are being displayed for sale.

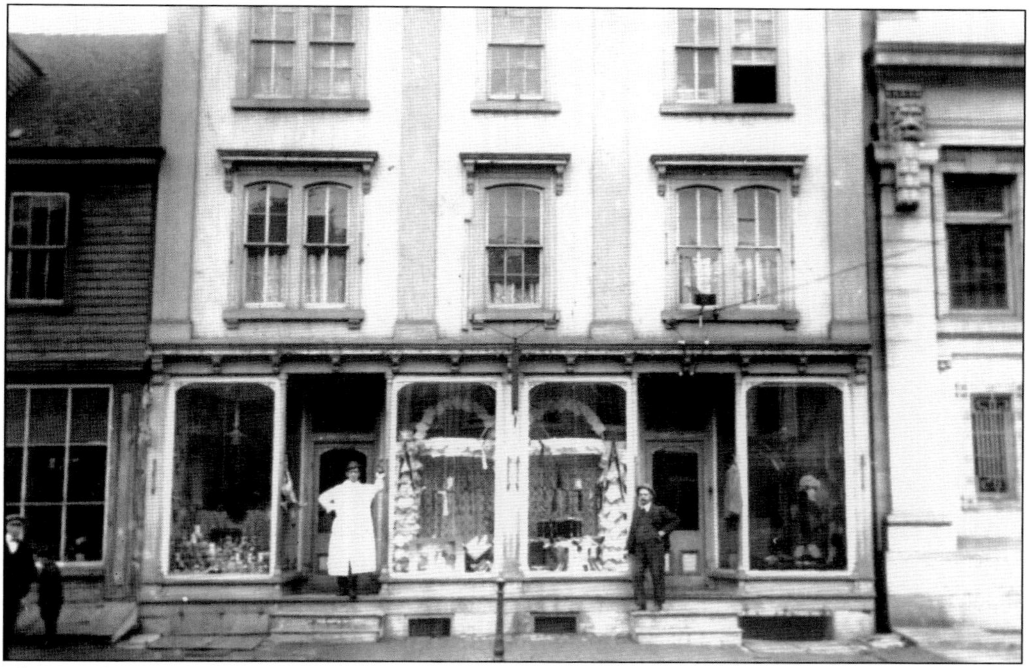

The Hooker Company store was located on the east side of North Second Street. In 1908, I. D. Beahm and Company acquired the mining lease for the Hooker Colliery. The colliery closed in 1918, but the store continued on as I. D. Beahm and Company. Notice the tree of ladies' hankies displayed in the front window.

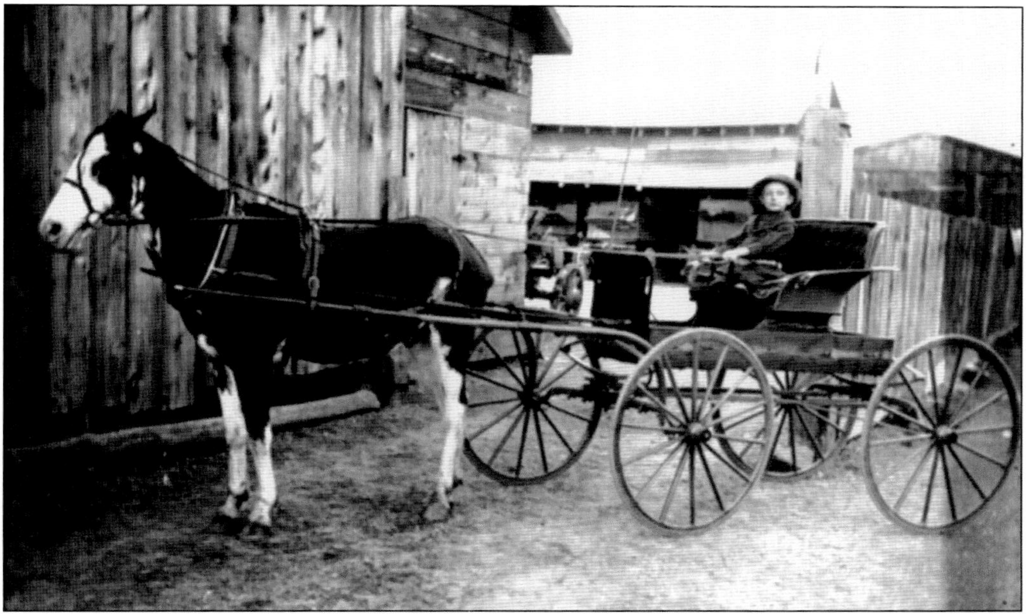

Albert Mettam established a lumber business on Third Street in 1887. Mettam was a well-known journeyman carpenter born in Hucknall, Torkard, Nottingham Shire, England, and he immigrated to St. Clair in 1884. Upon Mettam's death, the business passed to two of his remaining sons and then their children. The business remains in the family today.

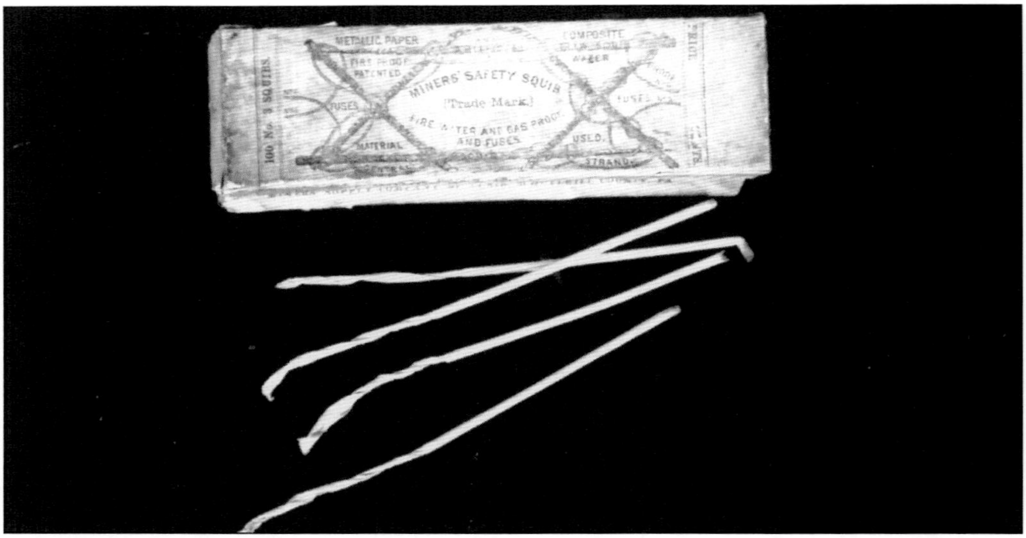

S. H. Daddow and Jesse Beadle invented and perfected a product that was used by the miners for firing dynamite, called a squib. Their squib was patented on September 6, 1870. Their squibs became more economical for the miners to purchase than to make on their own. In 1866, the partnership opened the Miners Supply Store to provide the squibs and other mining equipment, including a shovel made in St. Clair by another Daddow factory.

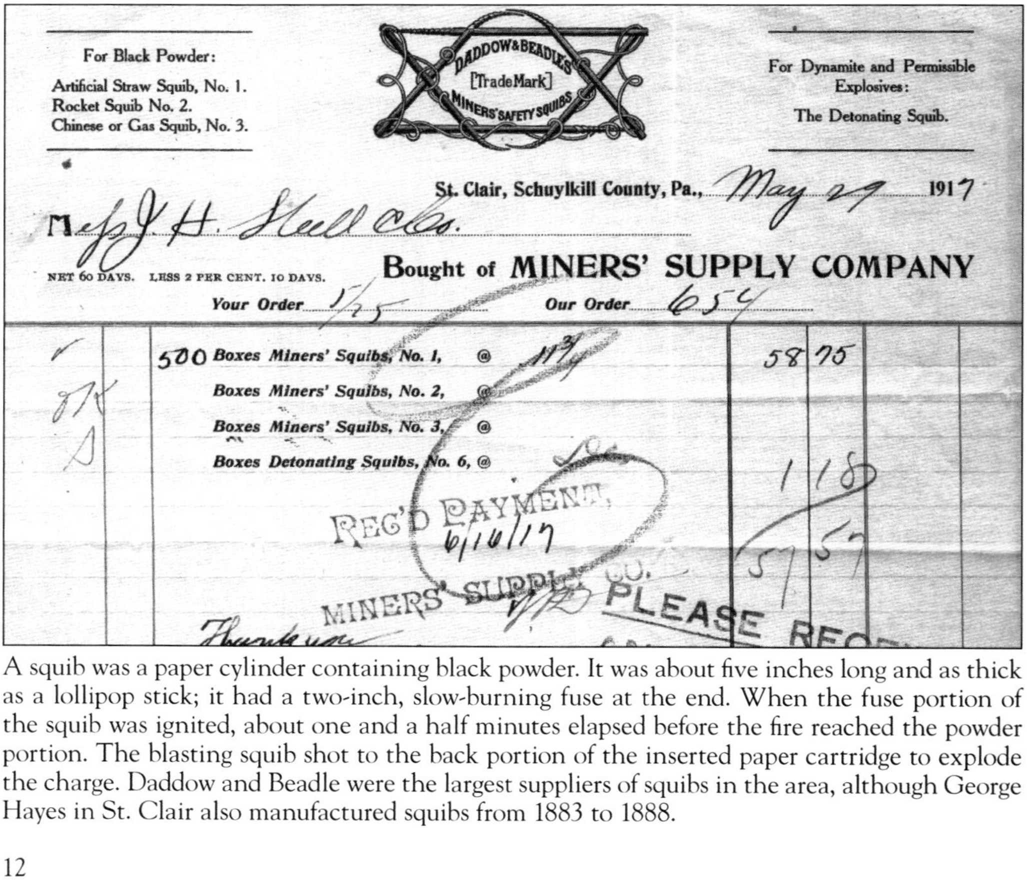

For Black Powder:
Artificial Straw Squib, No. 1.
Rocket Squib No. 2.
Chinese or Gas Squib, No. 3.

DADDOW & BEADLE'S [Trade Mark] MINERS' SAFETY SQUIBS

For Dynamite and Permissible Explosives:
The Detonating Squib.

St. Clair, Schuylkill County, Pa., May 29 1917

M J. H. Hell Co.

NET 60 DAYS. LESS 2 PER CENT. 10 DAYS.

Bought of MINERS' SUPPLY COMPANY

Your Order 175 Our Order 654

500	Boxes Miners' Squibs, No. 1, @ 11¾	58	75
	Boxes Miners' Squibs, No. 2, @		
	Boxes Miners' Squibs, No. 3, @		
	Boxes Detonating Squibs, No. 6, @	1	18
		57	57

REC'D PAYMENT, 6/16/17
MINERS' SUPPLY CO.
PLEASE REC

Thank you

A squib was a paper cylinder containing black powder. It was about five inches long and as thick as a lollipop stick; it had a two-inch, slow-burning fuse at the end. When the fuse portion of the squib was ignited, about one and a half minutes elapsed before the fire reached the powder portion. The blasting squib shot to the back portion of the inserted paper cartridge to explode the charge. Daddow and Beadle were the largest suppliers of squibs in the area, although George Hayes in St. Clair also manufactured squibs from 1883 to 1888.

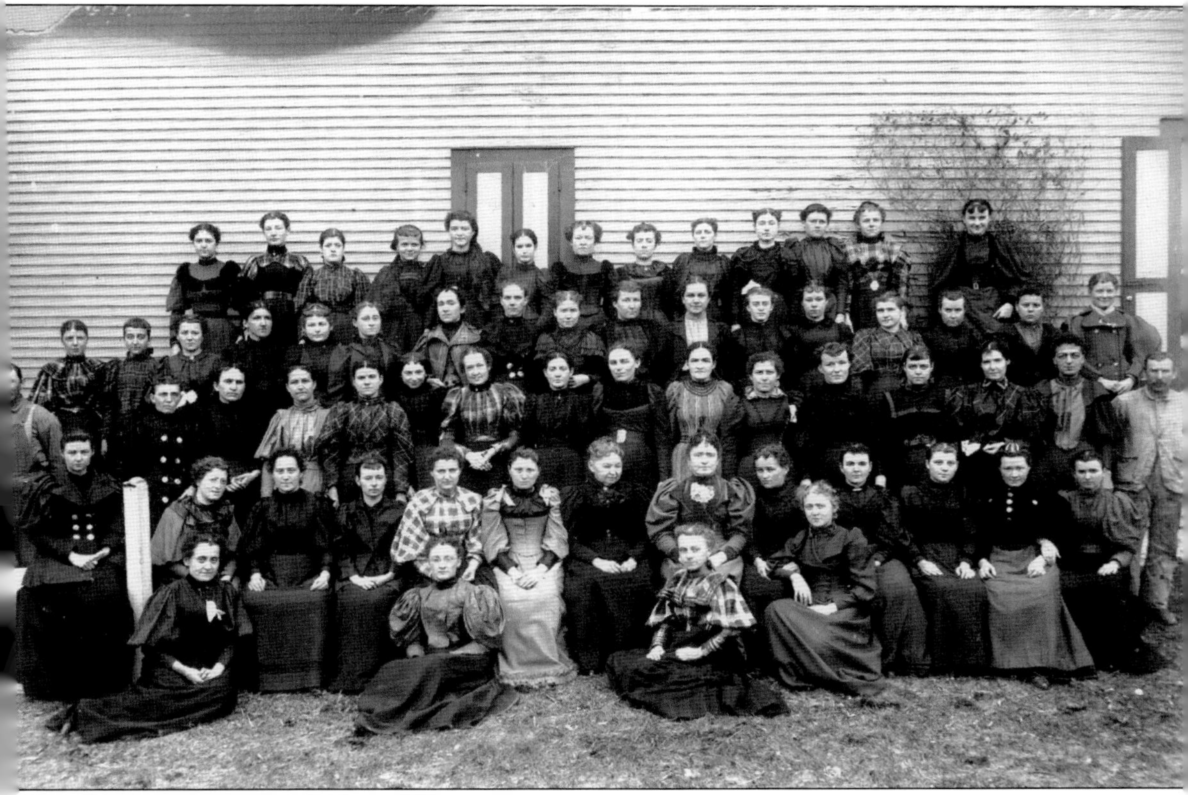

Squibs were made and packed by hand; all work was done by women workers seen in front of the factory. Located on Franklin Street, the squib factory produced 30,000–40,000 squibs daily that were sent to nearly every mining district in the United States. The Daddow and Beadle Squib Factory produced squibs twisted to the right while another factory in town, the Hayes factory, produced the left-sided squibs. In the 1880s, 90 percent of the squibs used in the United States were manufactured in St. Clair. Daddow's Squib Factory closed on February 9, 1929.

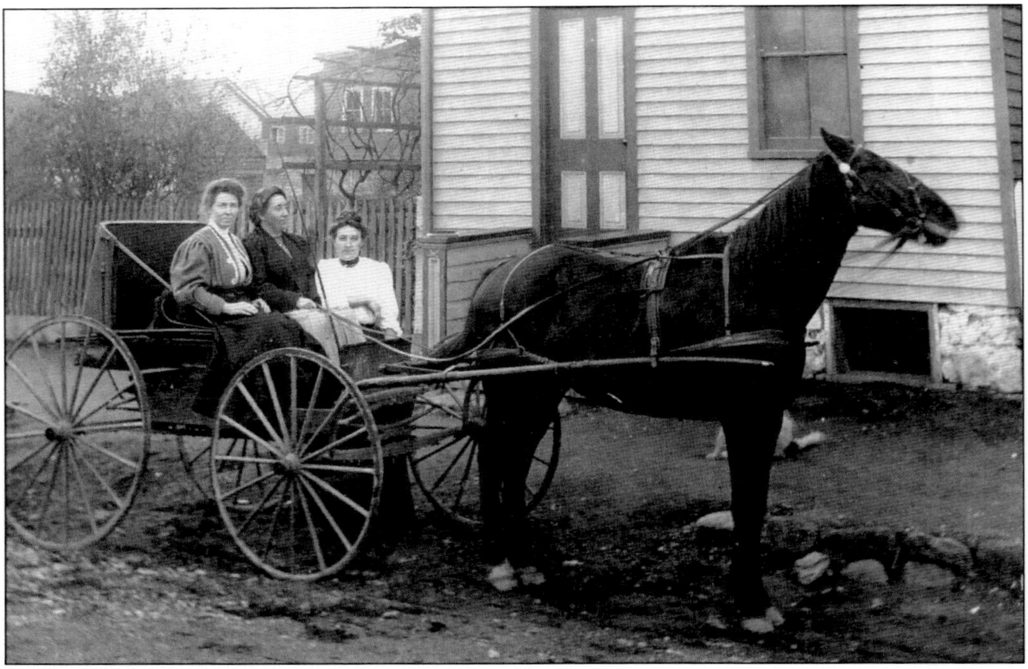

Seated in the carriage are Lizzie Gaynor and Annie Wench on the 400 block of South Nichols Street. The horse's name is Bill and belonged to their mother "Jolly Granny Jones," who sold milk throughout the town for 52 years, retiring at age 83. She could be found on the street on the severest winter days, serving her customers. (Courtesy of Bonnie Baker and Peg Frantz.)

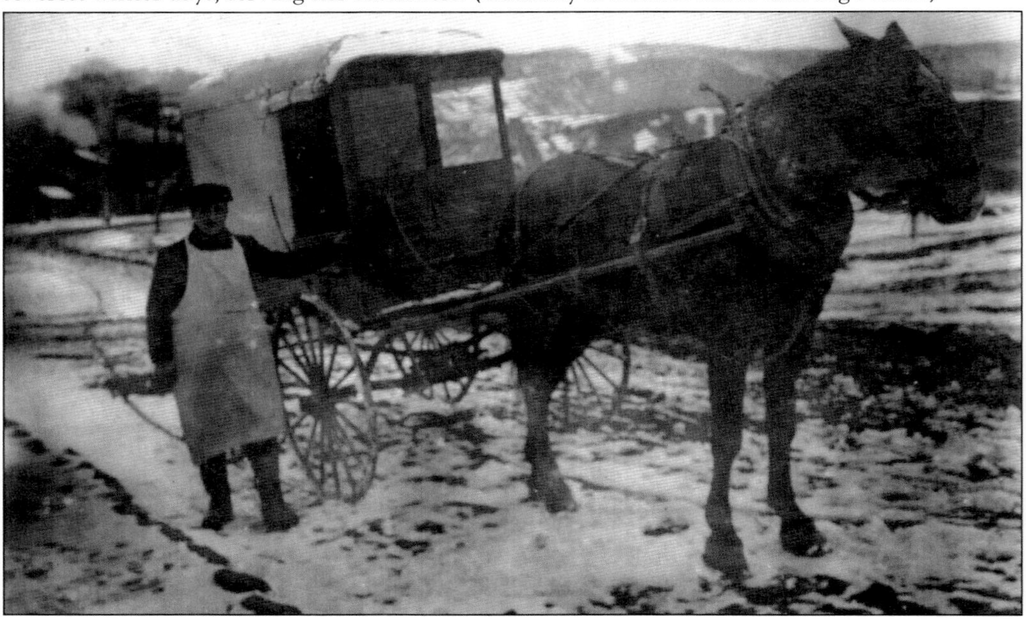

Many of the merchants in town traveled throughout surrounding rural areas of the town selling their wares to families. Businesses like Carpency's and Schmeltzer's maintained their own livery stable for their horses used with their delivery wagons. Shown in the picture, taken in 1909, is Joseph Carpency, out making his deliveries on a snowy winter day.

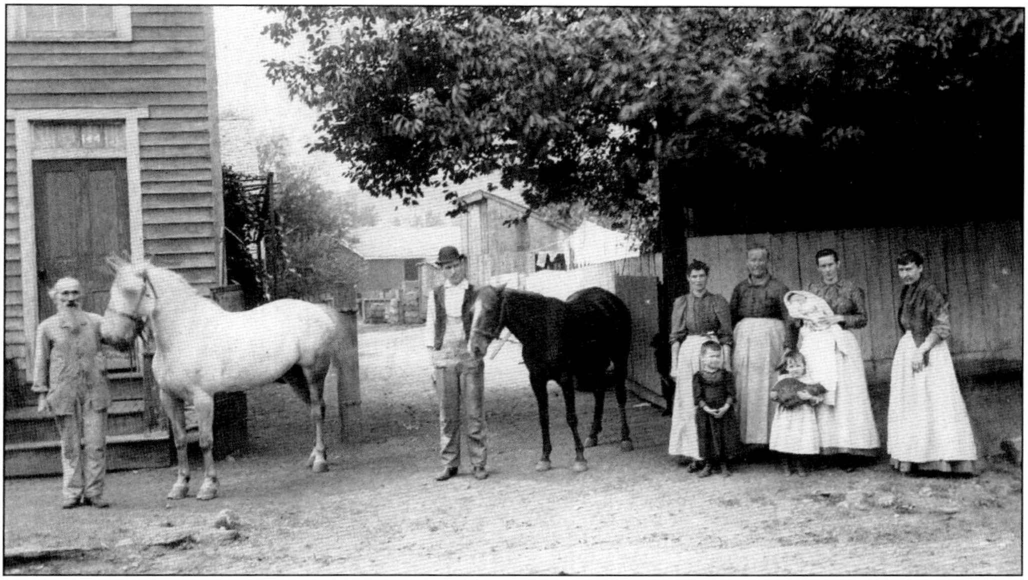

A longtime meat market operated by German immigrant Peter Schmeltzer was operated on the end of Mill and Franklin Streets. Schmeltzer is shown standing on the left with his family; an unknown worker holds the horse. Being a successful businessman, Schmeltzer was able to maintain a livery stable next to his business. A family story relates Schmeltzer paying children to herd the cattle from the train station in town to his place of business for slaughter. (Courtesy of Richard Leibel.)

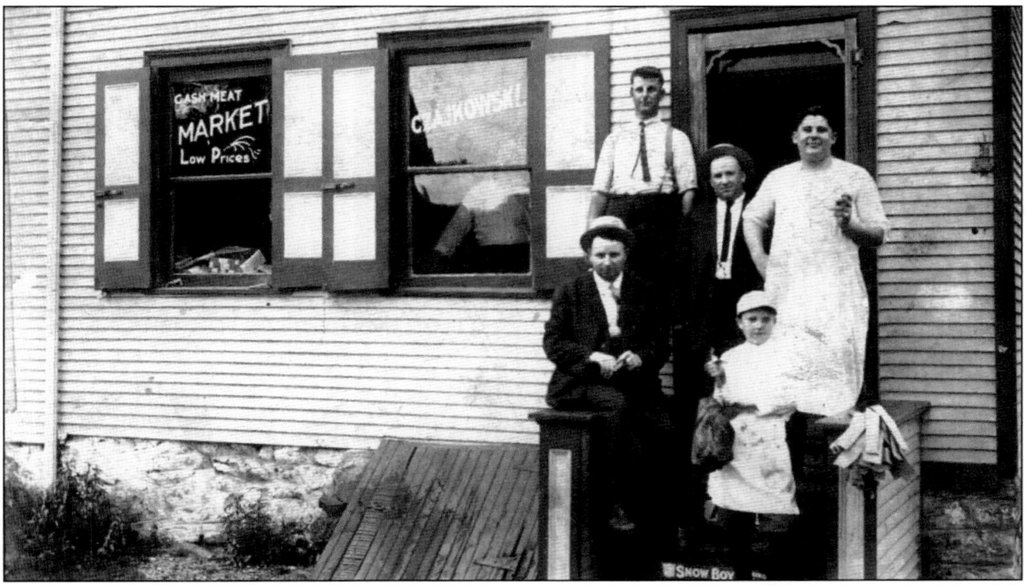

On the southwest corner of Nichols and Lawton Streets was Frank Czajkowsky's Meat Market. Czajkowsky was born in Lithuania and came to this country in 1907. He started the grocery business in 1910, and he continued until his death in 1936. Notice the sign in the window on the left, reading "Cash Meat Market." Sometime in the 1930s or 1940s, it passed into the hands of Helen Gustitus of Minersville and after the war opened as Whitey's Sea and Food Emporium. (Courtesy of Betty Gustitus.)

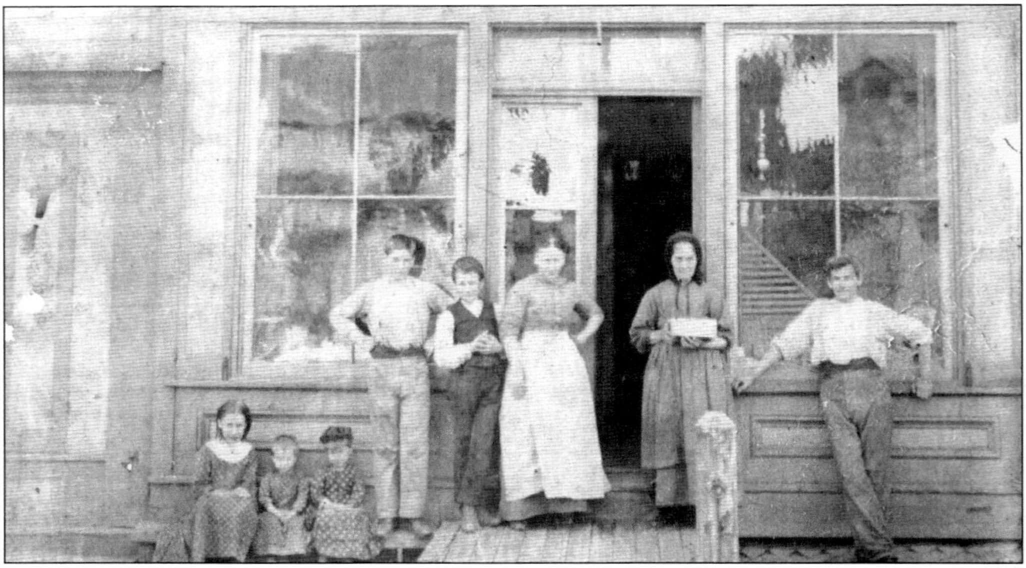

Wellner's Confectionary was founded in the 1870s by German immigrants John and Margaret Wellner. John Wellner Jr. continued with his father's business at 124 South Second Street, while his brother Nicholas ran a grocery and candy store just one block north. John's grandson Albert Burke and his wife, Mabel, carried on the family business changing the name to Burke's Candy in the 1940s. They made a variety of hard candy including clear toys, peppermint, cinnamon, wintergreen-striped pretzels and muffs, and a unique candy apple with a birch stem. (Courtesy of Mabel and Elizabeth Burke.)

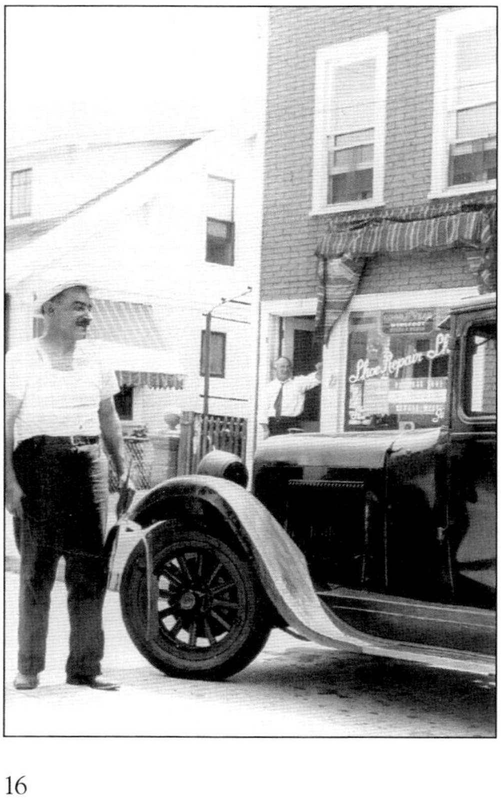

This shoe repair shop was owned and operated by Attilio DeMarkus. It was located on Hancock Street between Second Street and Front Street. This 1936 photograph shows John Mozloom near the car and Joe Bonanno in the doorway. DeMarkis later moved his shop to the first block on South Front Street. Shoe repair businesses thrived when times were tough but declined during times of economic growth. The recent recession has caused a new resurge of the cobbler business. (Courtesy of George Mozloom.)

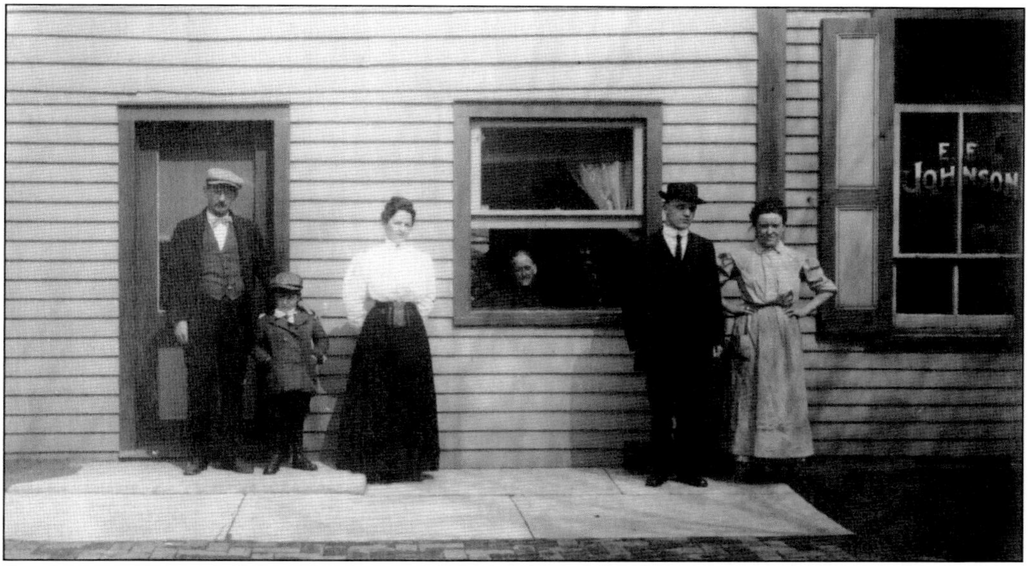

The E. F. Johnson hotel was located on North Second Street and served as an early meeting place for community leaders during the incorporation of the town of St. Clair. The first voting place in town was the tavern operated by Jonathan Johnson. Voting was held the first Monday in May every year.

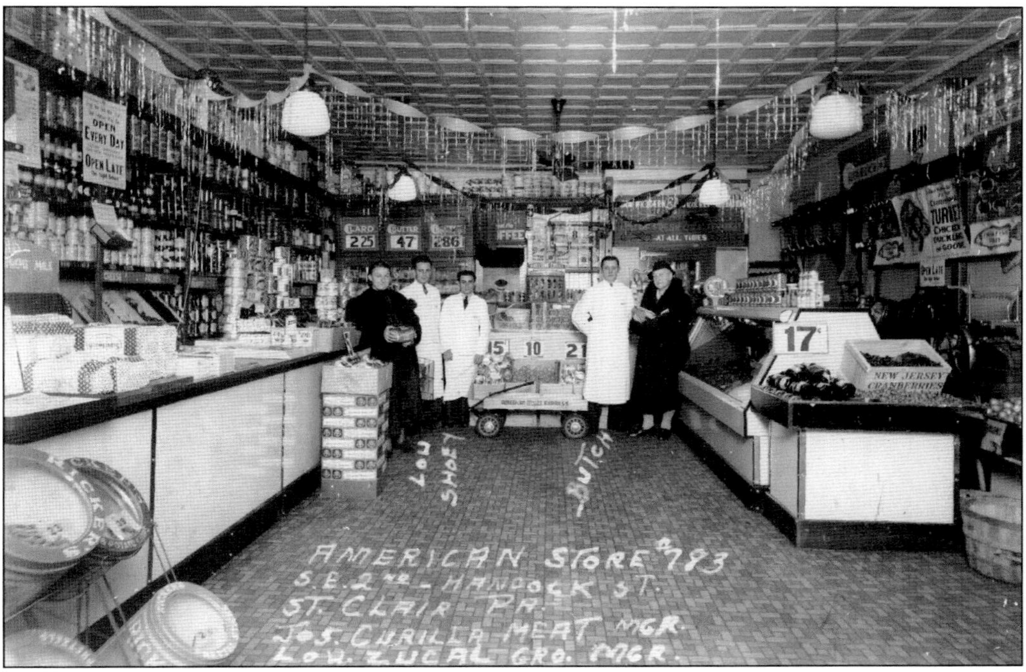

This picture of a local grocery store, located on the southeast corner of Second and Hancock Streets, was taken sometime in the 1930s or 1940s. It was known as the American Store. The photograph, taken around Christmastime, shows tinsel hanging from the ceiling and signs for turkeys and boxes of cranberries for sale. Underneath their image, the men are identified as Lou, Shoey, and Butch; Lou Zucal was the grocery manager and Jos. Chrilla the meat manager.

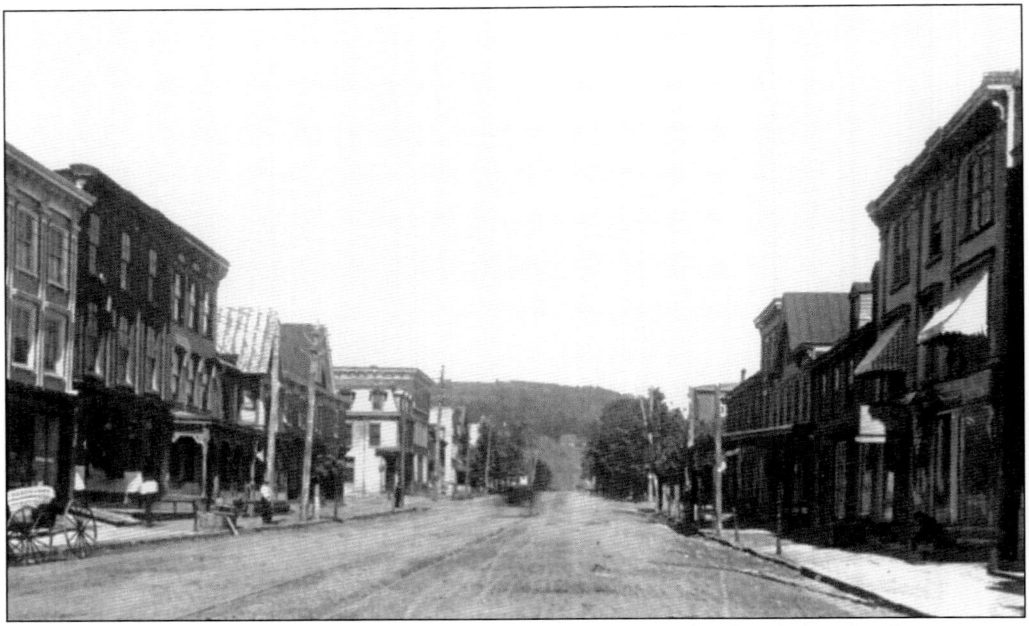

From the early 1800s to the late 1960s, the main street of St. Clair bustled with a large variety of small businesses. Almost every block had some type of barber, shoemaker, tinsmith, millinery, pharmacy, meat market, grocery, dry goods, or shoe store. Hotels and taverns populated nearly every street in town. George Gwinner on North Second Street had the leading bakery in town in the early years. Other bakeries and confectionery stores in the early 1900s were the Silver Bakery, Mahoney Bakery, and Raudenbush's Bakery.

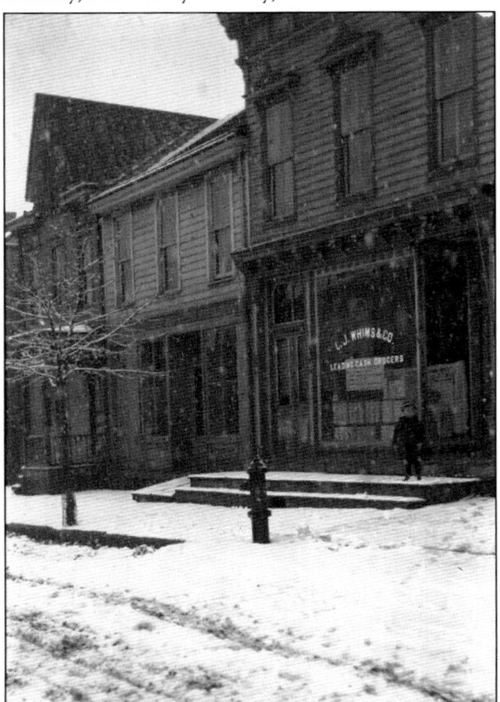

The picture of the Whims Store, taken on a cold snowy day, was located at 40 South Second Street. The owner and operator of this store was Lawrence J. Whims, son of a Civil War veteran who served in Company K, 190th Regiment of the Pennsylvania Infantry. Notice the small child on the step and also the one in the store window behind him. It is believed the store closed shortly after the 1929 stock market crash. (Courtesy of Larry Hyer.)

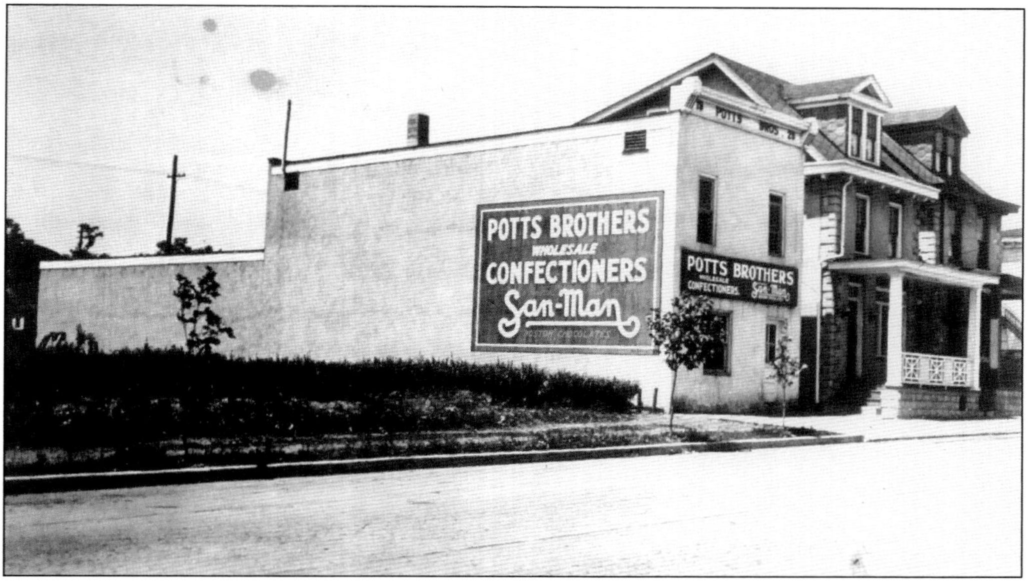

The Potts Brothers Wholesale Confectioners was started by Andrew and Nicholas Potts in February 1923. Andrew was a fire boss at the St. Clair Coal Company, and Nicholas was a motorman who decided to leave the mine and bought a candy business from Lester Clay of Pottsville. Andrew died in a mine accident one week before the day he was scheduled to leave the mines. Candy was first sold off a truck and warehousing done in the Potts home in Arnots Addition with candy stored in the living room, attic, and cellar. Years later, land was purchased from the Reading Coal Company, and a new two-story warehouse was erected to be a candy, tobacco, and cigar product store. It was the first warehouse in the eastern part of Pennsylvania to have air-conditioning, humidifying, dehumidifying, and automatic heating systems.

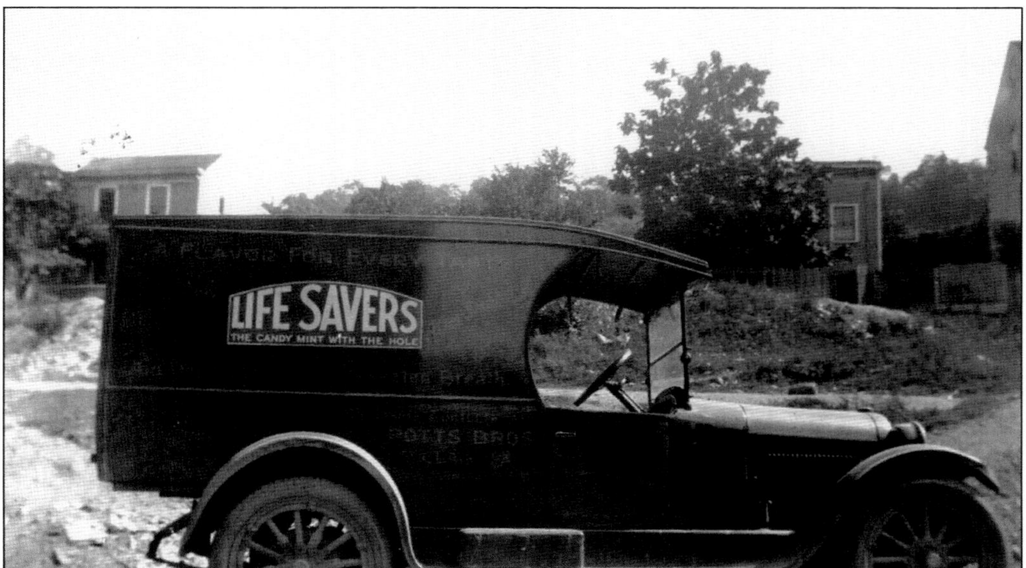

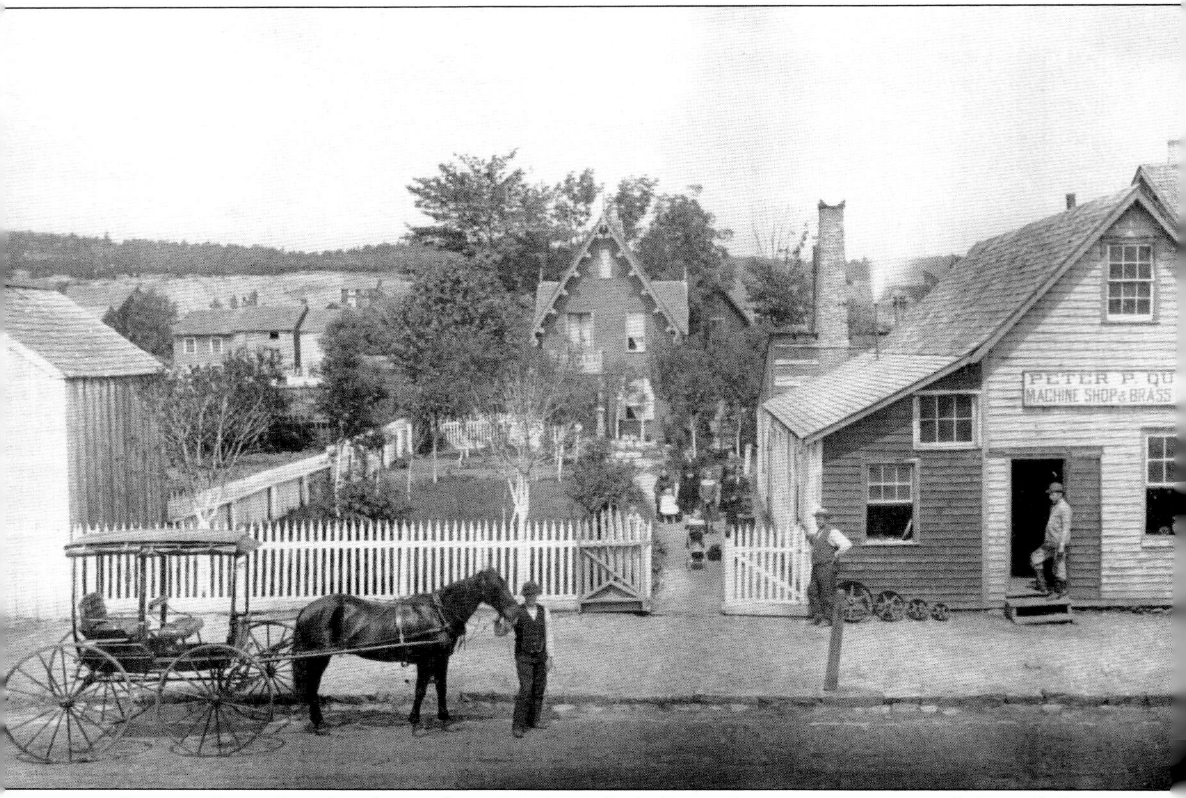

Quirin's Brass foundry, located on South Nichols Street between Lawton and Carroll Streets, was the first location of a family-run business that continues to operate in St. Clair. Peter P. Quirin, an immigrant from Bavaria, settled in St. Clair in 1854. An inventor, he owned and operated the foundry until his death in 1891. Two of his more popular inventions were the Quirin's Safety Lamp and a nonfreezing fire hydrant.

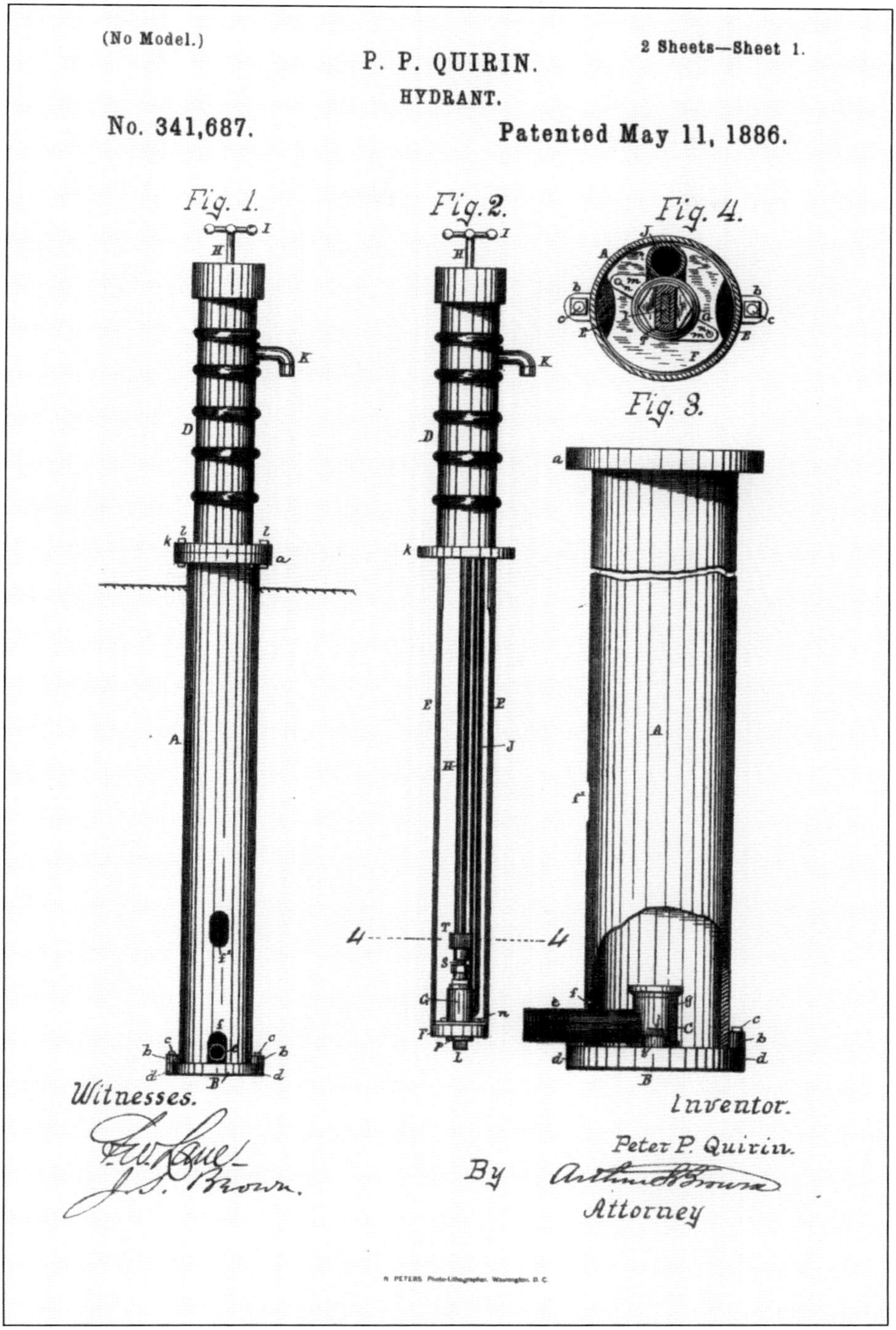

Quirin's hydrant was patented on May 11, 1886, No. 341,687. He invented this nonfreezing hydrant to be easily drained and ventilated with an improved cutoff valve and waste valve that prevented it from freezing. It was also constructed to enable the body of the hydrant to be easily detached from the water-supply pipe for cleaning and repairs without having to dig it out of the ground.

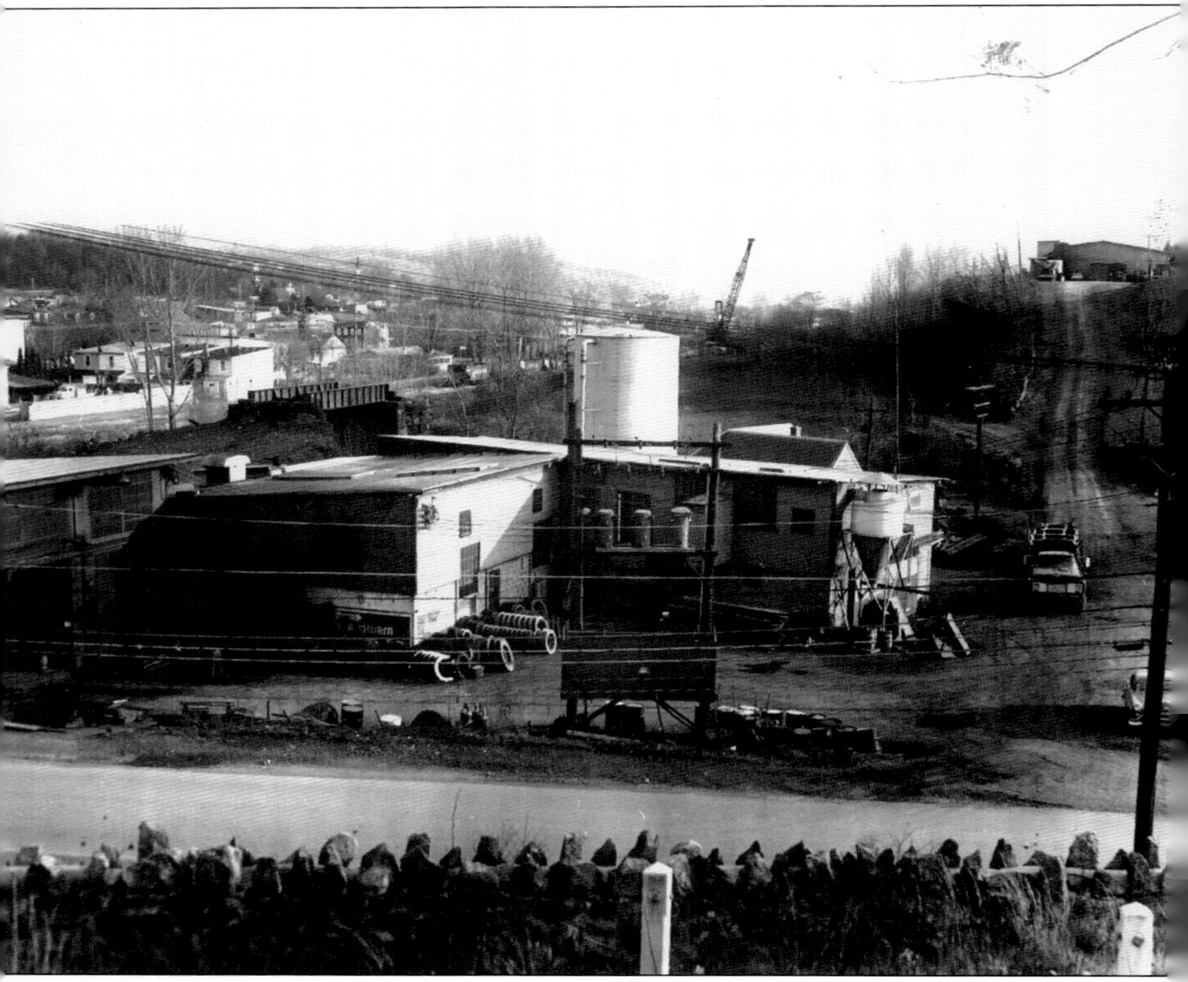

This machine shop, operated by the Quirin family, was located on Wade Road leading west from St. Clair toward the village of Wadesville. In 1945, the name was changed to the Leed Foundry, derived from the first names of Edmund and Leona Quirin. The machine shop moved to the foundry site in 1986.

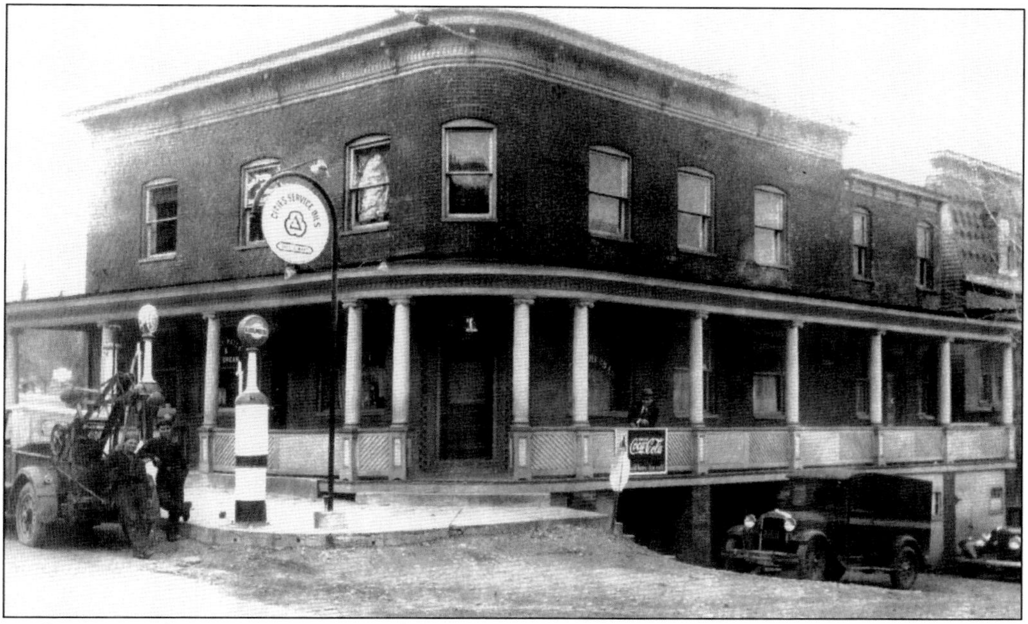

In the 1800s, this tavern was named the Dormer-Canfield Hotel. Catherine Canfield ran the hotel in the absence of her husband, a canal boatman. In 1856, she was convicted of keeping a "disorderly house," which as another name for brothel. Early in the 20th century, the hotel section burned to the ground and was reconstructed in 1913 with the present brickwork. At the time of the picture, the building was owned by the Penkunas family, who operated a tavern and automobile service business.

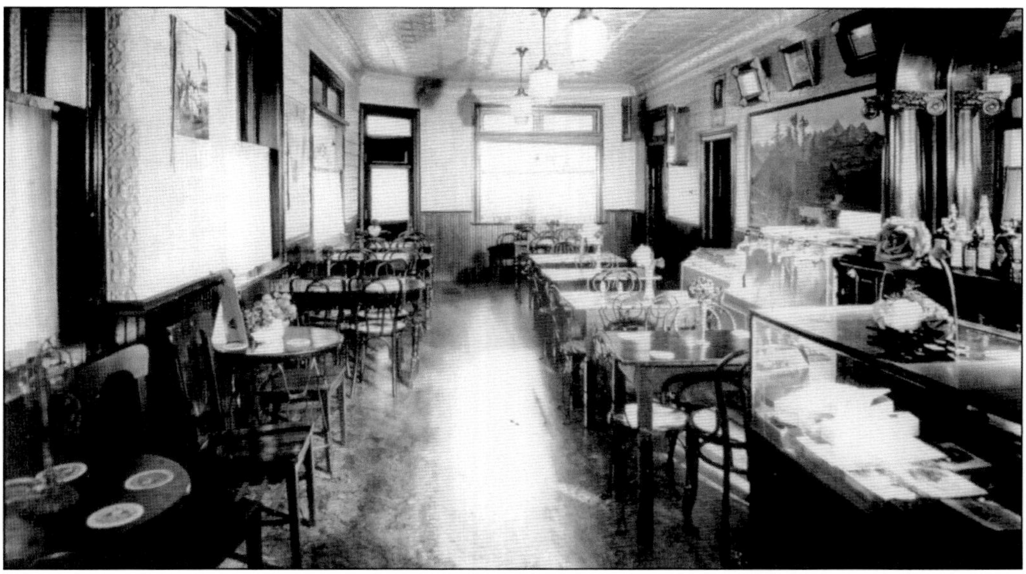

The Dormers operated a brewery across the street from their tavern. They also had a popular picnic area next to the brewery called the Atlantic Gardens. Starting in 1918, the building changed owners and was known as Penkunas's and then Micky Snyder's Bar. The building still operates as a popular restaurant and tavern. At the present time, original parts of the bar interior are the pressed tin ceiling, wainscotings, and door.

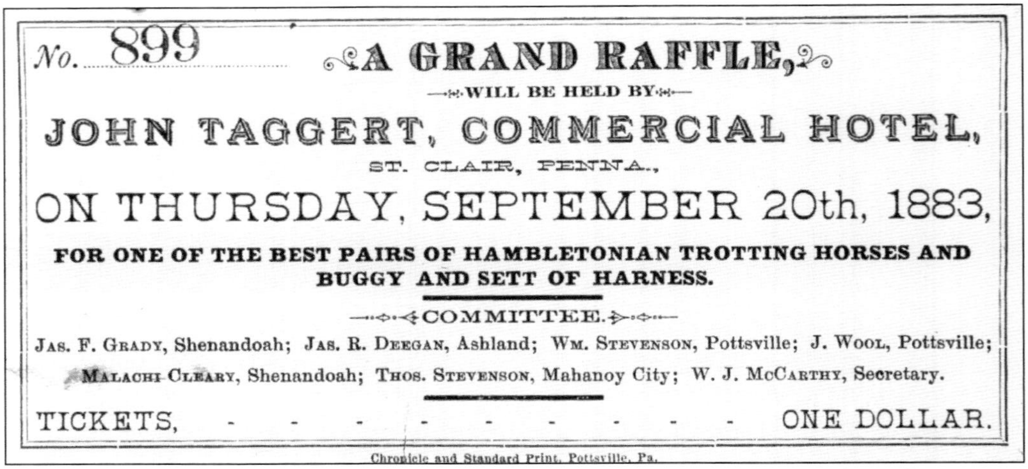

No. 899

A GRAND RAFFLE,

WILL BE HELD BY

JOHN TAGGERT, COMMERCIAL HOTEL,

ST. CLAIR, PENNA.,

ON THURSDAY, SEPTEMBER 20th, 1883,

FOR ONE OF THE BEST PAIRS OF HAMBLETONIAN TROTTING HORSES AND BUGGY AND SETT OF HARNESS.

COMMITTEE.

JAS. F. GRADY, Shenandoah; JAS. R. DEEGAN, Ashland; WM. STEVENSON, Pottsville; J. WOOL, Pottsville; MALACHI CLEARY, Shenandoah; THOS. STEVENSON, Mahanoy City; W. J. McCARTHY, Secretary.

TICKETS, - - - - - - - - - - ONE DOLLAR.

Chronicle and Standard Print, Pottsville, Pa.

Raffle tickets and lotteries were as common 100 years ago as they are today. The Taggert Commercial Hotel, located on the corner of Second and Carroll Streets, was previously known as the Betz Hotel and later the Boone building. John Taggert entered the hotel business by marrying the widow of the Betz Hotel owner. Taggert caused headlines in the local newspaper during 1860 when he was accused of dynamiting several locations in town, including the Baptist church.

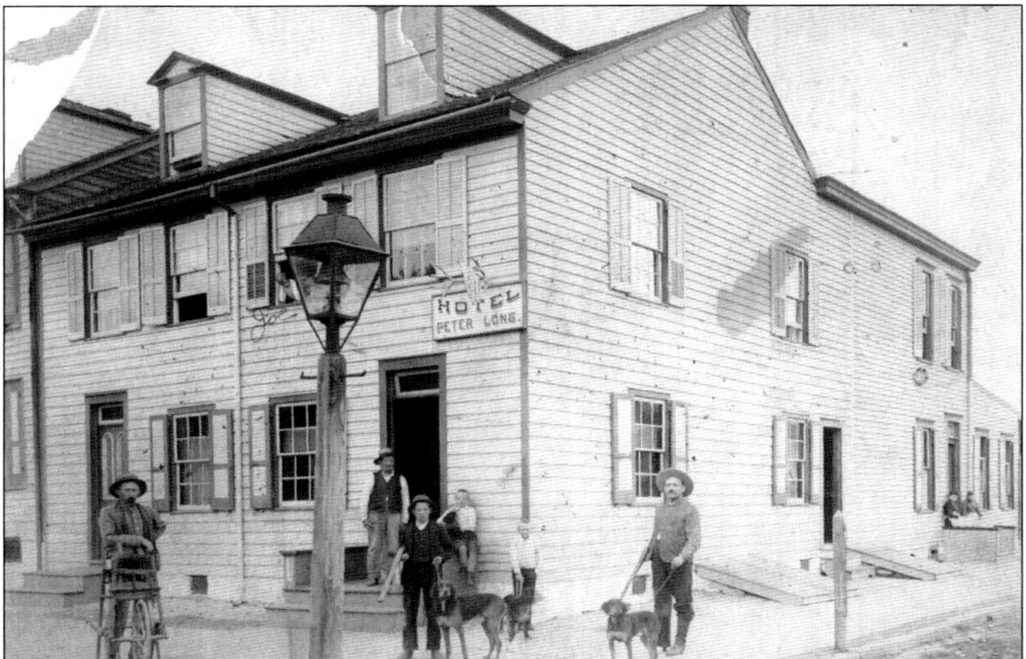

Michael Long settled in this area during the 1840s, when it was nothing more than swamps, farms, and forests. He opened the Long Hotel, later known as the Buck Horn Hotel, Tavern, and Livery Stable, located on the corner of Lawton and Front Streets. It was for many years a well-known gathering place of hunters and farmers of the county. This photograph was taken during the early 1900s with Peter Long being the owner of the establishment. Peter Long was electrocuted by a fallen wire while working at the hotel during a rainstorm around 1921.

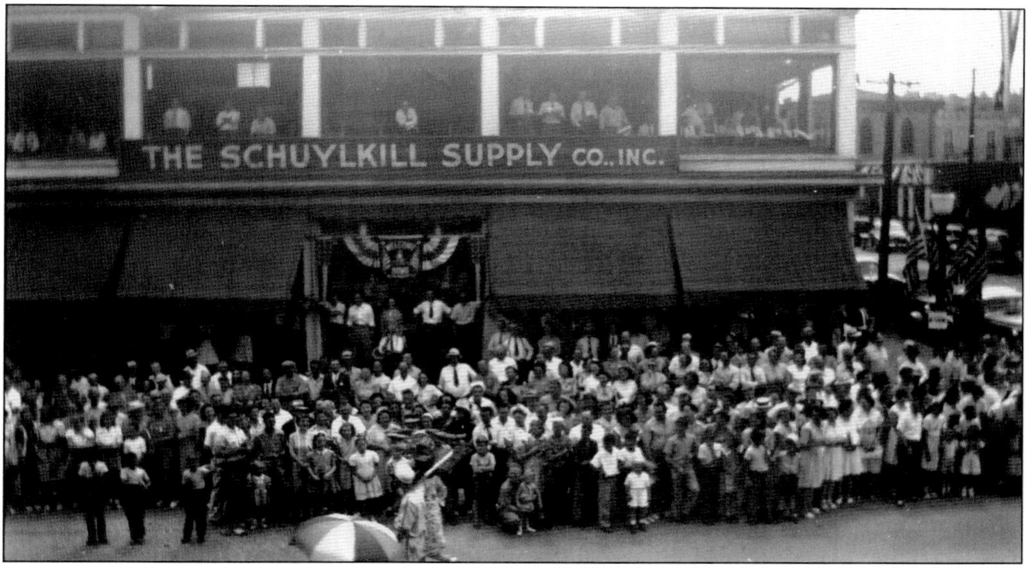

The Schuylkill Store, located on the southwest corner of Second and Carroll Streets, was operated by the local colliery owners. The photograph of the store was taken in the 1940s. Miners and their families were often required to shop here at prices controlled by the colliery owners. Their purchases were made on an account that was deducted from their earnings at the mines. In an earlier photograph, the manager and workers, dressed neat and uniformly, greet their customers while their dog takes a nap. Company stores were often known as the "pluck-me" store. A popular 1950s song refers to the company store in the chorus, "St. Peter don't call me cause I can't go I owe my soul to the company store."

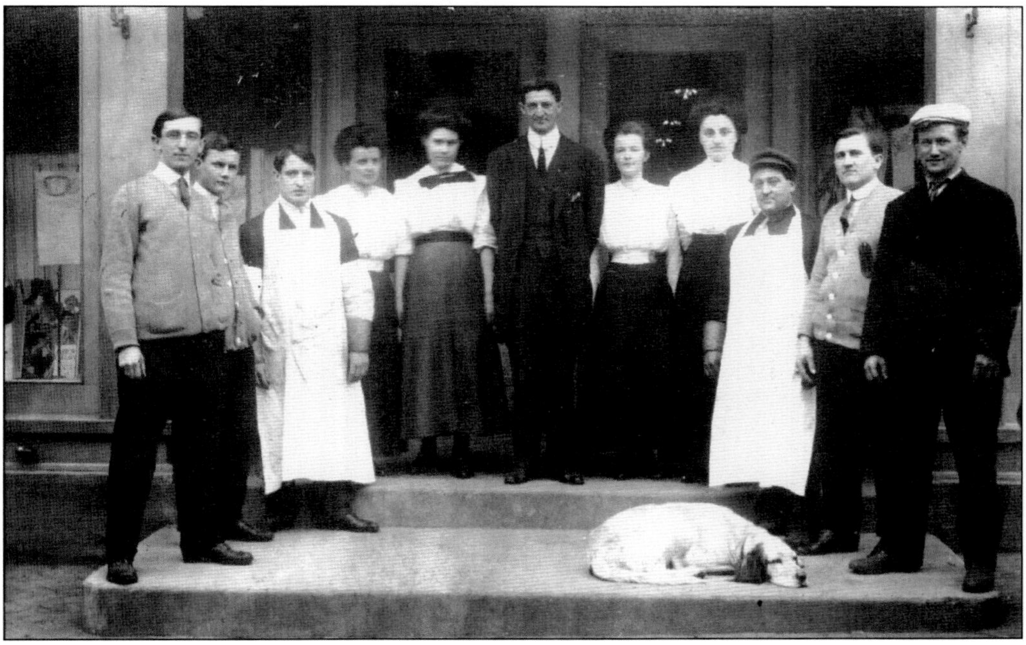

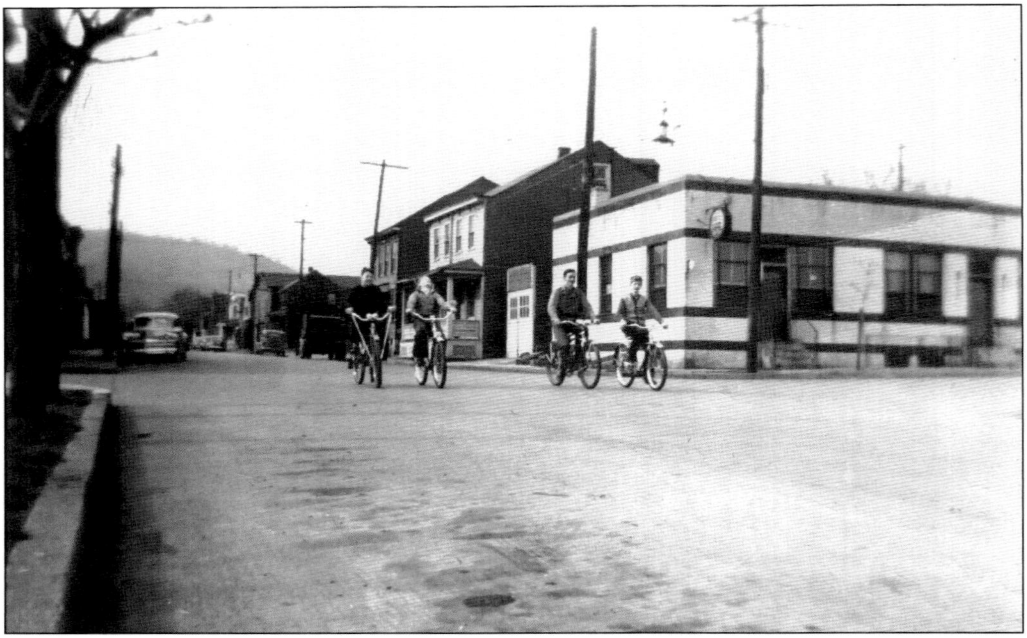

Gombar's bar, pictured in 1947, was located on the corner of Carroll and Third Streets. The bar was opened by Joseph Gombar and was later passed to his nephew Francis Gombar and his wife, Helen Melnic Gombar, who operated it until the mid-1960s. The Gombars still operate a fabric and costume shop in the building.

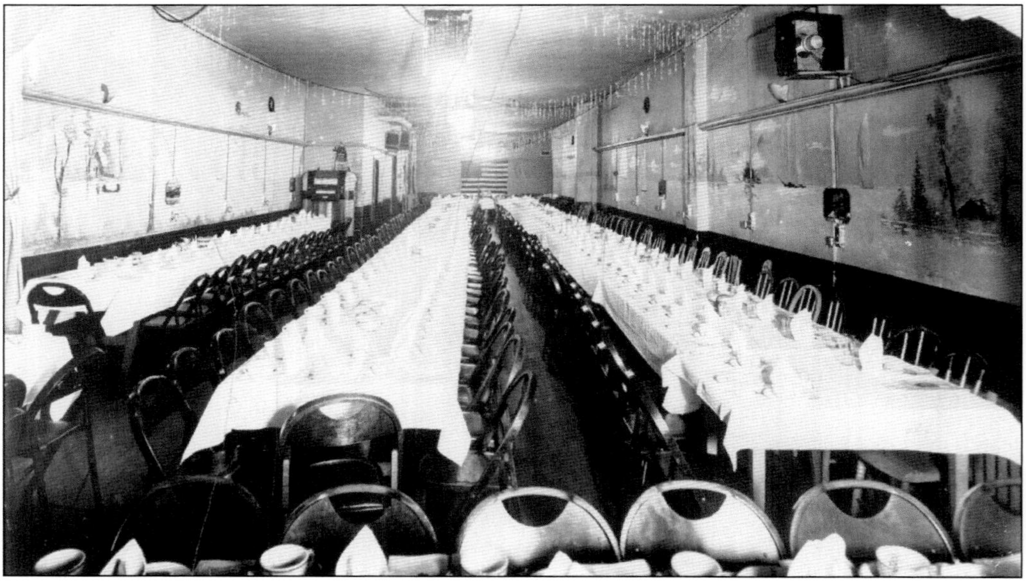

Located at the corner of Carroll and Second Streets, Gilmartin's Grille and Restaurant, previously known as the Boone Hall, was one of the more popular gathering places during World War II. Large numbers of soldiers from Fort Indiantown Gap could be found there every weekend, when it was usually standing room only in this 250-person-capacity hall. For over half a century, this building was either known as Bretz or Taggert Hotel, Boone Hall, Gilmartins, Peter and Paul's, or the Towne House.

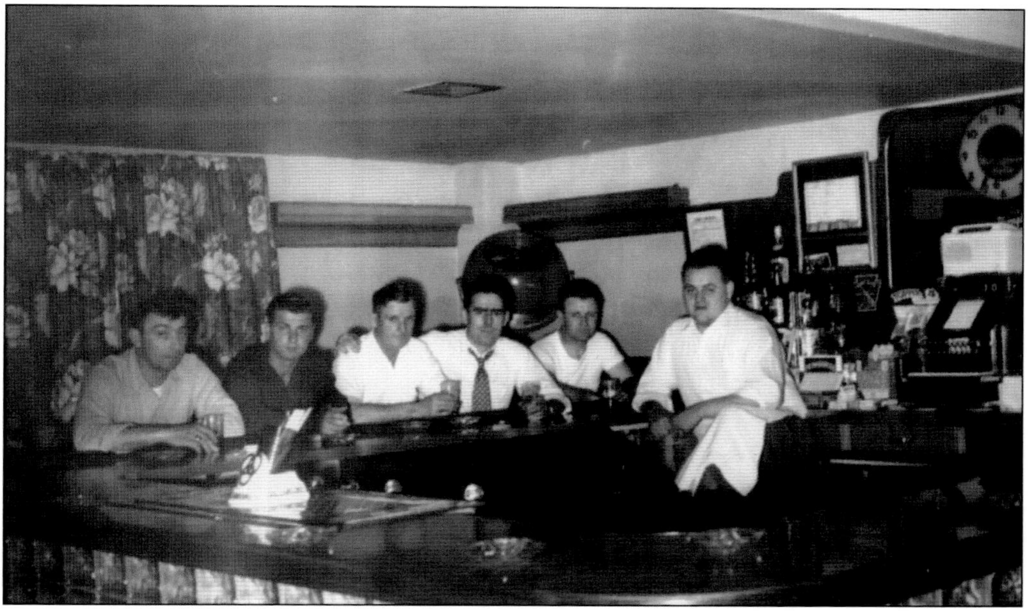

On the south corner of Lawton and Nichols Streets was a popular restaurant and bar called Whitey's Sea and Food Emporium. The bar became one of the original sports bars in the area and supported many of the sports teams in town. William and his wife, Betty Gustitus, were owners of this business until retirement in 1986. They were known for the best crab cakes in the county. The building was razed in 2006. (Courtesy of Betty Gustitus.)

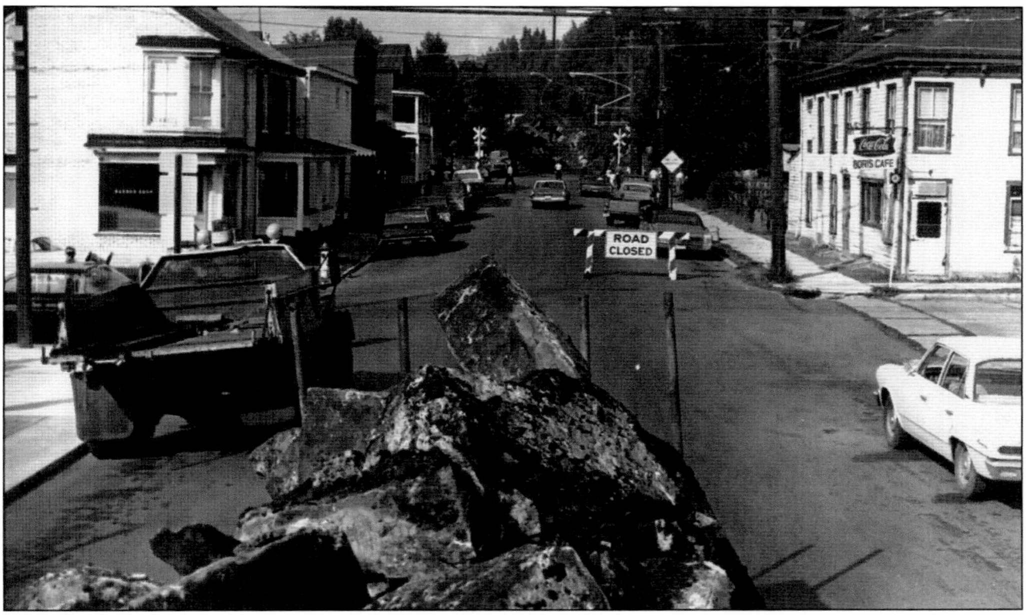

The economy was growing, and the availability of automobiles grew with it. This growth meant the inevitable decline of passenger rail services. During the 1960s, the stone railroad arch and overpass on Hancock Street leading to Arnots Addition and Wadesville was torn down. Boris Café, on the right, was the lot next to the site of the first hotel in town built to house workers of the Girard Tunnel.

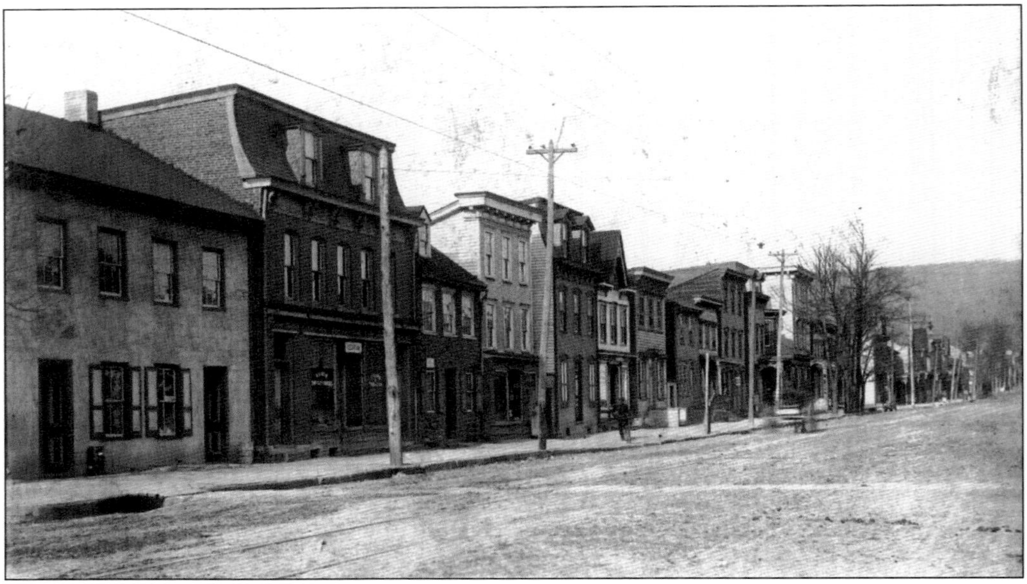

This *c.* 1905 picture looks north on Second Street and shows many of the stores that lined the main street of town. Second Street was still dirt until 1927, when it became the first street in town to be paved. The streets of St. Clair were laid out and given names by Henry C. Carey, Isaac Lee, and Abraham Hart around the mid-1830s. All streets were planned to run parallel or at right angels to Nichols Street.

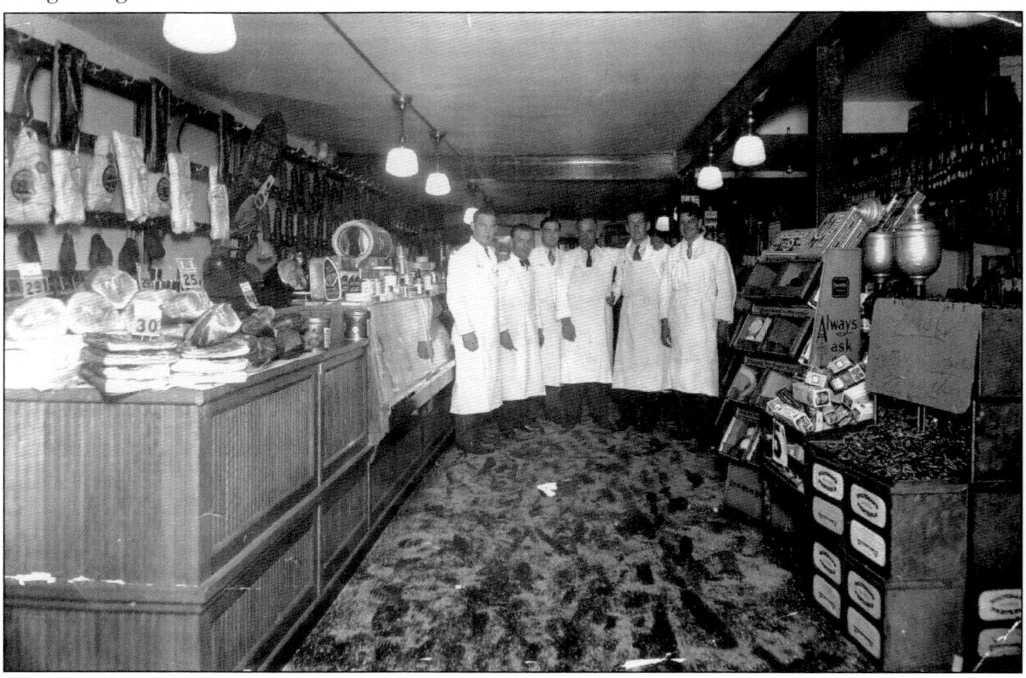

The last grocery store to occupy the former I. D. Beahm store on North Second Street was a Pennsylvania chain grocery store, the A&P. The gentlemen standing proudly in their long aprons, on a floor sprinkled with sawdust, were photographed around 1929. David Jones was remembered as a longtime butcher in this store.

Two

Coming Together with Organizations

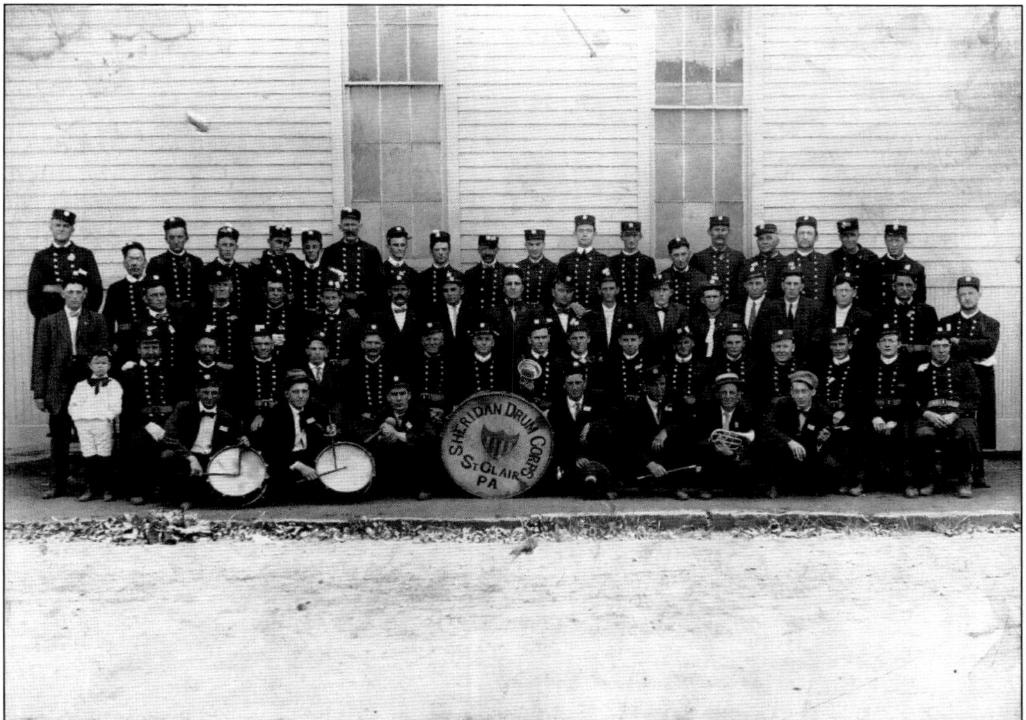

St. Clair took music to its heart as marching bands and ensembles filled everyone's need for dancing, marching, competitions, and listening. One of the earliest bands in St. Clair was the Sheridan Band, pictured here.

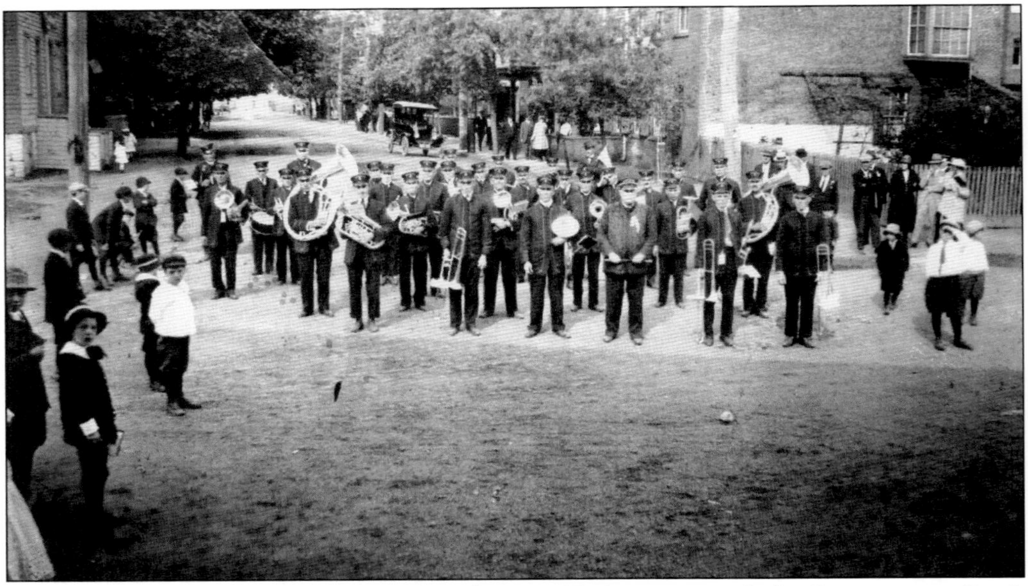

In 1884, Peter Schuster, Elmer Boyer, and James Tucker organized the Perseverance Band, directed by William H. Badge. The Perseverance Band was selected to lead the 1919 welcome home parade honoring the World War I veterans. Spectators lined the streets, porches, and roofs of the parade route, with an estimated 20,000 attending the parade.

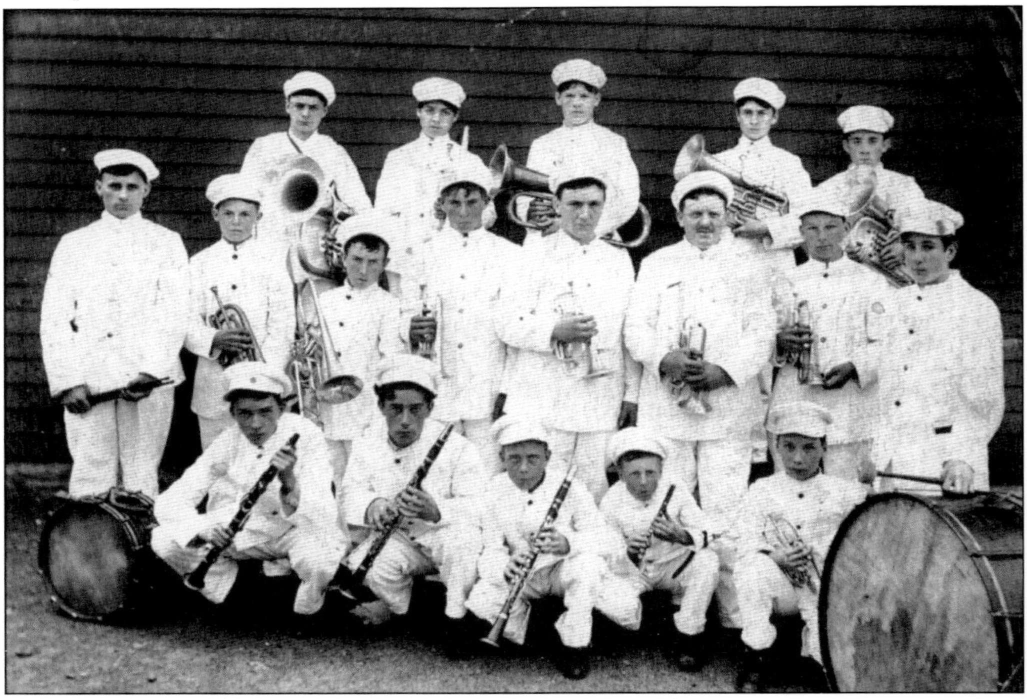

Wadesville, located in New Castle Township just west of St. Clair, was a thriving active mining "patch" up to the 1930s. The Wadesville Colliery gave employment to a wide area, and those who lived here had pride in their many social activities. The only identified Wadesville band member is Harry Scherr, front row fourth from left.

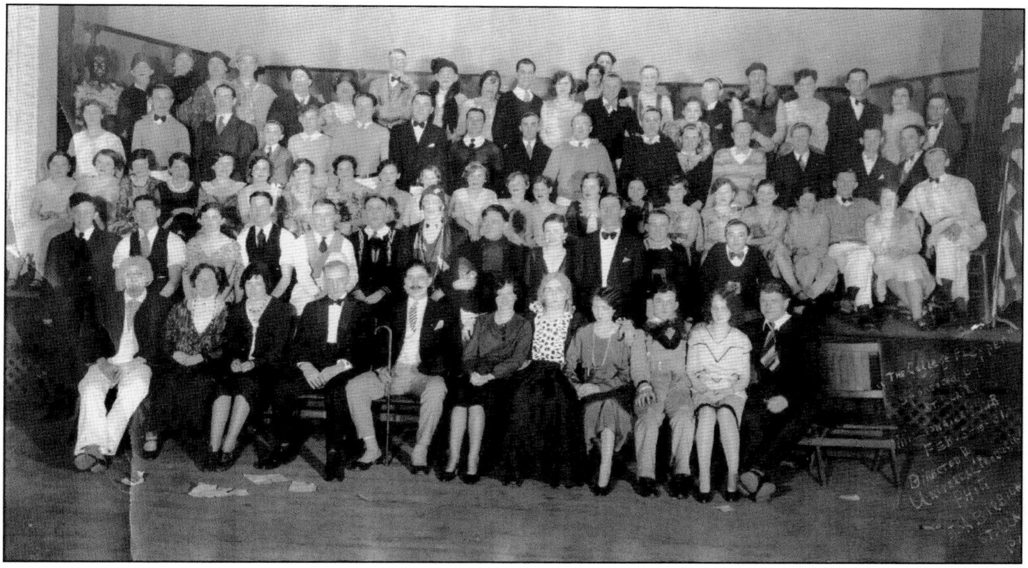

The Millionaires were a group of young men organized by Harry T. Plappert around 1925 to represent and advertise St. Clair in other communities by competing in their mummer's parades and putting on skits and plays in town. As mummers, they dressed up as hobos carrying a kerchief on a stick. This group won many prizes in local competitions, and in 1928, they won honors in the Philadelphia New Year's Mummer's Parade. The group photograph shows the cast of the play *The College Flapper.*

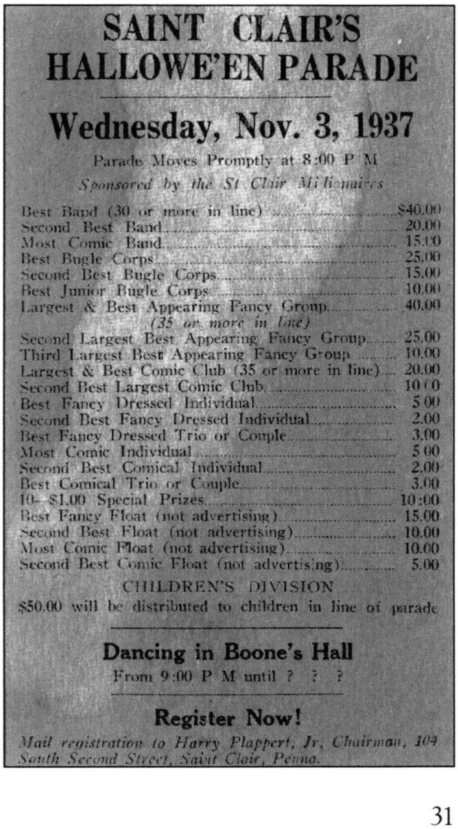

SAINT CLAIR'S
HALLOWE'EN PARADE

Wednesday, Nov. 3, 1937

Parade Moves Promptly at 8:00 P M

Sponsored by the St Clair Millionaires

Best Band (30 or more in line)	$40.00
Second Best Band	20.00
Most Comic Band	15.00
Best Bugle Corps	25.00
Second Best Bugle Corps	15.00
Best Junior Bugle Corps	10.00
Largest & Best Appearing Fancy Group (35 or more in line)	40.00
Second Largest Best Appearing Fancy Group	25.00
Third Largest Best Appearing Fancy Group	10.00
Largest & Best Comic Club (35 or more in line)	20.00
Second Best Largest Comic Club	10.00
Best Fancy Dressed Individual	5.00
Second Best Fancy Dressed Individual	2.00
Best Fancy Dressed Trio or Couple	3.00
Most Comic Individual	5.00
Second Best Comical Individual	2.00
Best Comical Trio or Couple	3.00
10—$1.00 Special Prizes	10:00
Best Fancy Float (not advertising)	15.00
Second Best Float (not advertising)	10.00
Most Comic Float (not advertising)	10.00
Second Best Comic Float (not advertising)	5.00

CHILDREN'S DIVISION

$50.00 will be distributed to children in line of parade

Dancing in Boone's Hall

From 9:00 P M until ? ? ?

Register Now!

Mail registration to Harry Plappert, Jr, Chairman, 104 South Second Street, Saint Clair, Penna.

The St. Clair Halloween parade, once sponsored by the St. Clair Millionaires club, provided various prizes for the different divisions in the parade. The group ended the evening with dancing later in the night at Boone Hall. The parade continued on in the town after the Millionaires disbanded, sponsored by the Kiwanis and Woman's Club.

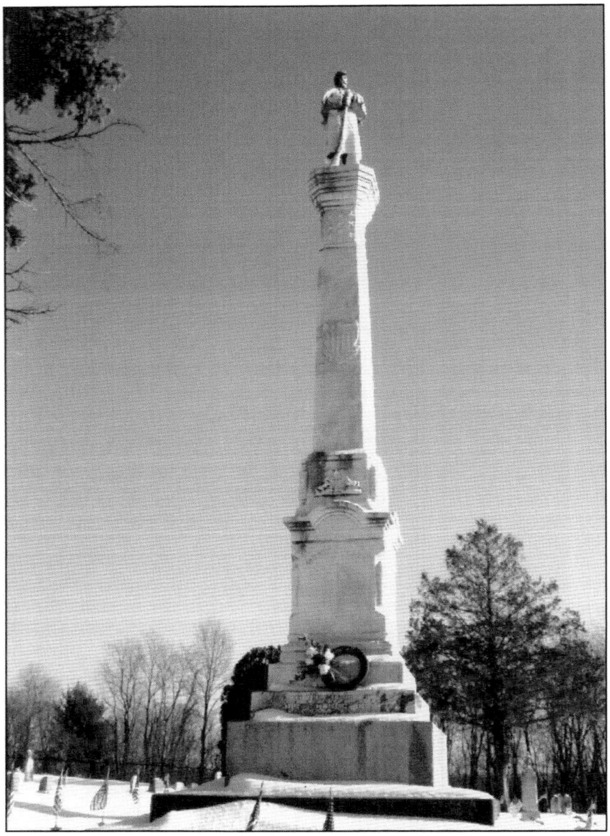

The Grand Army of the Republic (GAR) monument, honoring Civil War veterans, was dedicated on Thanksgiving Day of 1874, with speeches presented by local dignitaries, clergy, and even the governor of Pennsylvania. The Civil War Monument is located at the Odd Fellows Cemetery on top of Lawton's Hill, which overlooks the town of St. Clair. The hill is known today as the Gun Club Hill.

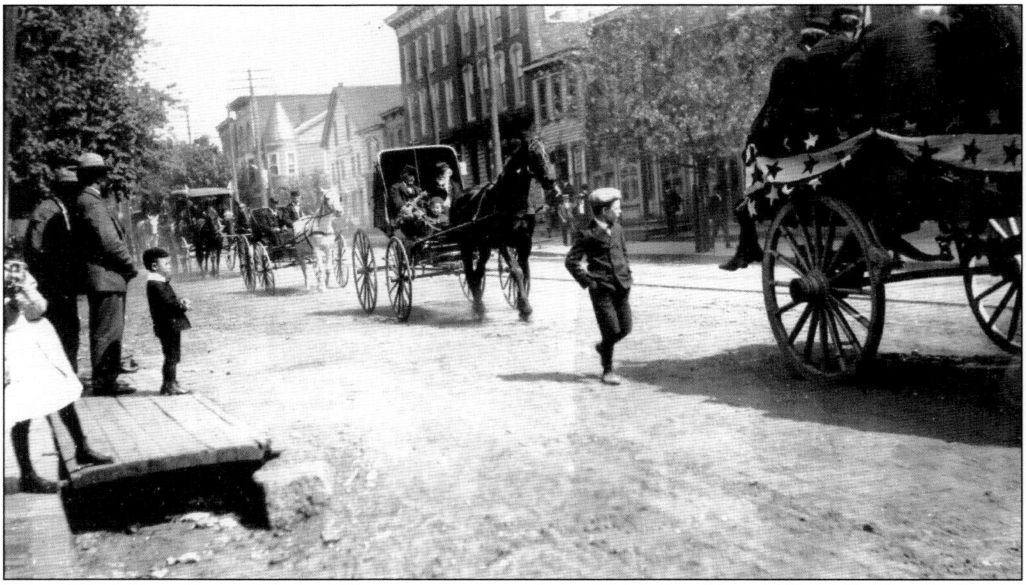

In the great parade of 1914, members of GAR traveled by horse and buggy throughout the parade route. The route stretched south on Second Street, turned onto Lawton Street, and ended up at the Odd Fellows Cemetery on top of the hill overlooking the town.

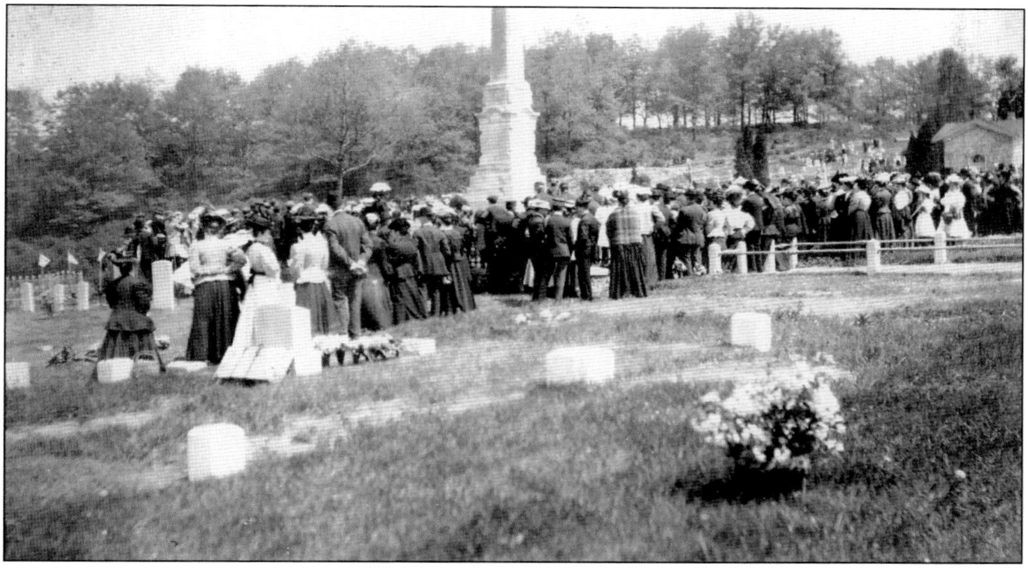

People followed the parade to the cemetery for the traditional GAR ceremony at the Civil War Monument. As seen on the photograph, many people carried baskets packed for a picnic after the ceremonies. During the Civil War, men from St. Clair had the highest percentage of volunteers in Schuylkill County and were awarded the Vicksburg Cane. This cane was reportedly made from a tree limb that hung over Ulysses S. Grant and Robert E. Lee at the time of the South's surrender.

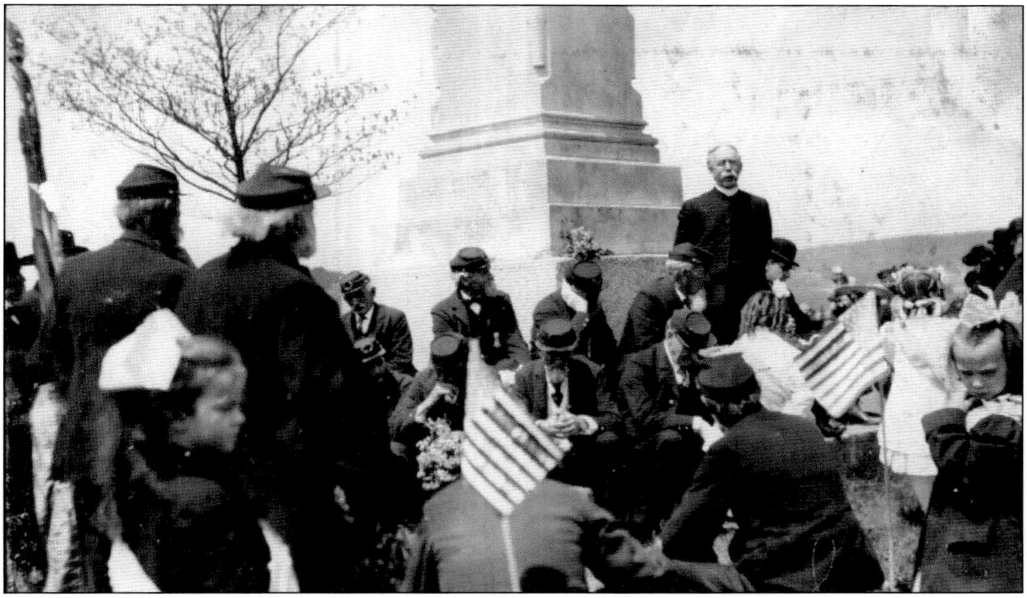

By 1914, there were only a few Civil War veterans remaining, and GAR Post No. 75 decided to turn its cemetery rituals over to another organization to be carried out going forward. With much celebration, GAR turned over its ritual to the honor students of the local high school, who still continue the tradition today.

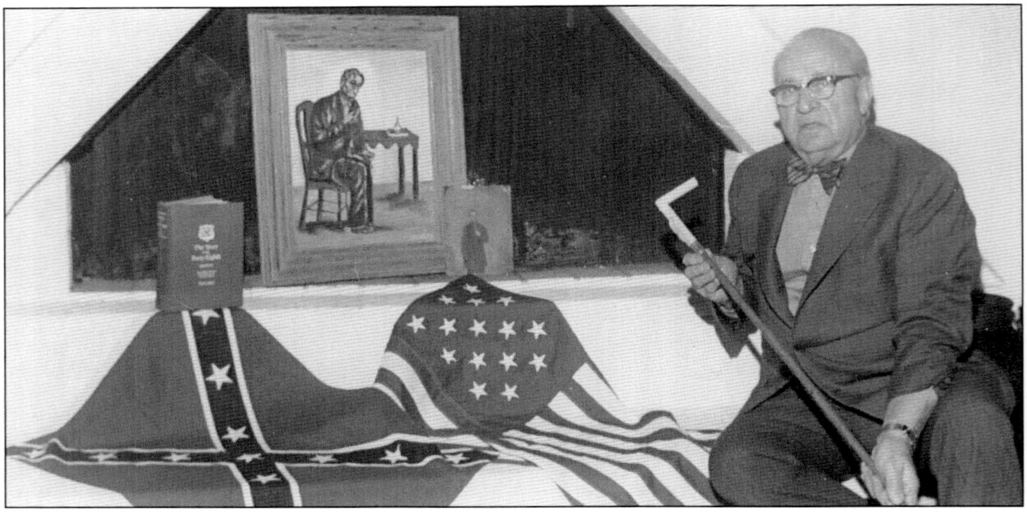

During the country's bicentennial in 1976, various Civil War memoirs were gathered and displayed for the town's celebrations. Sitting among Union and Confederate flags, the *History of the Forth-Eight*, a painting of Abraham Lincoln, and a tintype of Cpl. Richard Brown is Dr. Charles W. Delp holding the Vicksburg Cane. Corporal Brown, a St. Clair native, lost his right arm during the war carrying a comrade from the field of battle and was recuperating when the Confederate surrender came. Perhaps because of the service St. Clair gave to the country, Gen. Ulysses S. Grant presented Brown with the famous Vicksburg Cane, the branch of the elm tree that General Grant used as a walking stick when Confederate general Robert E. Lee surrendered at Appomattox Court House. Brown was a corporal in the war serving with the 48th Regiment Pennsylvania Veteran Volunteer Infantry. The cane is currently believed to be in the possession of the Brown family.

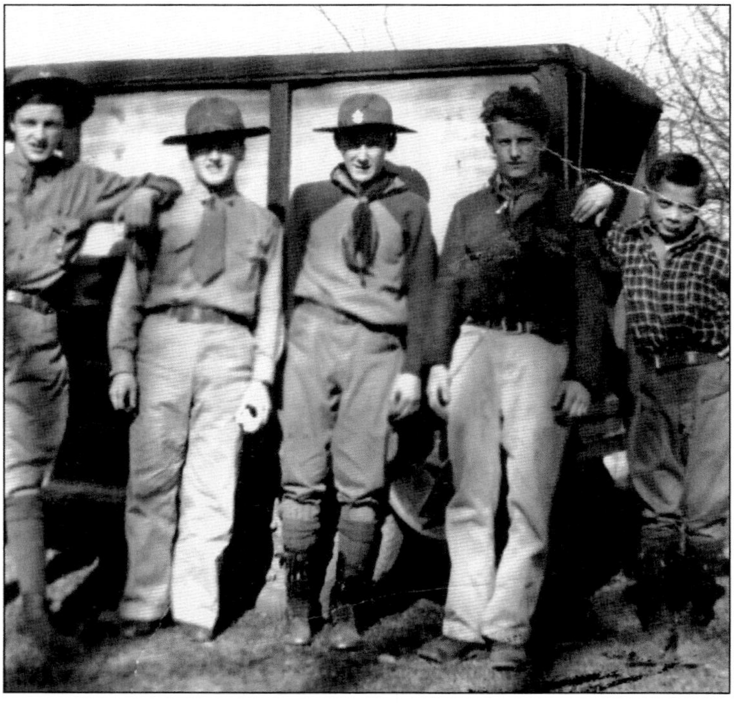

In 1910, the Boy Scouts organization spread over England and America. By the fall of that year, plans were being made to organize a troop in St. Clair. They recruited boys whose ages ranged from 10 to 18 years. Several prominent citizens in town financed the movement. There were several troops in town, the last being Troop 190, which was organized in 1952 and continued to 1995. Early members of the initial Troop 17 from 1939 are Bob Frantz, Frank Frantz, Theodore Donald Thorn, John Sich, and Allan Crawshaw.

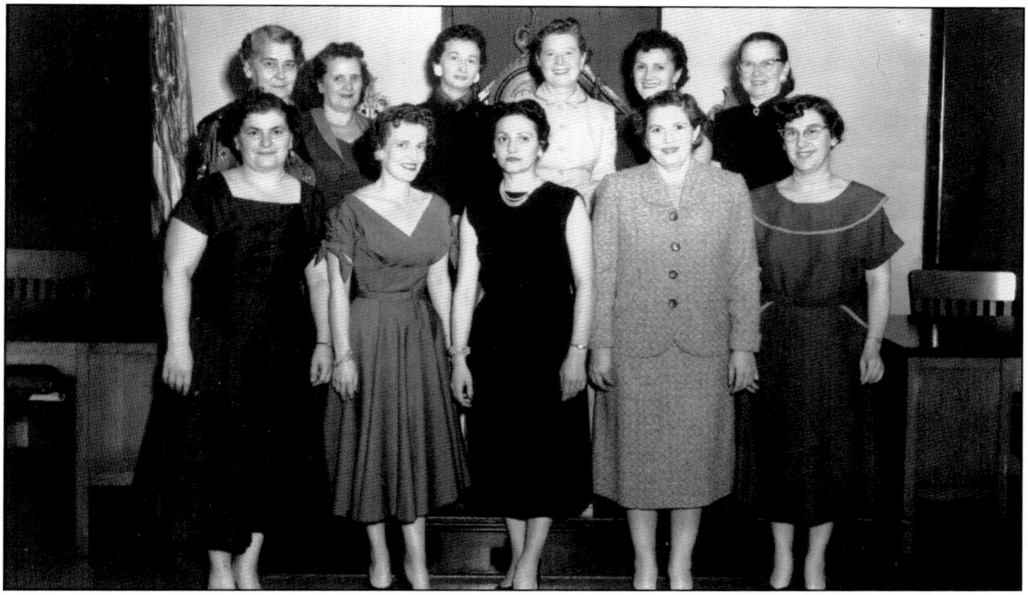

Phoebe Tomko was the first president of the St. Clair Woman's Club, which was organized in 1938. Its purpose was to promote good will and friendship and support projects aimed at community improvement. The members hosted a "senior tea" for the graduating class of St. Clair High School and sponsored awards at graduation. The club cosponsors the annual St. Clair Halloween parade.

In 1975, a skeleton was found in a mahogany casket under a false floor on the second floor of the former International Odd Fellows Lodge in St. Clair by the building's owner, pharmacist David Buchanan, during renovations. Metal insignias found on the coffin and tips of the finger bones were of those used by the Independent Order of Odd Fellows. During the ritual of initiation, the new member was blindfolded and placed in chains while the members marched around the room. When the blindfold was removed, he had to look at this human skeleton, illuminated by torchlight, and meditate about death.

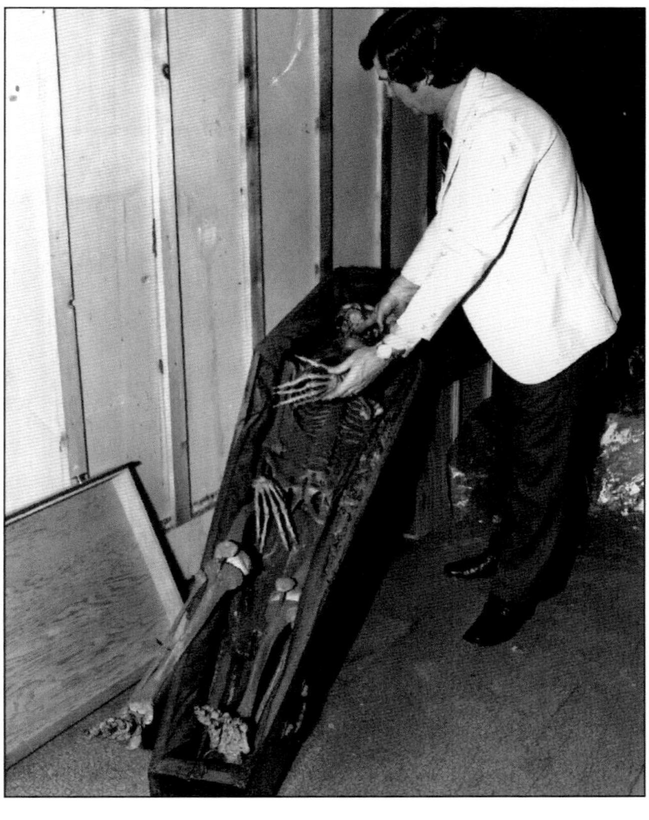

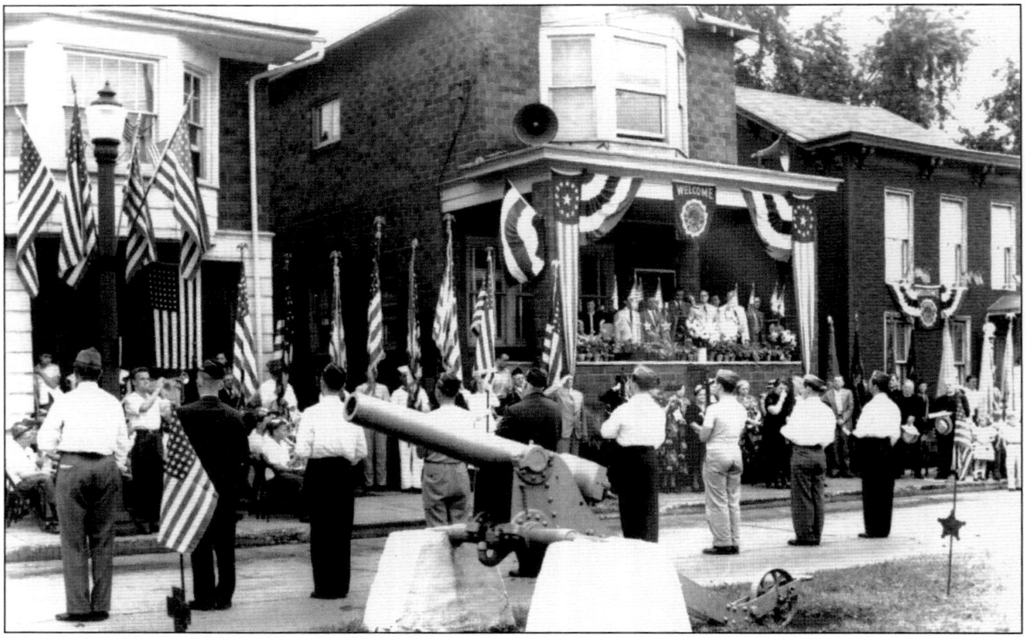

The first building that housed the American Legion was on South Second Street and included a bowling alley in the basement. At that time, there were no automatic pinsetters, and young boys would set up the pins after each frame. In front of the building, in the middle of Second Street, was an island that displayed the town's war memorials and cannons. Not long after the photograph was taken in the 1950s, the island was removed, and the memorials were taken to the Veterans Memorial Football Stadium.

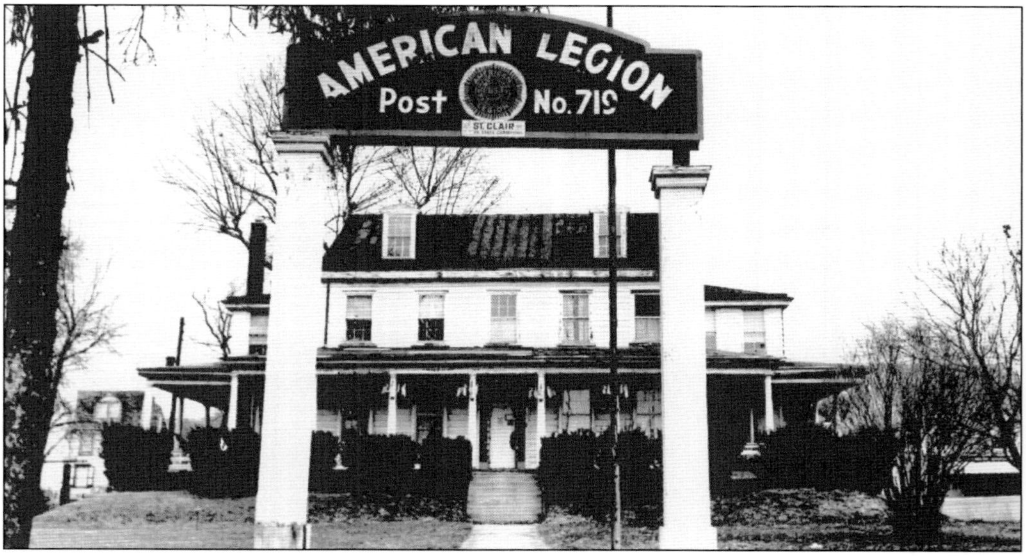

This mansion was built by the Lawton family after 1850, and it was built on an embankment so the cellar was not below ground level since this area of town was swampy. In the early 20th century, the mansion became the Mansion House Hotel, operated by then owner William Gittens. During the Depression, the mansion remained empty until the 1950s, when the members of the American Legion purchased it after outgrowing their building on South Second Street.

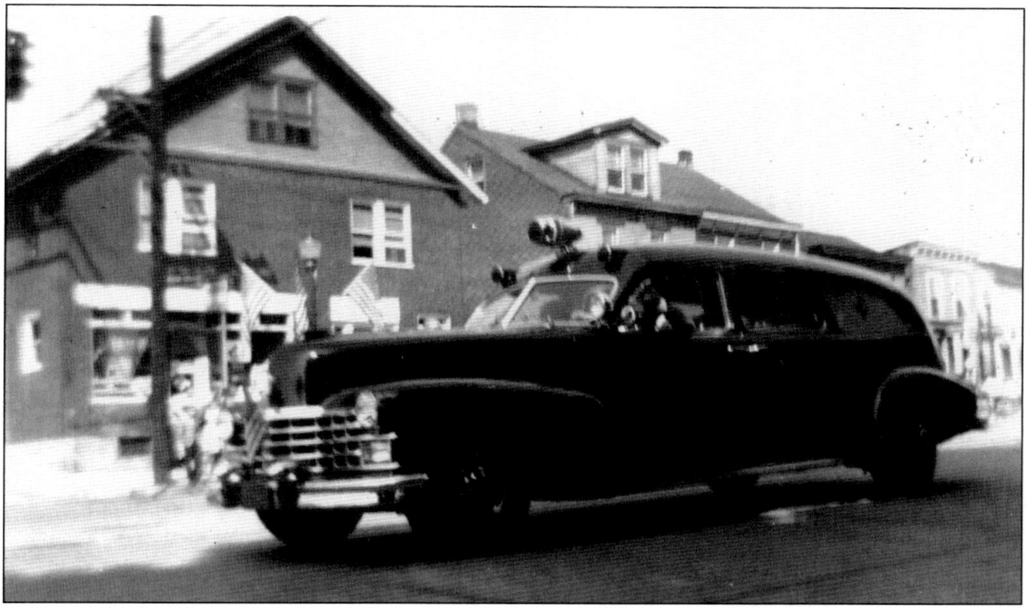

The first ambulance in St. Clair was a hearse purchased by the local miners to transport injured miners to local hospitals. It later grew into an organization called the Veterans Memorial Ambulance, which serves the local St. Clair Area. The photograph of this early ambulance, a 1948 Cadillac, was taken during the Memorial Day parade in 1948.

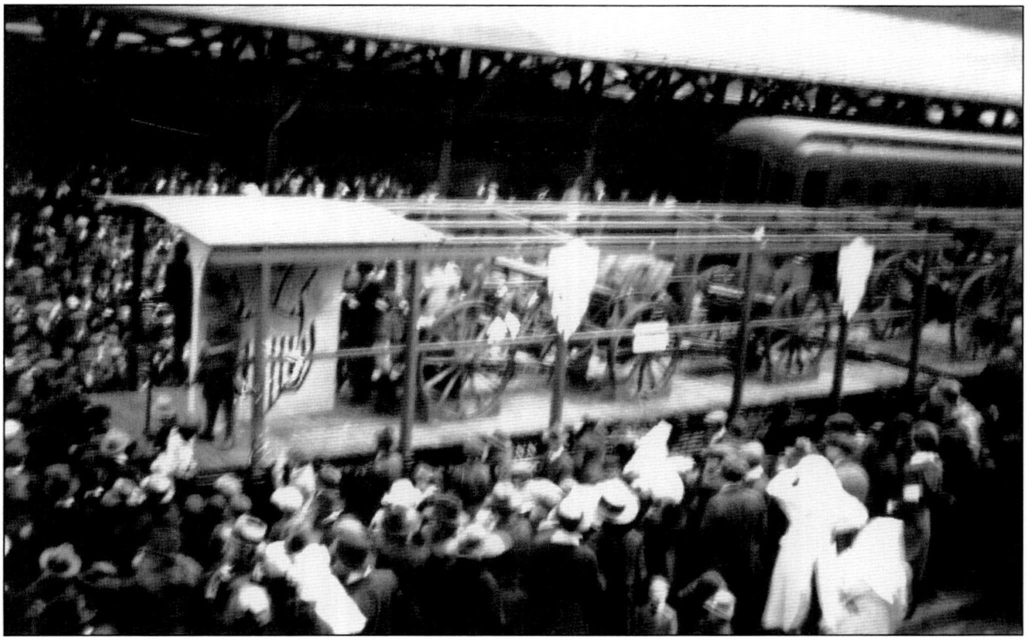

This picture displays the great pride people took in celebrating military accomplishments by Schuylkill County people. This picture is believed to be at the Pottsville railroad station around the World War I era. The history of how or when two post–Civil War cannons came to St. Clair is still unknown, but this photograph may help to unlock the mystery. The cannons sat on the "island" for many years until moved to the stadium with the war memorials.

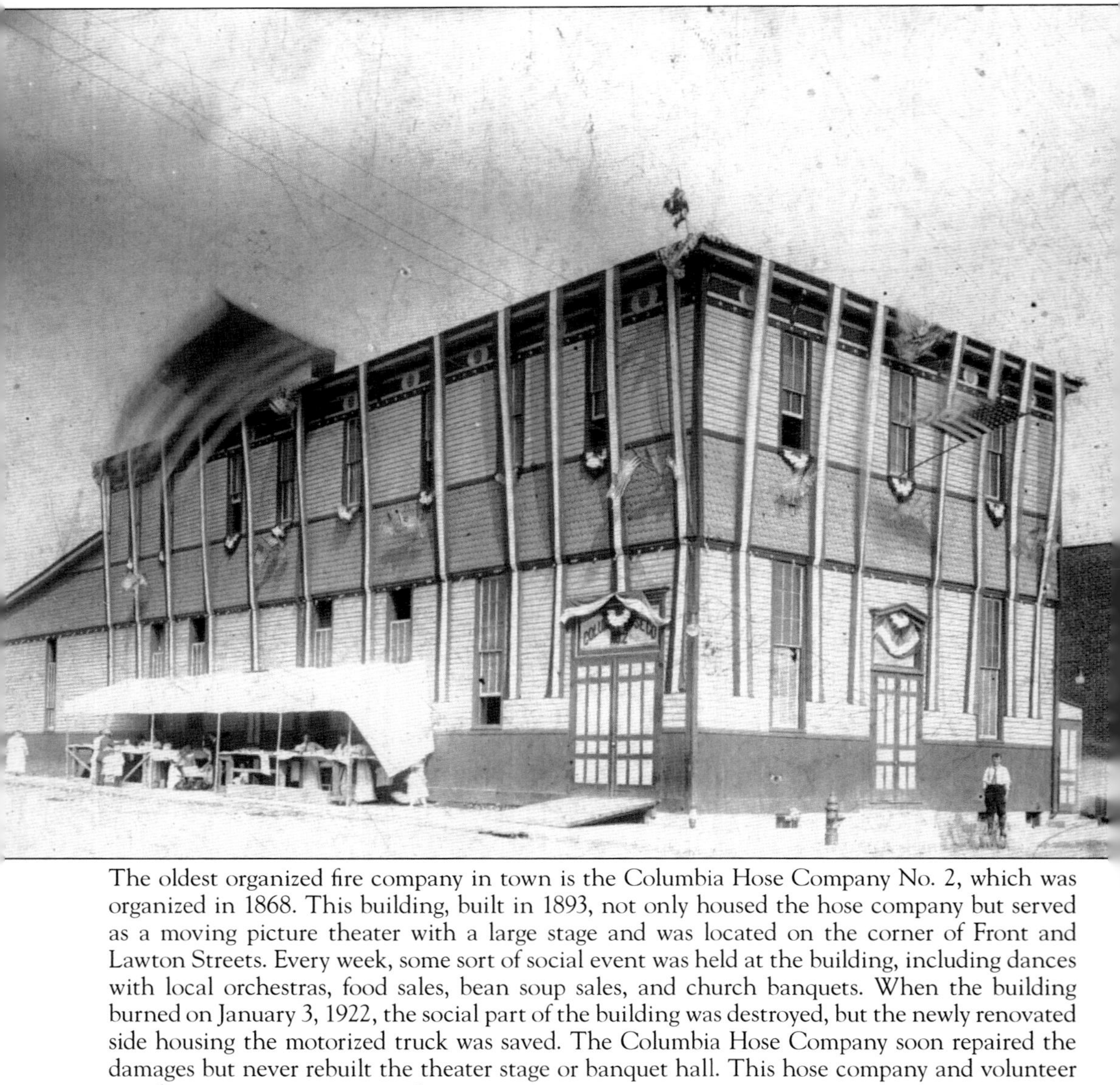

The oldest organized fire company in town is the Columbia Hose Company No. 2, which was organized in 1868. This building, built in 1893, not only housed the hose company but served as a moving picture theater with a large stage and was located on the corner of Front and Lawton Streets. Every week, some sort of social event was held at the building, including dances with local orchestras, food sales, bean soup sales, and church banquets. When the building burned on January 3, 1922, the social part of the building was destroyed, but the newly renovated side housing the motorized truck was saved. The Columbia Hose Company soon repaired the damages but never rebuilt the theater stage or banquet hall. This hose company and volunteer members remain in service today.

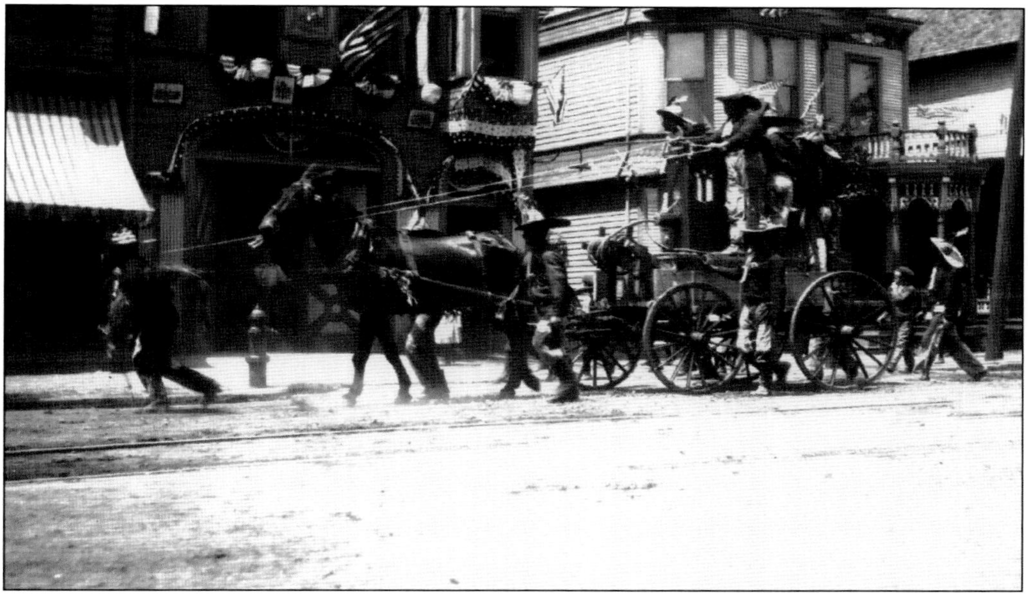

Volunteer firefighters have been a part of St. Clair since 1867, when Hope Fire Company No. 1 was first organized. Early fire apparatus of the first companies were hand pumpers pulled by mules, such as the one in this photograph taken from a grand parade held in 1914. This pumper with the rubber hose was most likely an antique piece at the time of the photograph. (Courtesy of Larry Hyer.)

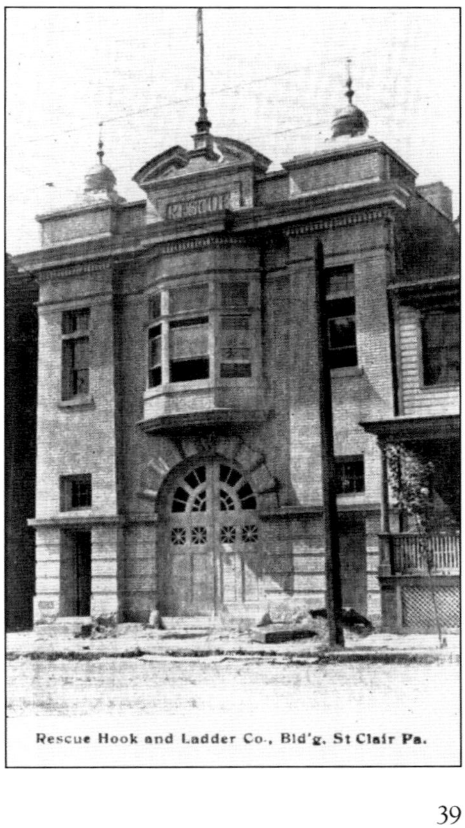

The Rescue Hook and Ladder Company was first organized on January 10, 1898, and its meetings held at the home of W. W. Thorn. The borough purchased a truck and ladder apparatus for this group in March 1898 and allowed the group use of the town hall for storage of the truck. In September 1904, the company decided to build a brick-and-tile building on a plot of land purchased from W. A. Boone on North Second Street. The Rescue Hook and Ladder Company operates out of the same location today.

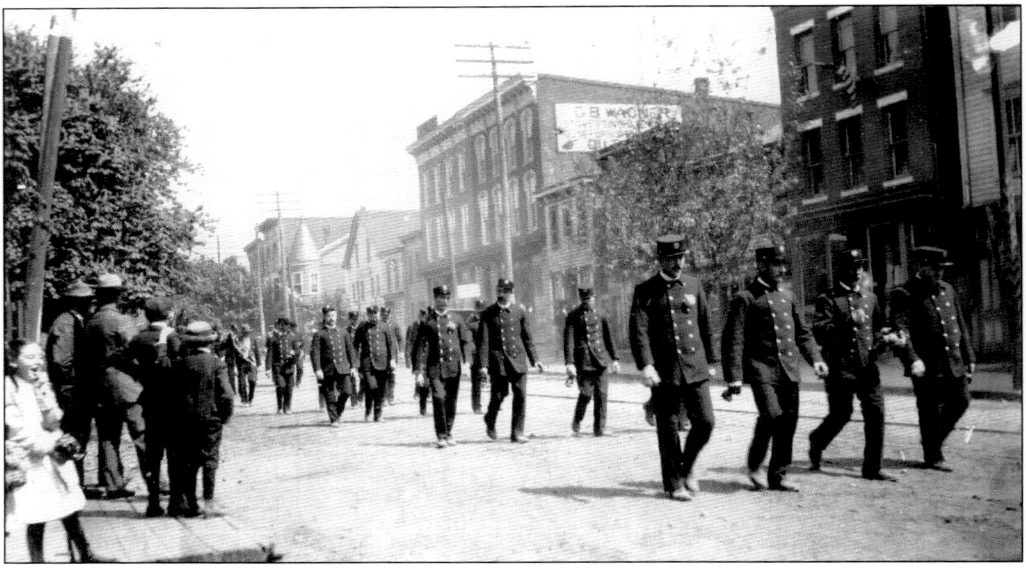

Early volunteer fire companies had highly decorative uniforms used for the many parades, competitions, and conventions. The companies would travel throughout the state for competitions and have won many trophies for the town. This photograph was taken during a parade in St. Clair in 1914. (Courtesy of Larry Hyer.)

HANG UP WHERE HANDY

SAINT CLAIR FIRE ALARM SIGNALS

Box No.	Location	Box No.	Location
12	Kubitska-Pine St.	32	Second & Carroll Sts.
13	Gogotz-Arnout & Dick Sts.	34	Third & Lawton Sts.
14	Balsis-Wade Rd.	35	Nichols & Lawton Sts.
15	William Mick-Shaft Hill	36	Morris & Railroad Sts.
16	Parvin's Hill	41	Second & Railroad Sts.
21	Third & Hancock Sts.	42	Third & Patterson Sts.
23	Second & Franklin Sts.	43	Second & Russell Sts.
24	John's Patch	45	Thwing St.
25	Mill & Sherman Sts.	46	Mill & Patterson St.
26	Nichols & Franklin Sts.	48	Nichols & Russell Sts.
27	Mill & Hancock Sts.	52	East Lawton St.
28	Johnnie's Esso	61	East Mines
31	Morris & Carroll Sts.	62	Rennick's-Diener's Hill

'One Blast' - Line Out of Order

COMPLIMENTS OF:

ALERT FIRE CO. No. 1

"JOIN A VOLUNTEER COMPANY OF YOUR CHOICE ....

BUT....JOIN ONE"

In Case of Fire, Need of Police, Ambulance, or any Emergency, Call

Police Dept. 429-2240 or 628-3792

Electric Light Dept. 429-0640

FIRE DEPARTMENTS

Alert Fire Co.	429-0530
Columbia	429-2350
Rescue	429-0860
Phoenix	429-1180
West End	429-0420
Wadesville	429-9991
Independence	429-0867

This card was a popular handout for fire companies, businesses, and politicians and was the key to the fire alarms in town. Whenever there was a fire, the horn would blast out the number corresponding to the street or area where the fire was located. For example, for number 14, it would be 1 blast, followed by a pause, and then followed up by 4 blasts.

Three

The Railroads

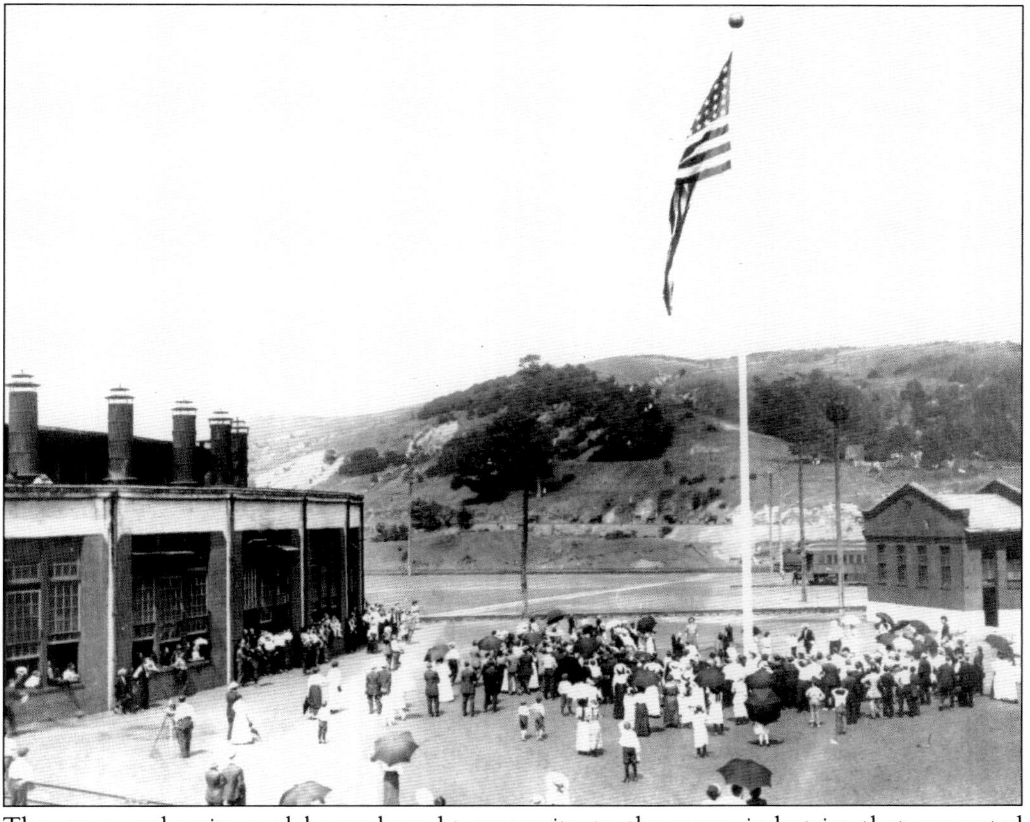

The great anthracite coal boom brought prosperity to the many industries that supported mining. The Reading Railroad expanded its repair shops and yards in St. Clair, creating the largest classified coal yards in the country. Construction of the St. Clair railroad yards was begun in 1909 and completed in 1912. A grand dedication with a formal ceremony was held on May 7, 1913.

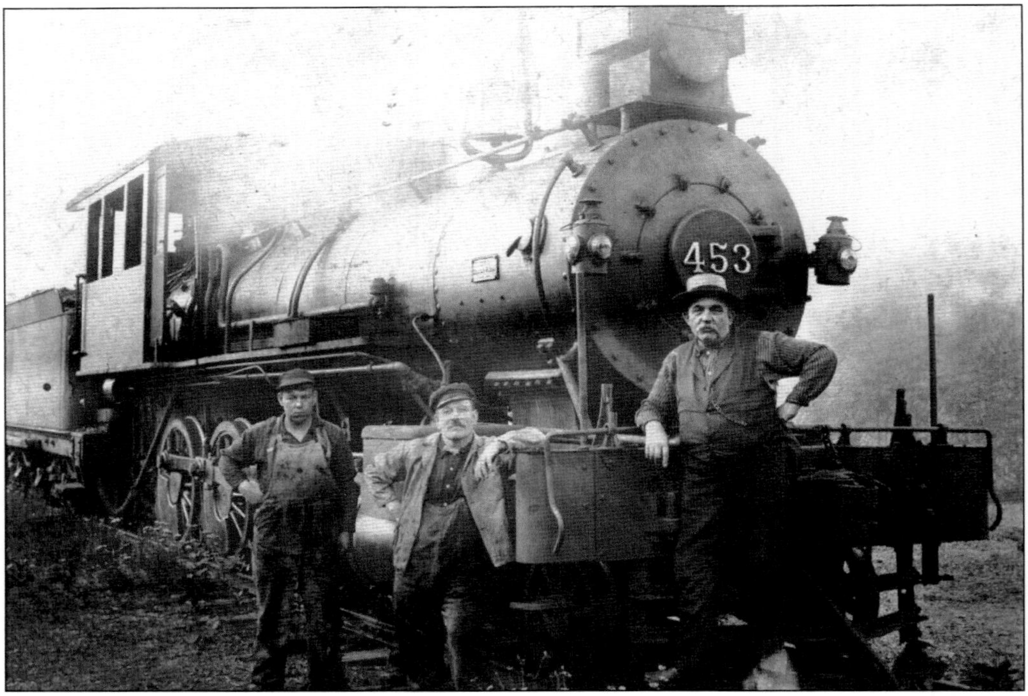

Engine No. 453 is shown with its crew in the St. Clair yards sometime in the late 1920s. The discovery of anthracite coal in Schuylkill County meant the need for transportation of the coal to Philadelphia. Canals were used until the 1860s and began competing with the railroads in the late 1840s. In the 1870s, the railroads won out by offering a faster more economical way to ship the coal to market.

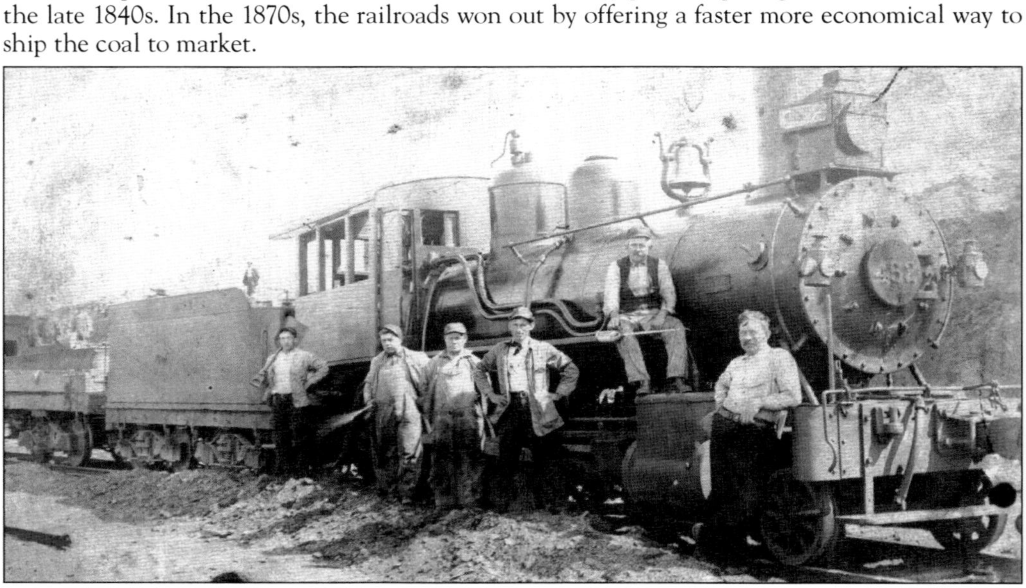

Over 1,200 men and 25 supervisors were employed at the St. Clair yards when working at full capacity. Workers are shown standing around engine No. 452 in the late 1920s. In the early 1960s, the Reading Company closed the once famous railroad yards. Car runners carried what appear to be baseball bats but were really sprag sticks used to manually operate car brakes on the gravity tracks.

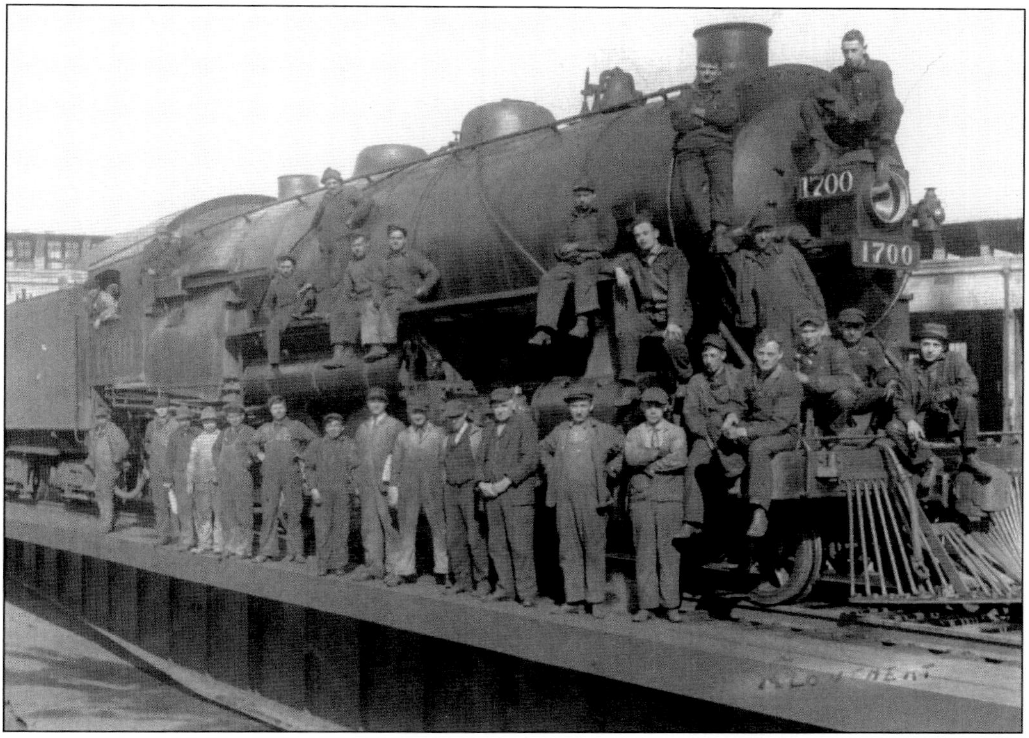

The demand for coal began to decline after World War II. New technologies and new transportation trends helped to change the coal regions and bring an end to the railroading in St. Clair. The last day for steam locomotives that pulled and pushed loaded coal cars to the scales for weighing was November 1, 1953.

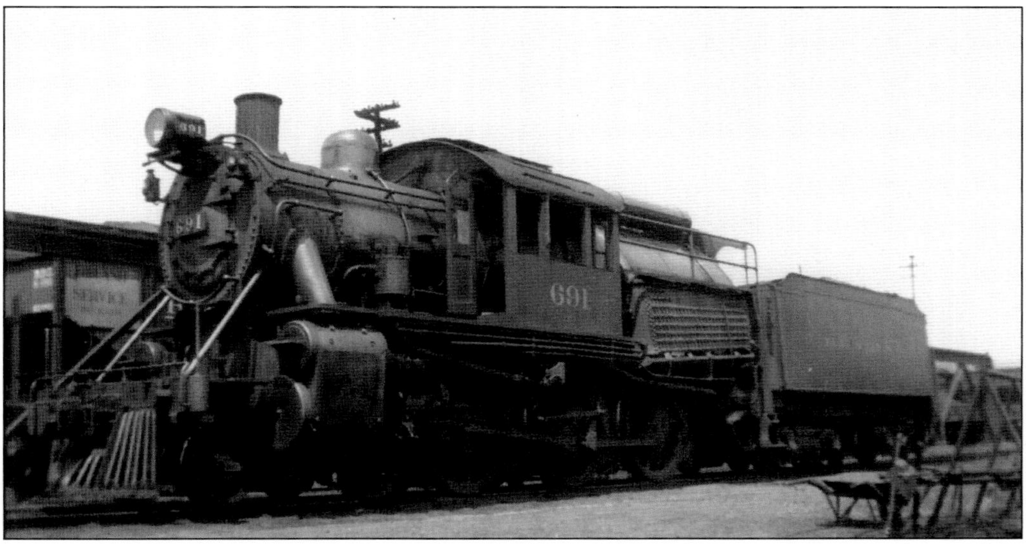

This steam engine photograph was taken at the St. Clair rail yards on June 13, 1937. The Reading Railroad became famous nationwide in 1935 when introduced as a property selling for $200 on the still-popular game Monopoly. One of the playing pieces is a steam train just like the one in this picture.

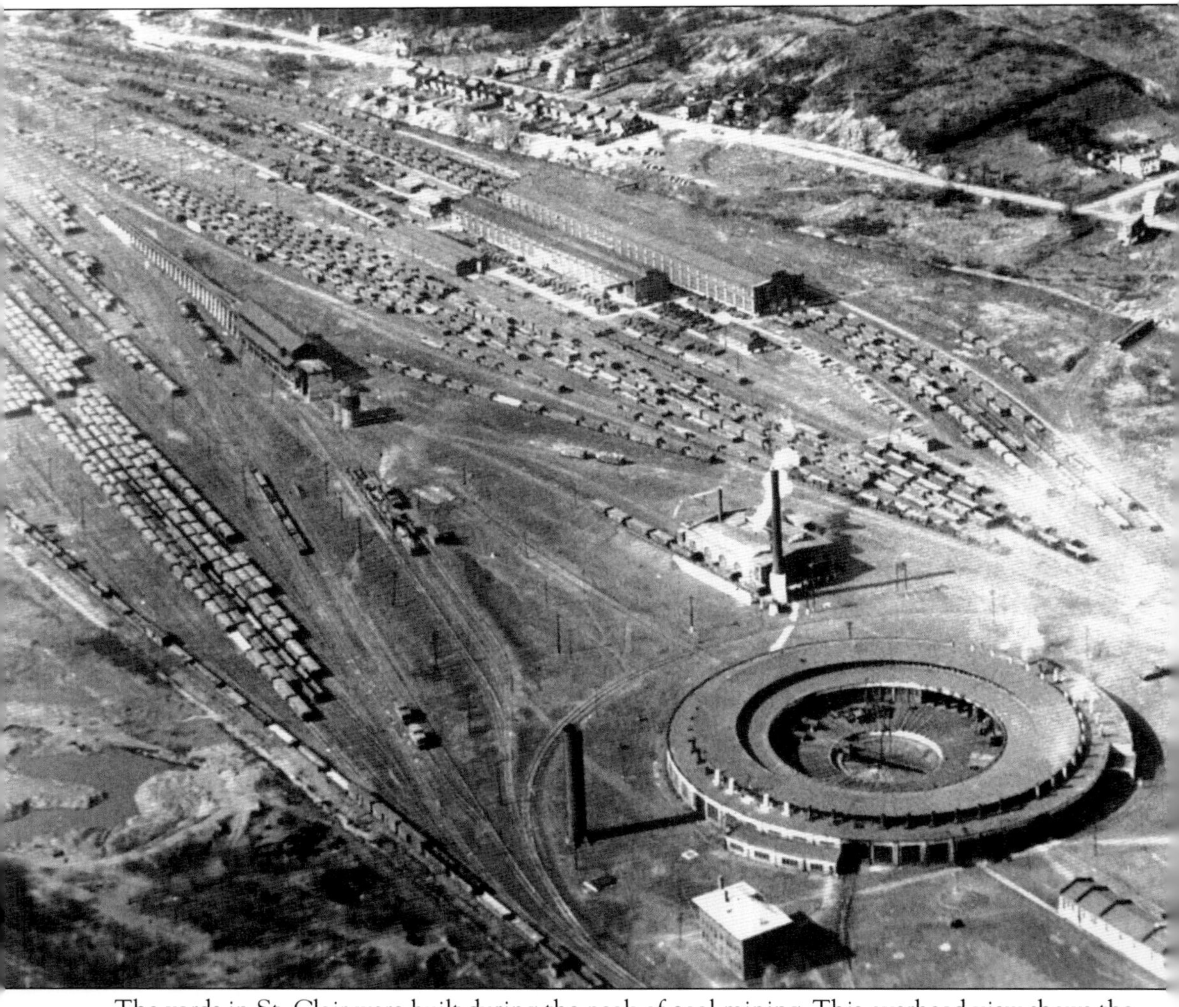

The yards in St. Clair were built during the peak of coal mining. This overhead view shows the St. Clair rail yards and the huge roundhouse located just south of the town. Being the largest coal yard in the world made St. Clair a target in World War II, since disrupting the rail lines would have a disastrous effect on the economy. The great roundhouse closed in 1964 and was demolished in 1972.

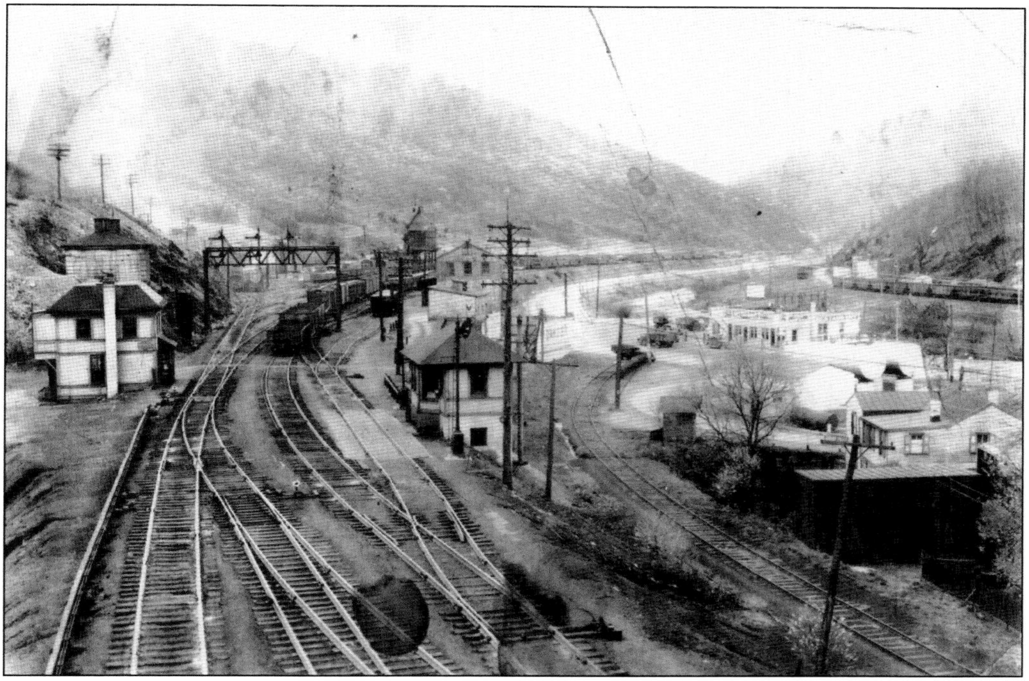

Shown are the Pennsylvania railroad yards at Mount Carbon just outside Pottsville. Visible are three major means of transportation, the train tracks and the main vehicle highway connecting the local towns in the county. The Reading Railroad is on the far right, and the Pennsylvania "Pennsy" Railroad is shown on the left.

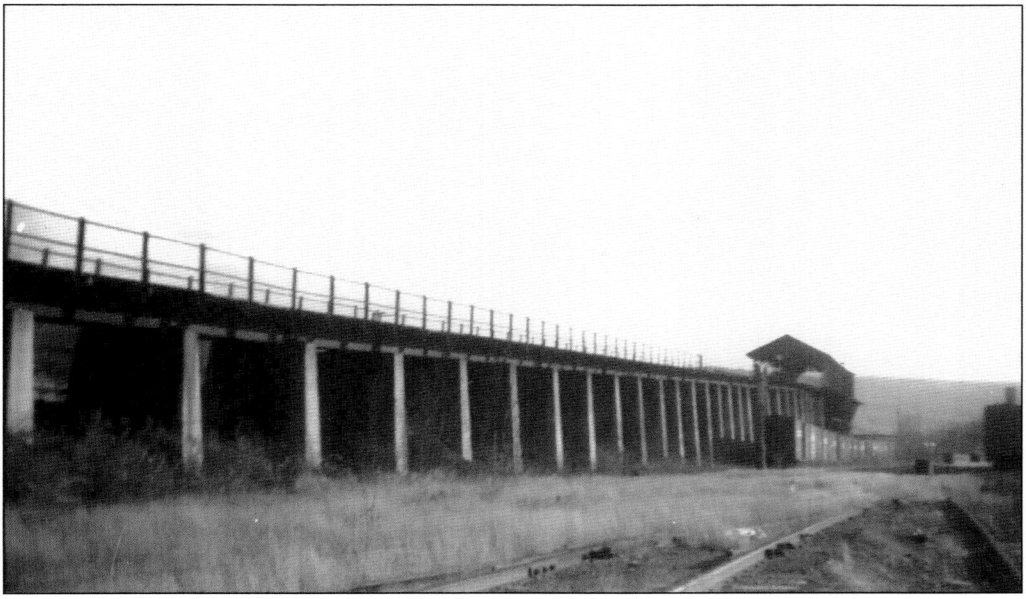

The coal docks shown in this photograph were used to supply coal for operation of the steam engines. In the 1930s, carloads of unprepared coal were moved from the mines to the breakers and loaded cars at the breakers were sent to St. Clair, grouped, and then sent to their market destination. Loaded coal cars carried about 80 tons of coal.

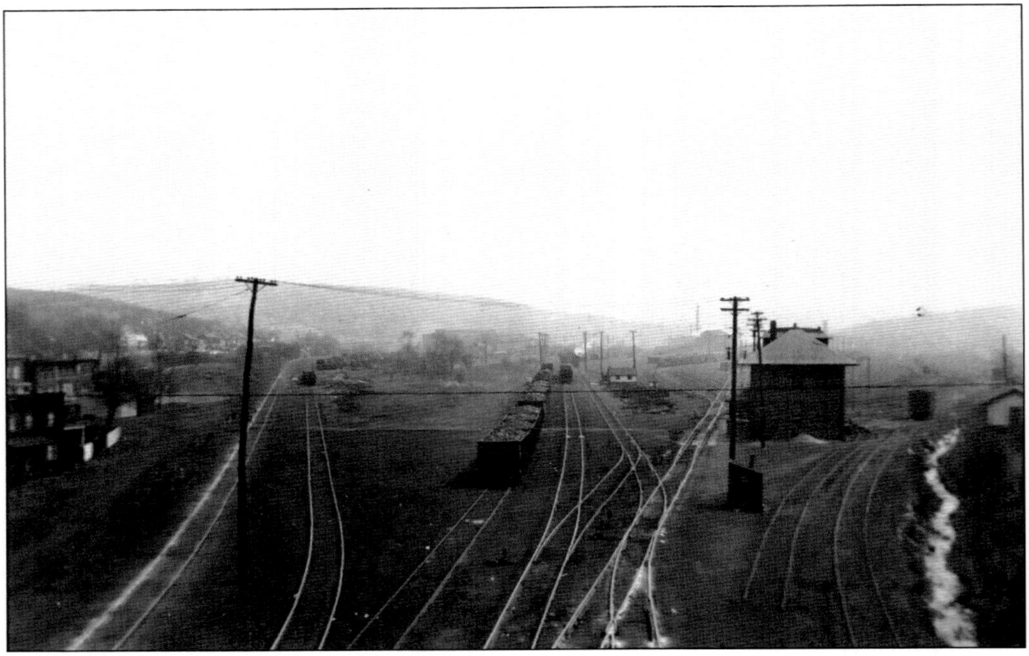

The office and scale are shown in this photograph of the yards. During the height of service of the St. Clair yards, the Reading Company employed over 1,000 men. All trains of empty cars were made up at the yards and dispatched to the northern collieries (north of the Broad Mountain), and all loaded cars were assembled and sent to the southern markets.

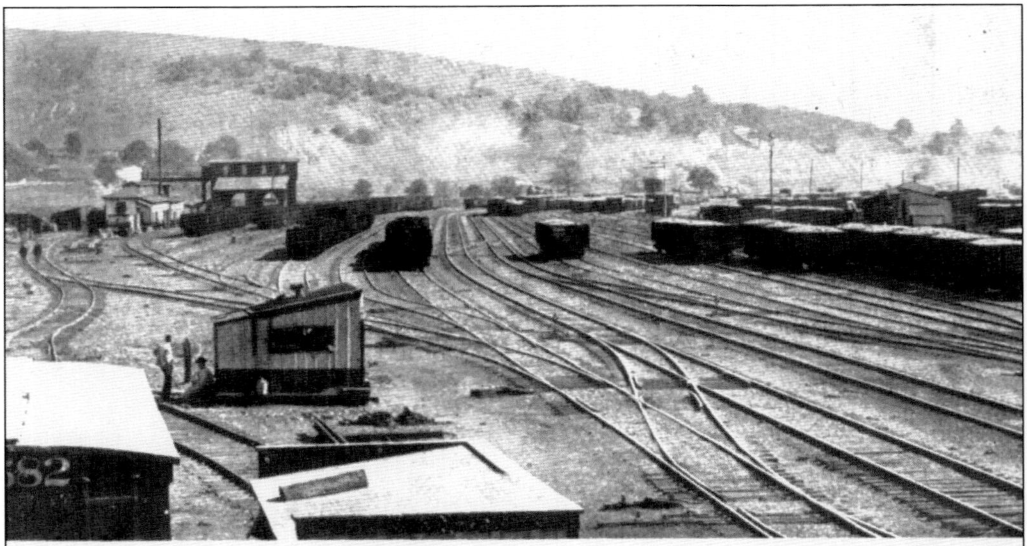

At the rail yards, there was a powerhouse; oil-house; warehouse; heavy, intermediate, and light car repair shops; coaling station; and ash pits, where the engines dropped their ashes. There were 63 tracks that covered 46.5 miles with a capacity for over 2,000 cars, and an engine house large enough to contain 52 locomotives.

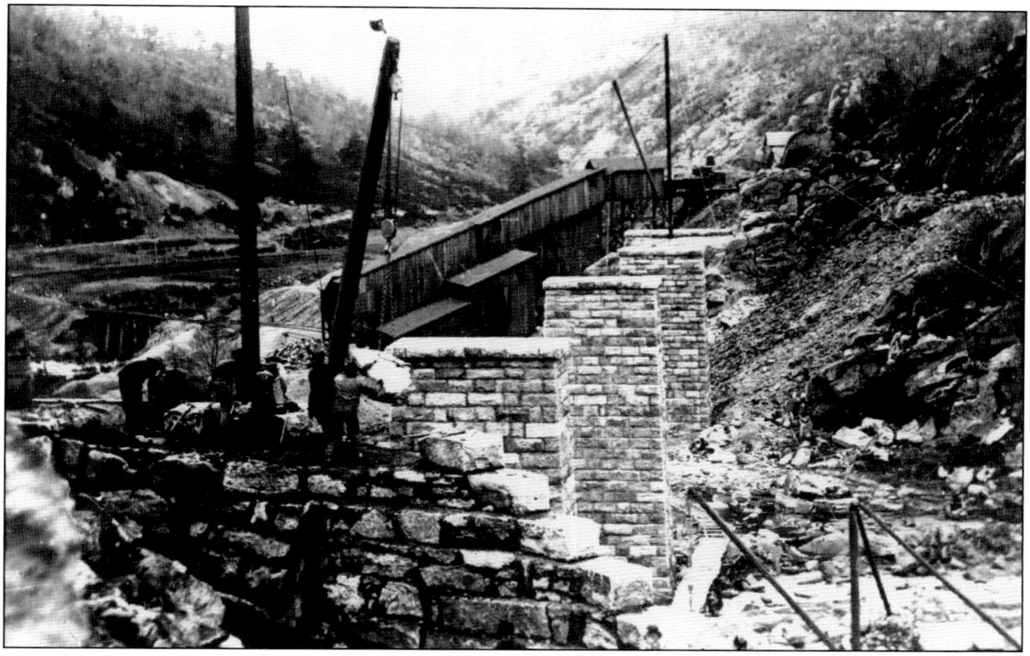

In 1887, about a year before the Pennsylvania Railroad tracks reached Pottsville from the south, the men were putting up the stone foundations for the imposing trestle that bridged the gorge above St. Clair. A little farther south, men were cutting a tunnel between St. Clair and Pottsville in preparation for the arrival of the first train of passenger cars over the new railroad at St. Clair. This train ran for the first time on September 4, 1886.

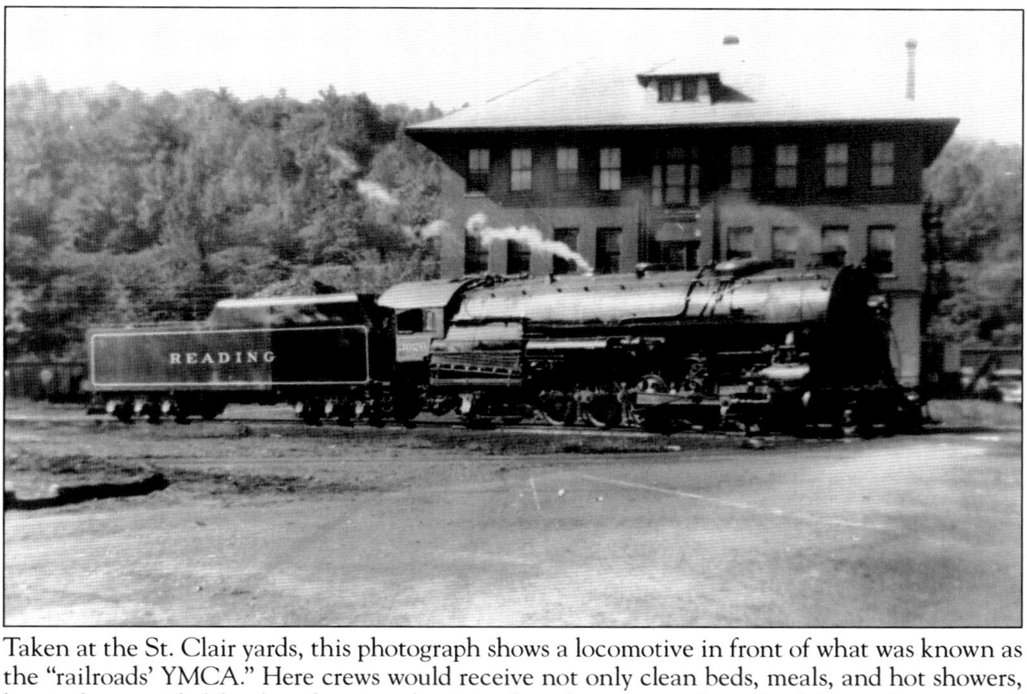

Taken at the St. Clair yards, this photograph shows a locomotive in front of what was known as the "railroads' YMCA." Here crews would receive not only clean beds, meals, and hot showers, but it also provided for the educational, spiritual, and recreational needs of the workers.

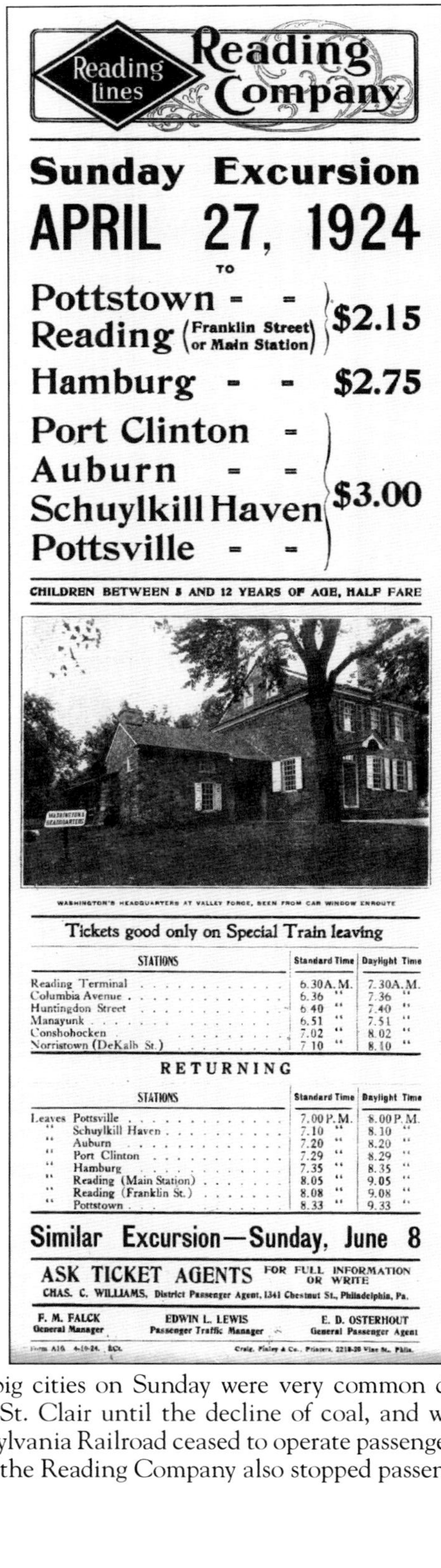

Reading Lines

Reading Company

Sunday Excursion

APRIL 27, 1924

TO

Pottstown - -	$2.15
Reading (Franklin Street or Main Station)	$2.15
Hamburg - -	$2.75
Port Clinton -	$3.00
Auburn - -	$3.00
Schuylkill Haven	$3.00
Pottsville - -	$3.00

CHILDREN BETWEEN 5 AND 12 YEARS OF AGE, HALF FARE

WASHINGTON'S HEADQUARTERS AT VALLEY FORGE, SEEN FROM CAR WINDOW ENROUTE

Tickets good only on Special Train leaving

STATIONS	Standard Time	Daylight Time
Reading Terminal	6.30 A.M.	7.30 A.M.
Columbia Avenue	6.36 "	7.36 "
Huntingdon Street	6.40 "	7.40 "
Manayunk	6.51 "	7.51 "
Conshohocken	7.02 "	8.02 "
Norristown (DeKalb St.)	7.10 "	8.10 "

RETURNING

STATIONS	Standard Time	Daylight Time
Leaves Pottsville	7.00 P.M.	8.00 P.M.
" Schuylkill Haven	7.10 "	8.10 "
" Auburn	7.20 "	8.20 "
" Port Clinton	7.29 "	8.29 "
" Hamburg	7.35 "	8.35 "
" Reading (Main Station)	8.05 "	9.05 "
" Reading (Franklin St.)	8.08 "	9.08 "
" Pottstown	8.33 "	9.33 "

Similar Excursion—Sunday, June 8

ASK TICKET AGENTS FOR FULL INFORMATION OR WRITE

CHAS. C. WILLIAMS, District Passenger Agent, 1341 Chestnut St., Philadelphia, Pa.

F. M. FALCK, General Manager — EDWIN L. LEWIS, Passenger Traffic Manager — E. D. OSTERHOUT, General Passenger Agent

Form A16 4-10-24. 8Ct. — Craig, Finley & Co., Printers, 2218-20 Vine St., Phila.

Train excursions to the big cities on Sunday were very common during the booming 1920s. The railroads thrived in St. Clair until the decline of coal, and with the dawning of trolley transportation, the Pennsylvania Railroad ceased to operate passenger service to the community in 1940. Eight years later, the Reading Company also stopped passenger service to the town.

Four

The Great Coal Era

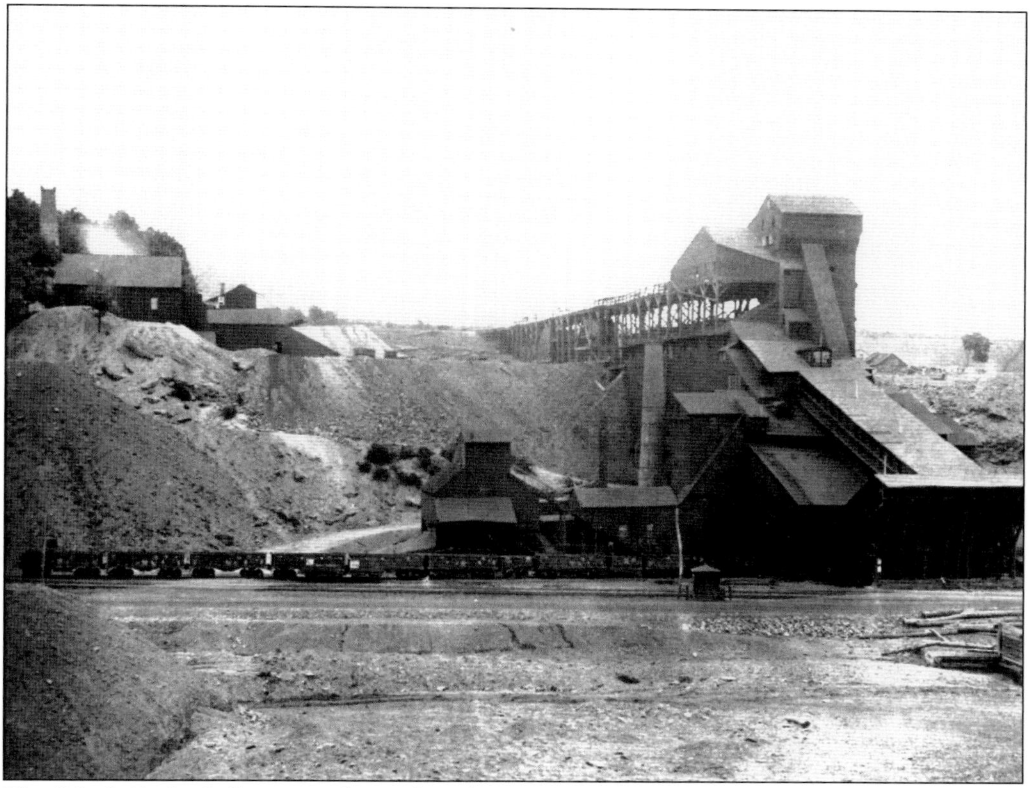

The John's Eagle Colliery was located at the northeastern end of town and was first opened around 1831 and worked to a limited extent. Thomas and William Johns made improvements to the colliery and operated it successfully for a quarter of a century. The Johns brothers were among the few prosperous mine owners who actually lived near their colliery. Their home was known as Johns Mansion until it burned in the 1980s.

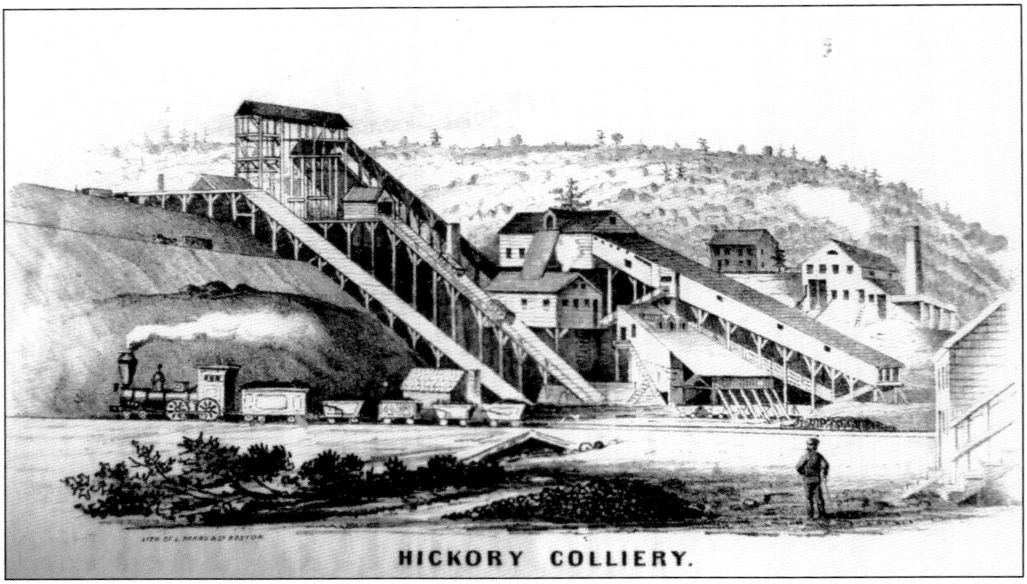

This sketch from 1866 shows the Hickory Colliery, which was located across the creek, southwest of the St. Clair Coal Company. It was operated by Beck and Woodside from 1825 to 1835. John Pinkerton ran it from 1835 to 1844. Pinkerton dug a ventilation tunnel north to an earlier drift. This mine at its prime produced 100,000 tons per year. Benjamin and William Milnes purchased the mine from Pinkerton and sank a new slope continuing westward.

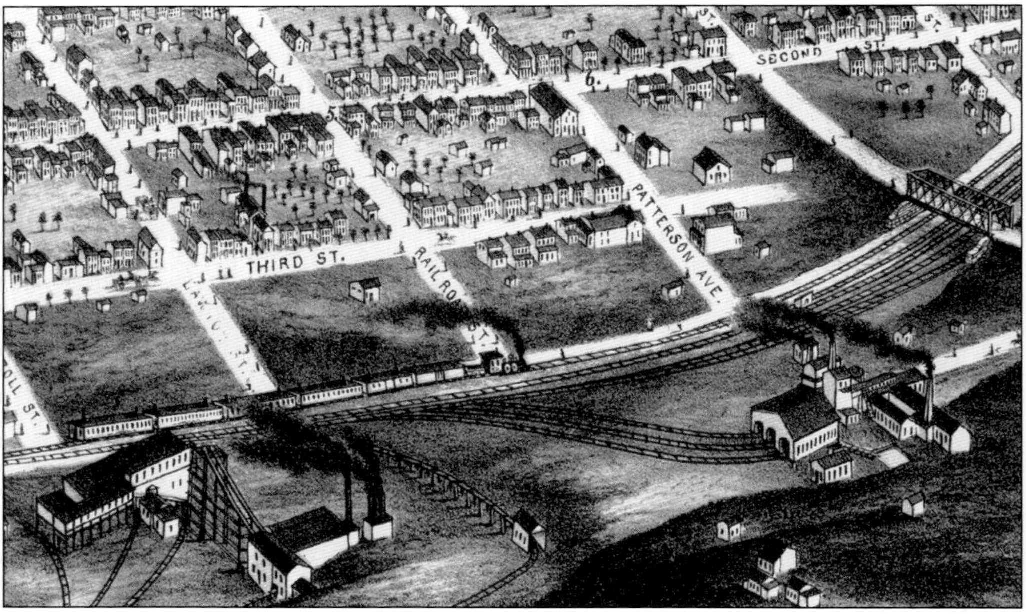

The town's early industrial growth began with the iron business located at the southwestern part of town on Second Street. The St. Clair Furnace, or Patterson Iron Furnace, owned by Burd Patterson, was put into blast in 1842 and was smelting 75 tons of anthracite iron per week. The St. Clair Shaft pictured on the sketch, located on the west side of town at the end of Carroll Street, was the first vertical shaft sunk to the Mammoth Vein in the anthracite region. The breaker was started up in October 1854 and was sunk to a depth of 30 feet of coal.

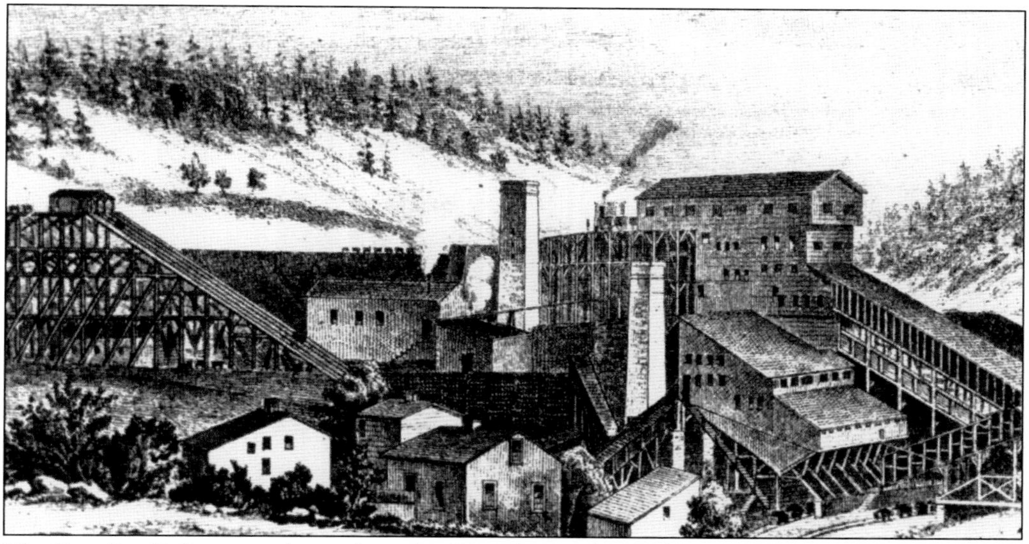

The Repplier Colliery was located north of St. Clair in the Darkwater–New Castle area. It began as a drift opened by the Neny brothers. Around 1840, Joseph Lawton began operations at that location and named it the Mammoth Colliery. In approximately 1850, a St. Clair merchant, George S. Repplier, purchased the colliery, renaming it the Repplier Colliery. The colliery operated off and on until closing sometime in the 1950s.

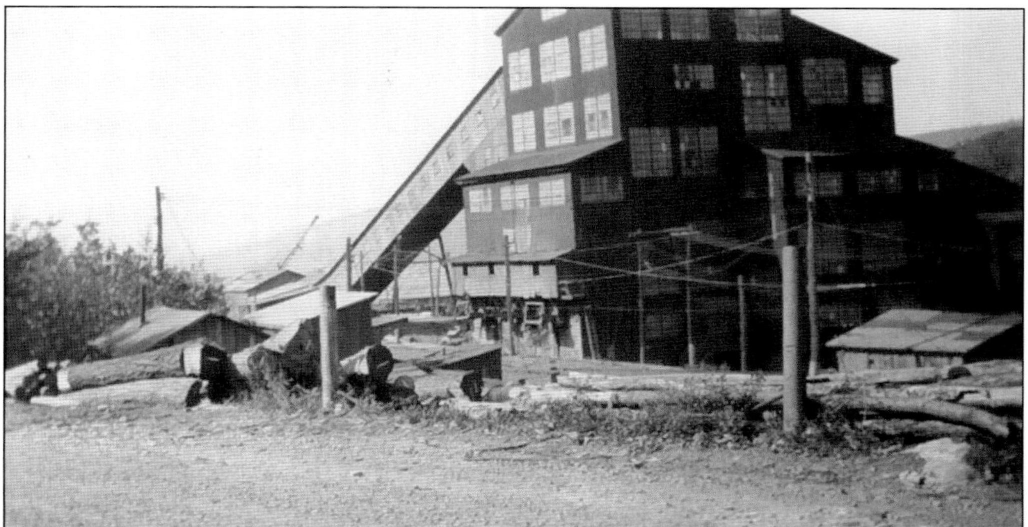

This picture of the Repplier Colliery was taken in the early 1940s, shortly before it was destroyed by fire in 1946. The Repplier was rebuilt and continued operation until the early 1950s. After closing, the entire area was strip-mined.

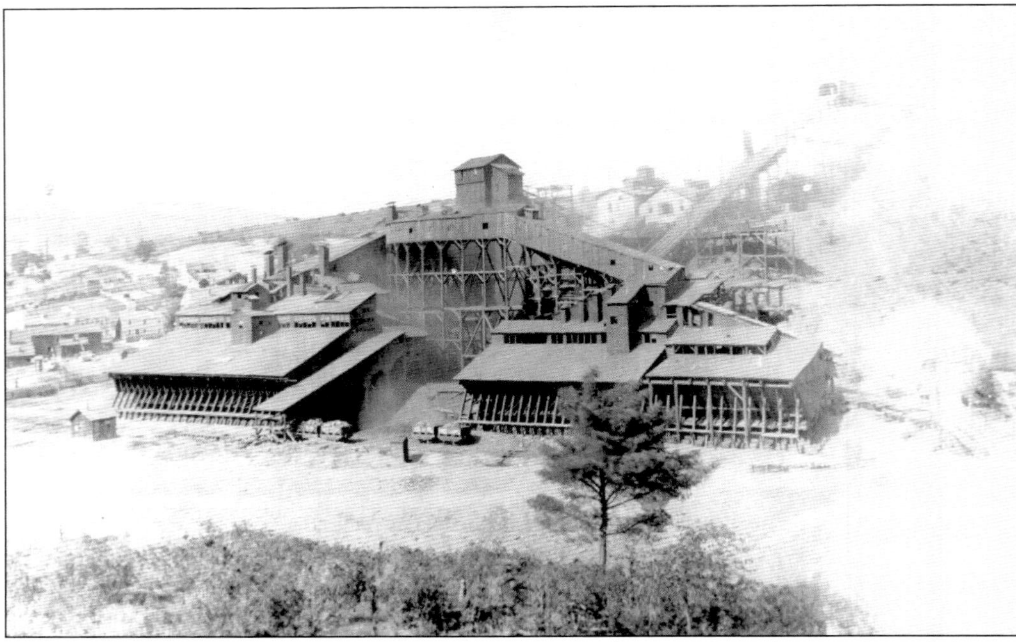

The Wadesville Colliery, located in the village of Wadesville west of St. Clair, was formerly known as the Hickory Shaft, which was a continuation of the Old Hickory Colliery water level workings and slopes. Excavations started on a shaft in 1864, when a depth of 666 feet was reached. The property was sold on September 25, 1876, by the sheriff to the Pennsylvania Reading Coal and Iron Company. The colliery operated only on Fridays for two years prior to it closing in March 1932.

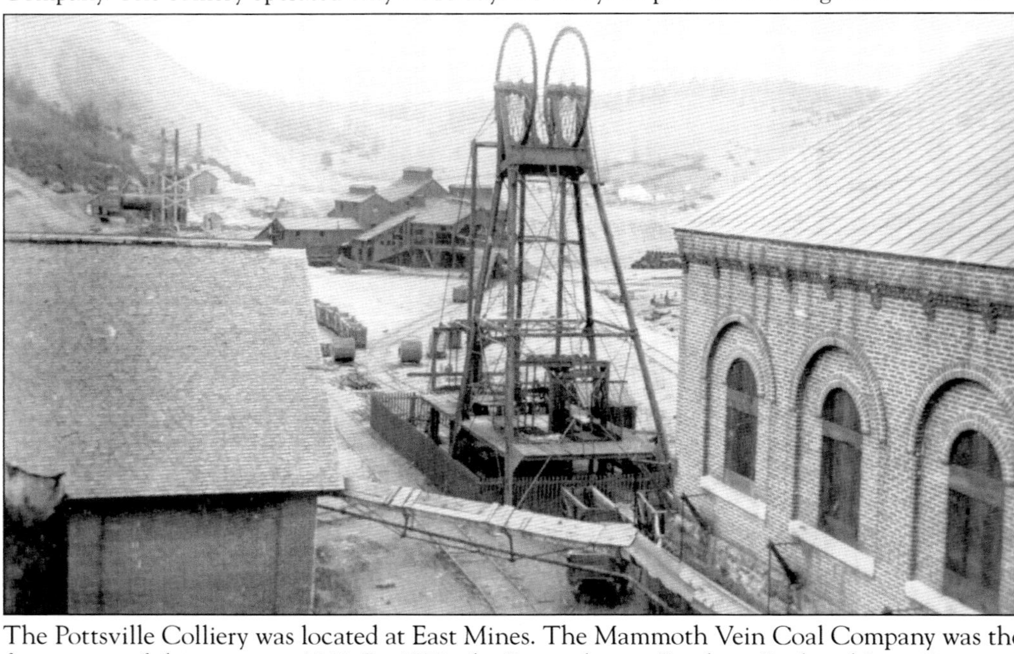

The Pottsville Colliery was located at East Mines. The Mammoth Vein Coal Company was the first owner of this mine in 1869. By 1870, the Pennsylvania Reading Coal and Iron Company gained control and continued mine operations. There were two shafts to this mine, and both were considered the deepest mine in the county at the time. The mine closed in 1884.

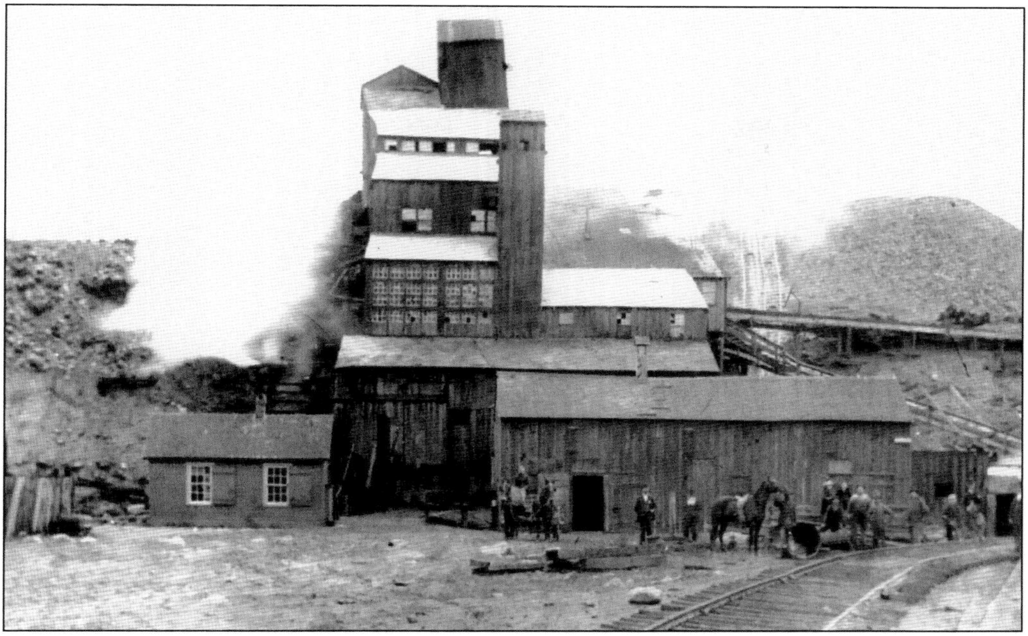

The Hooker Colliery was located at the end of East Carroll and Price Streets and was formerly known as the Jackson Colliery. It began operation in the early 1870s, and in 1908, the lease was taken over by I. D. Beahm and Company and operations ceased following World War I. At the south end of town, there was a huge bridge known as the White Bridge that crossed over South Mill and Nichols Streets, providing railroad service to the Hooker Colliery.

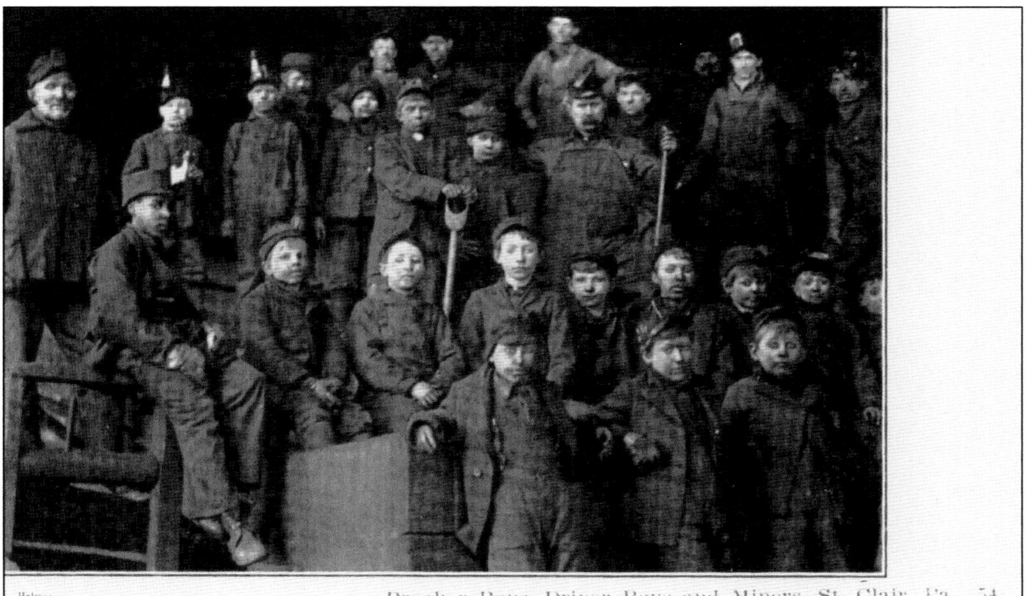

After the coal is brought to the surface, it goes through a machine called a breaker. Then the young boys, called "breaker boys," would separate the slate and rock from the coal. Older men who had injuries and could no longer do the work might end their mining career as they started, working above the ground as slate pickers.

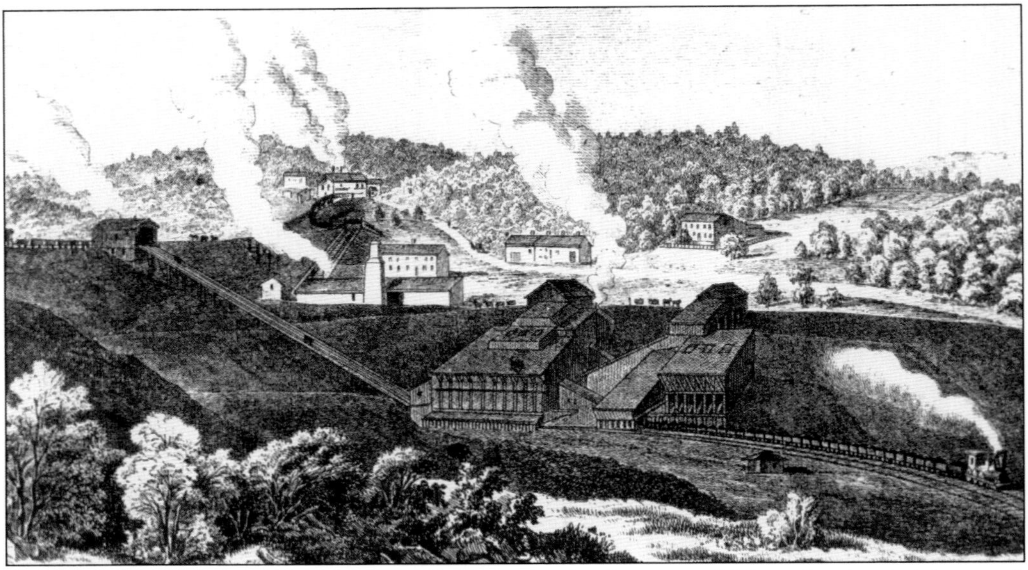

Pine Forest Colliery was opened in High Germany by Benjamin Milnes, Benjamin Haywood, and George Snyder in 1845 and was part of the Mammoth Vein. In November 1866, the owners sank a vertical shaft, but ventilation was a problem. In 1872, Snyder sold the colliery to the Philadelphia and Reading Coal and Iron Company. In 1890, the colliery was reopened but closed down again in 1899. Reading Anthracite operated the Pine Forest Colliery strip-mining until 1986.

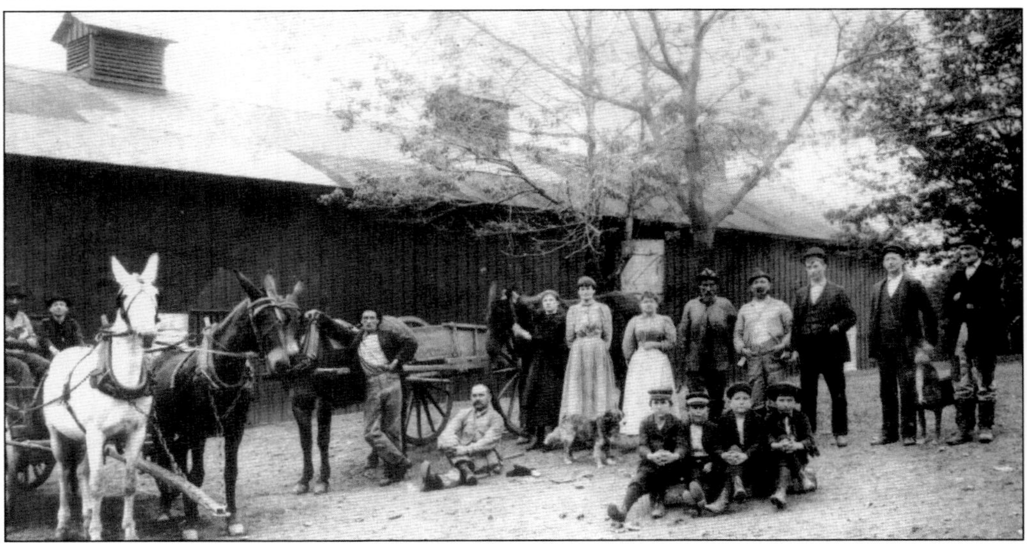

On March 19, 1898, Pine Forest Colliery was given orders to shut down. Foremen Tiley and Archibald McDonald had been sent instructions to suspend all work and prepare to remove the machinery. A few men finished out 1898 by removing boilers, pumps, and anything else that could be sent to another colliery. Between 400 and 500 men and boys were thrown idle. Most of them resided in St. Clair. Pictured are, from left to right, Doc Malia, ? Taylor, ? Wood, ? Betz, Cecelia McDonald, Kate McDonald, Mary (McDonald) Frew, foreman Archibald McDonald, foreman Tiley, James McDonald, Tim Clark, and Sam Seitzinger. In front are three Tiley boys and Joseph Frew.

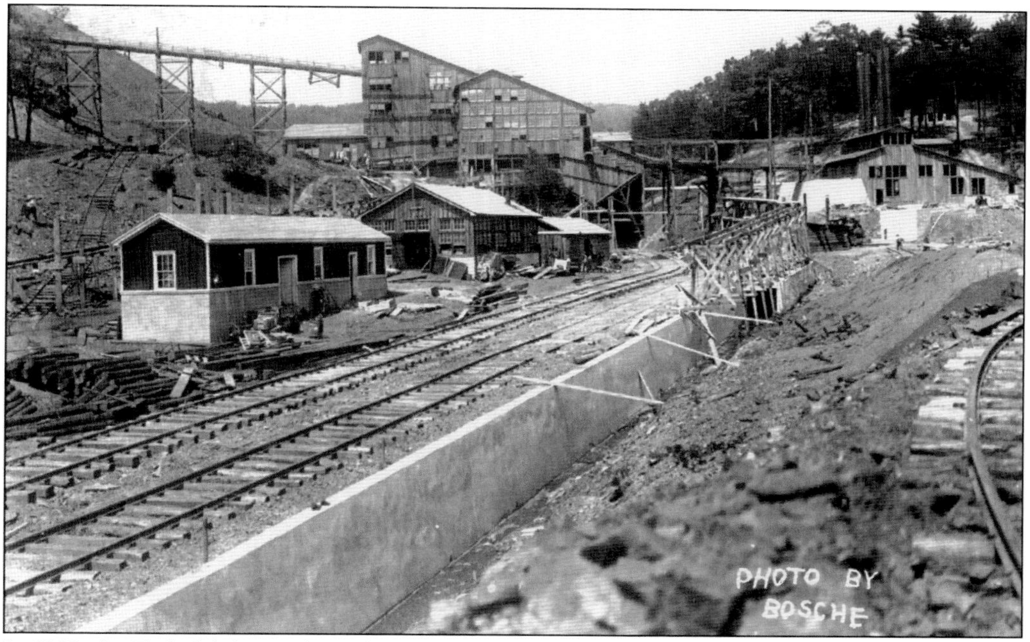

In 1889, the Philadelphia and Reading Coal and Iron Company reopened the Pine Forest Colliery after it was abandoned in 1885. Mining continued until 1898, at which time it was abandoned as "worked out." Later a washery was constructed, and the old Pine Forest Colliery culm banks were run through to reclaim fine coal that was discarded from the first mining operations.

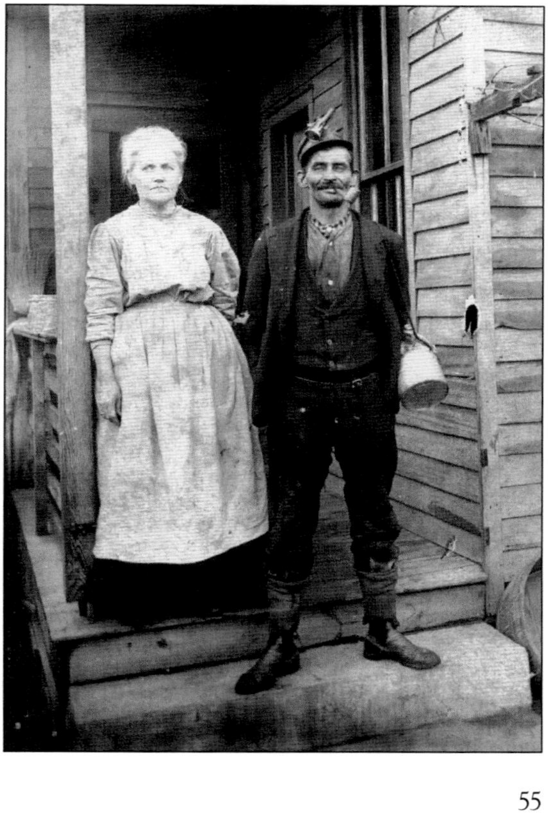

Posing on the back porch of their home located at 221 South Nichols Street are Joseph and Maryann (Roberts) Silcox. The photograph, taken in 1910, shows Joseph, a miner at the Hooker Colliery, still in his work clothes and carrying his lunch tin. Joseph died in 1913 of miners' asthma. (Courtesy of David Silcox.)

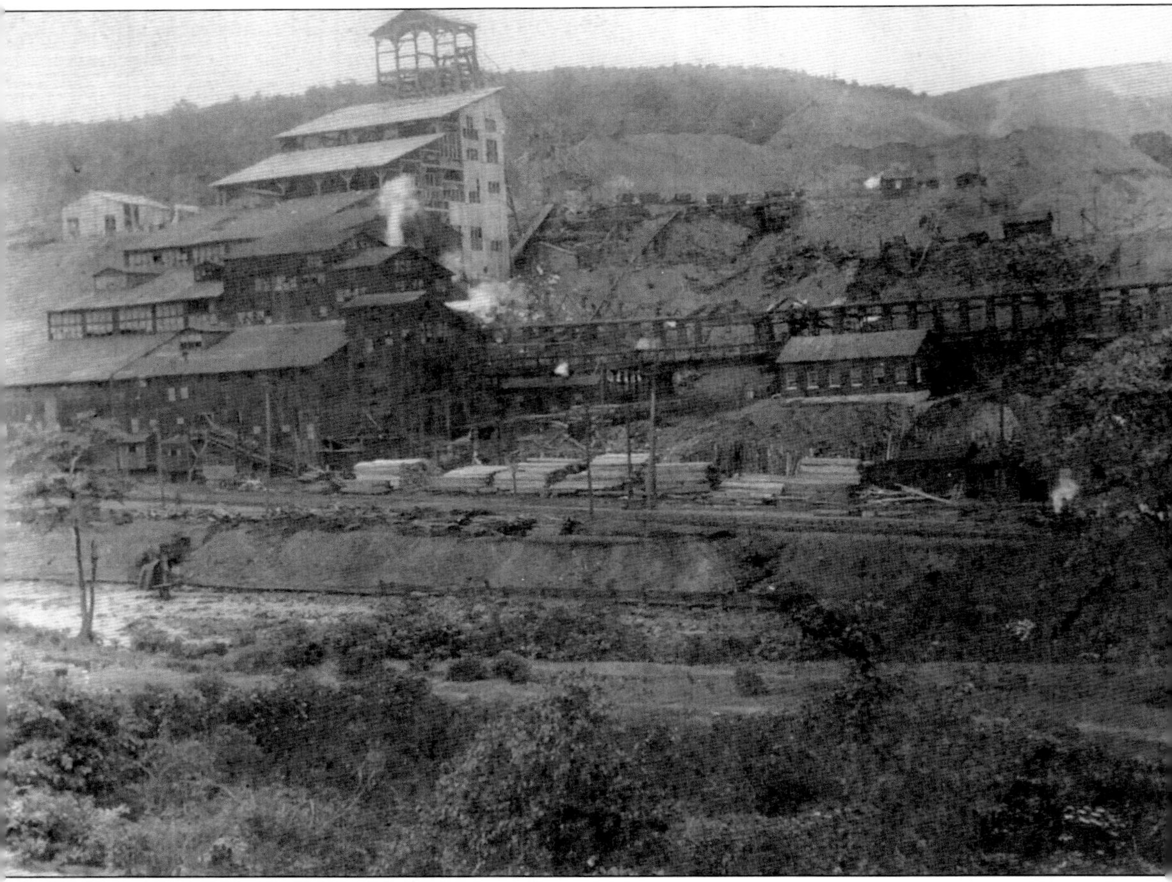

The Herbine Colliery was the former John's Eagle Colliery, located at the north end of town. The colliery was operated by the St. Clair Coal Company and employed 600 men and boys and shipped 2,000 tons of coal daily. This location was the longest-running coal-producing area in

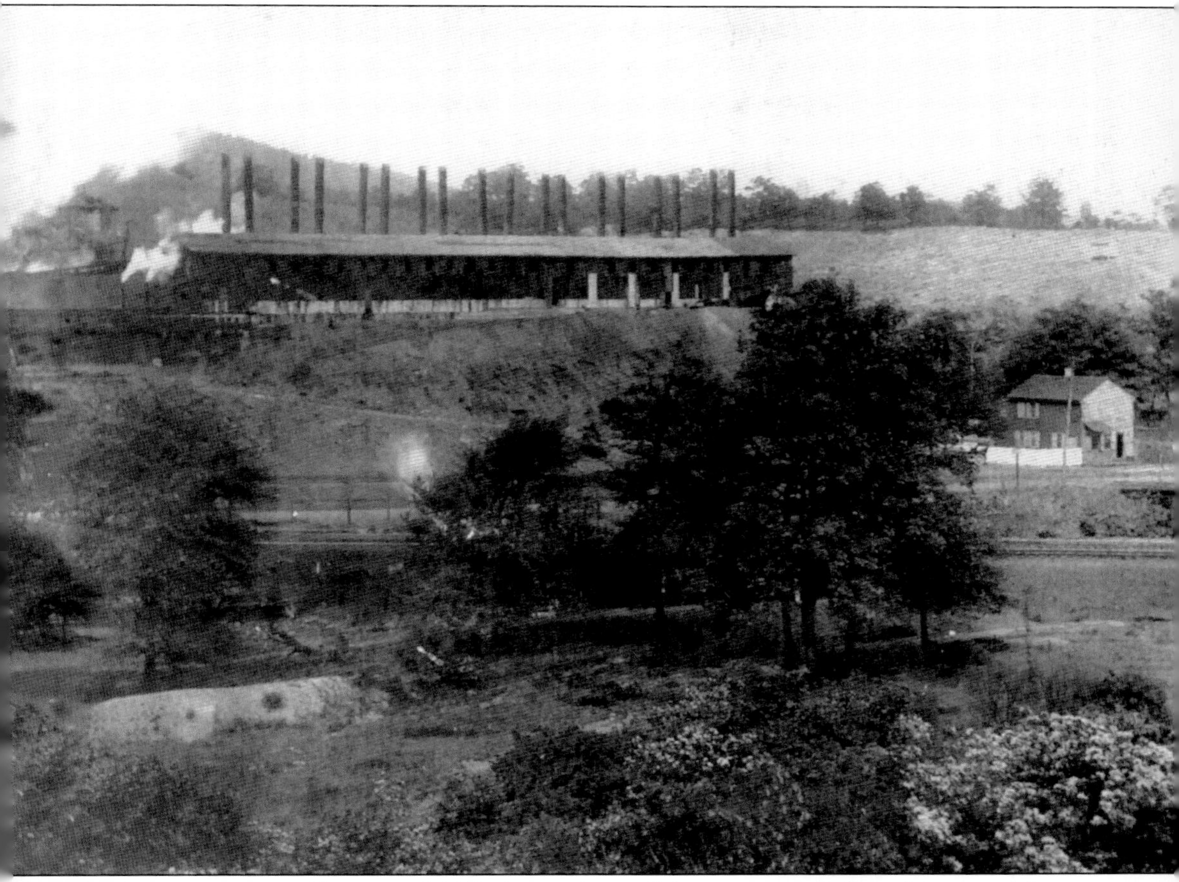

town. Operations existed here until 1957, but coal is still being removed from this area today. (Courtesy of Laura B. Davenport Thomas.)

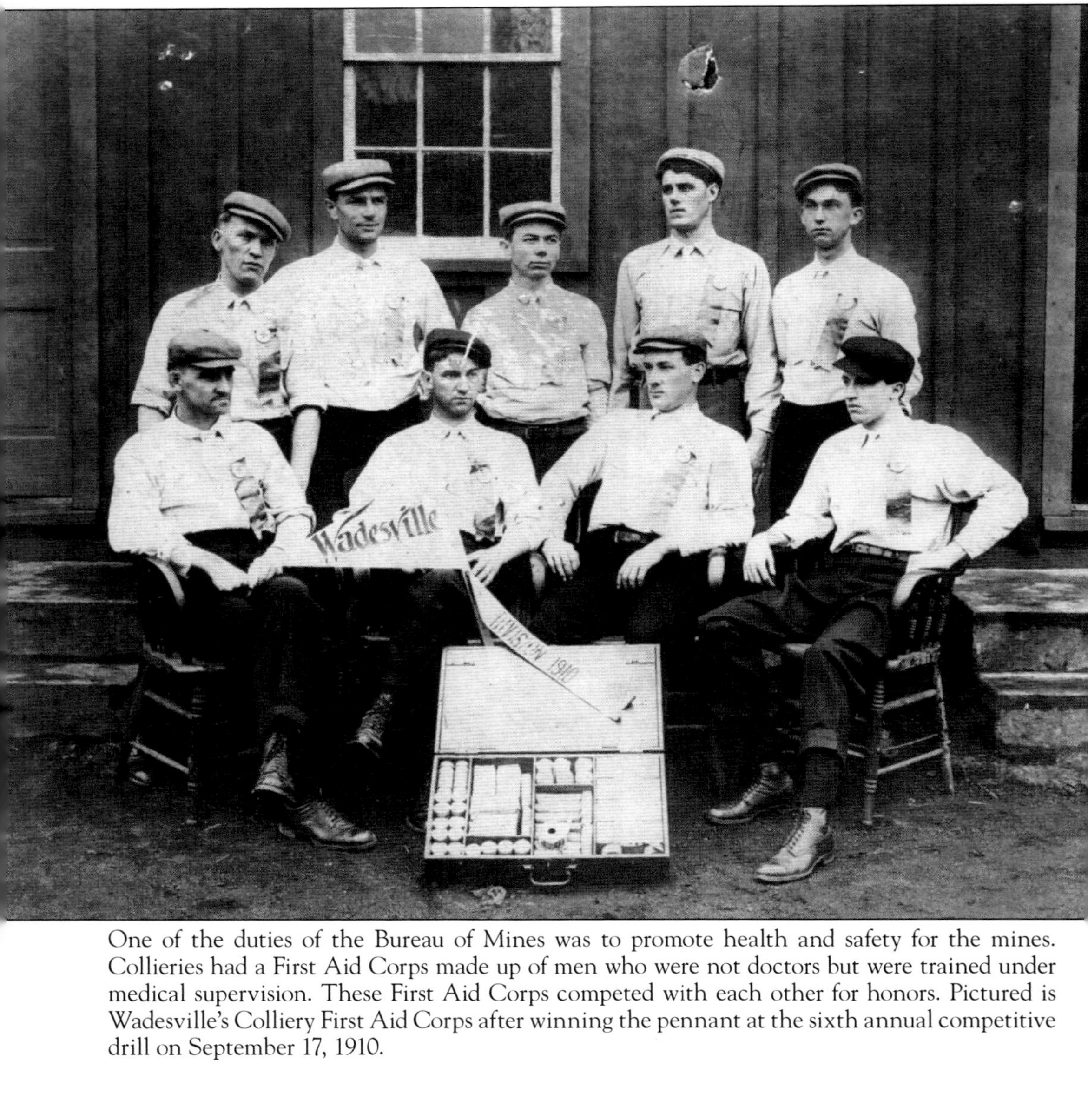

One of the duties of the Bureau of Mines was to promote health and safety for the mines. Collieries had a First Aid Corps made up of men who were not doctors but were trained under medical supervision. These First Aid Corps competed with each other for honors. Pictured is Wadesville's Colliery First Aid Corps after winning the pennant at the sixth annual competitive drill on September 17, 1910.

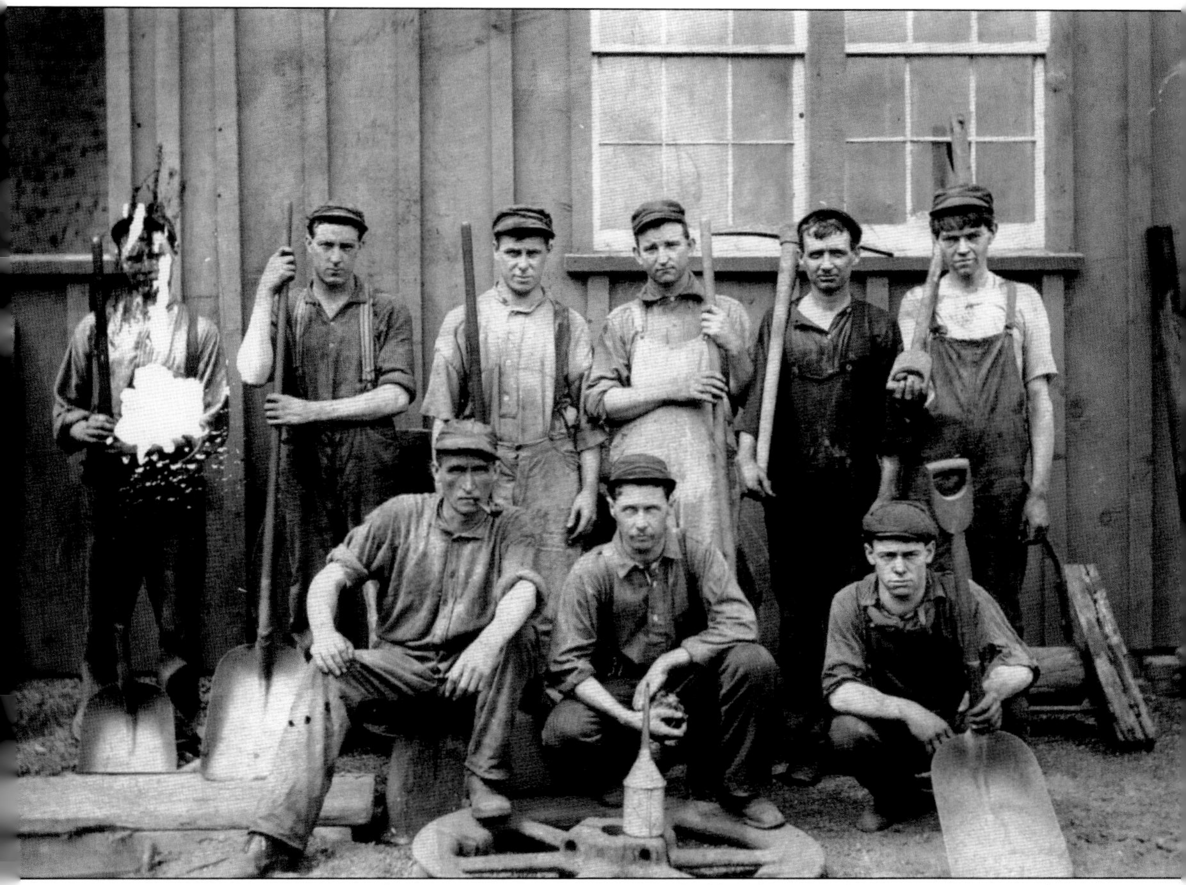

The Wadesville Colliery opened in May 1867 and continued off and on for the next 50 years. The picture was taken in the 1920s while operations were owned by the Philadelphia and Reading Coal and Iron Company. The miners are shown holding the tools of their trade. Only two of the men are identified, Thomas S. Lloyd in the back row and Noah Haslam in front.

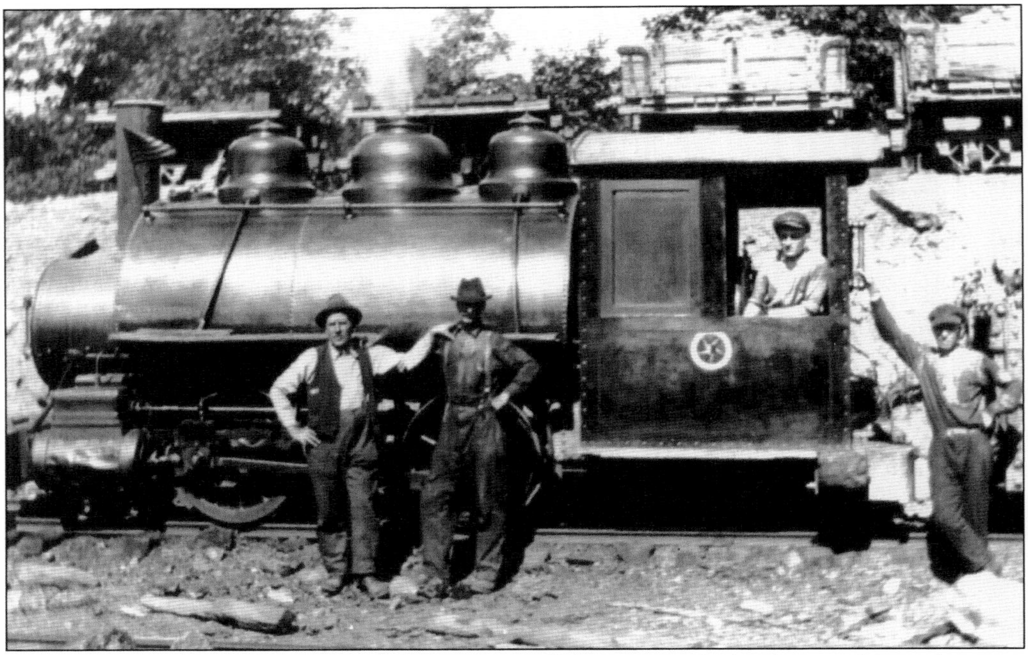

The mine lokie, also known as a dinkey, was a small locomotive for hauling coal from the mine to the breaker and removing ashes and rock refuse from the breaker. It was also used to transport freight such as timber and props for use in the mines. Shown standing in front of the locomotive are Harry Scherr, Fred Scherr, and Joe Lejko, all lokie engineers.

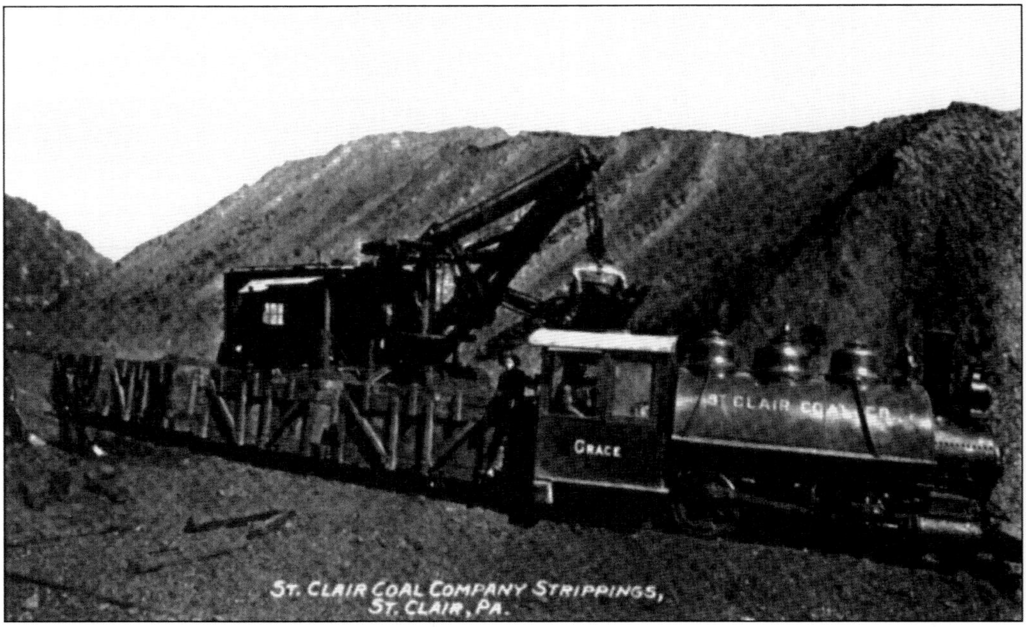

Lokie engineers for the St. Clair Coal Company felt pride in their machinery, enough to give this lokie a name, *Gracie*. Lokie engineers were required to take classes and apprentice before becoming certified to be an engineer. Locomotives were usually 12 feet long, 4 feet wide, and 6 feet from the rail to the top of the stack.

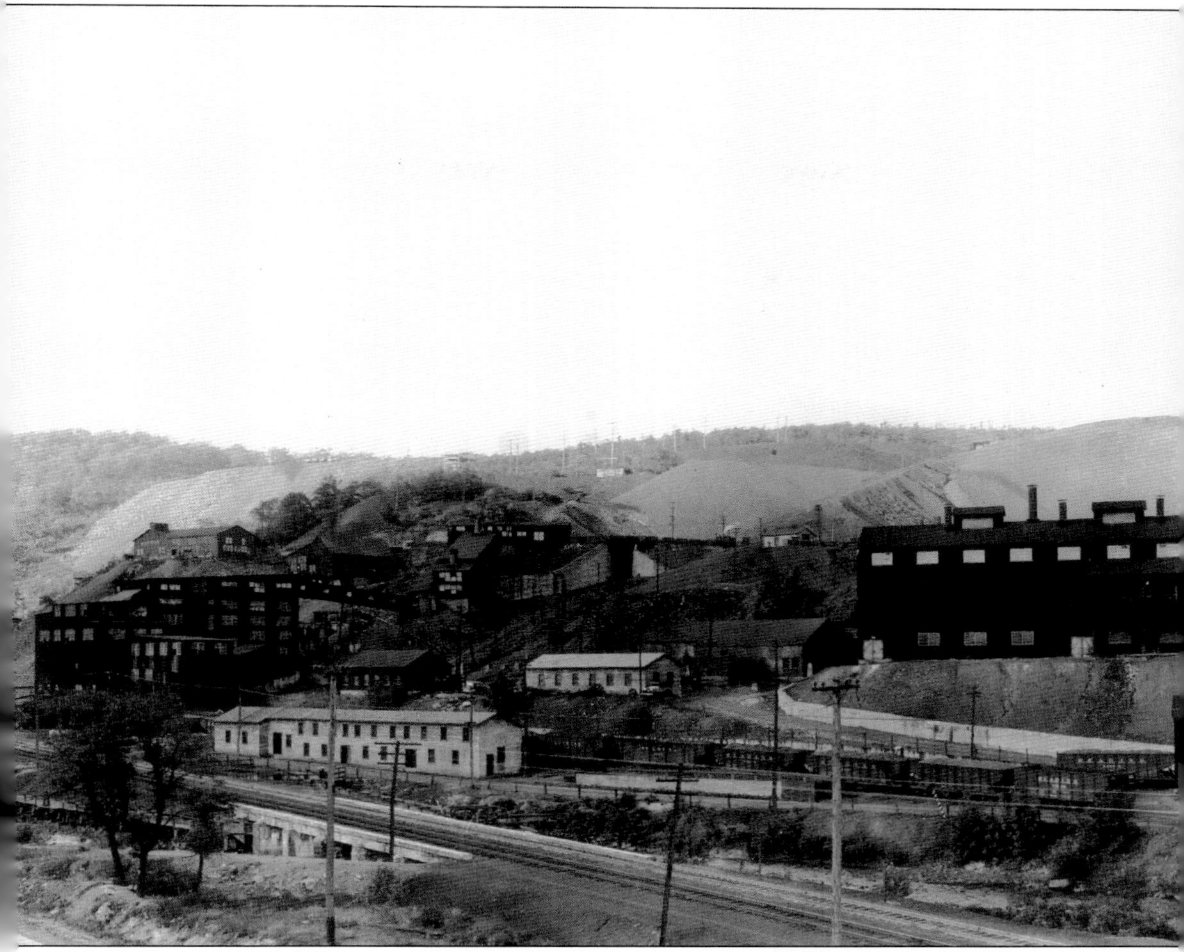

The St. Clair Coal Company breaker stood on the site of the former Eagle Colliery. A group of New York businessmen, led by William A. Taylor and the Patterson family, leased this colliery in 1885 and renamed it the St. Clair Coal Company or Herbine Colliery.

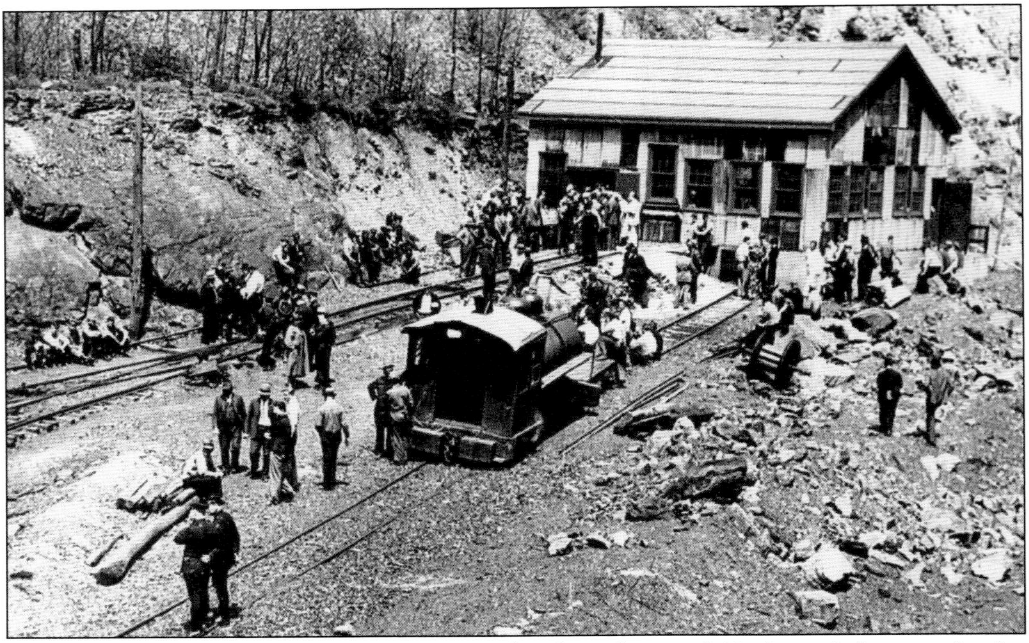

On April 27, 1938, blasts killed 7 men immediately and injured 11. An eighth man, the fire boss Andrew Potts, died during the night. Potts was scheduled to leave the mines the next week to work full-time at his candy distribution business. The explosion happened 500 feet underground and a mile inside the mine from the slope. Mine inspectors determined the first blast occurred from a carbide light igniting after a cave-in from a gangway that was idle since 1909. The workman wearing the lamp was killed immediately from the first blast; the other victims were caught by the second blast.

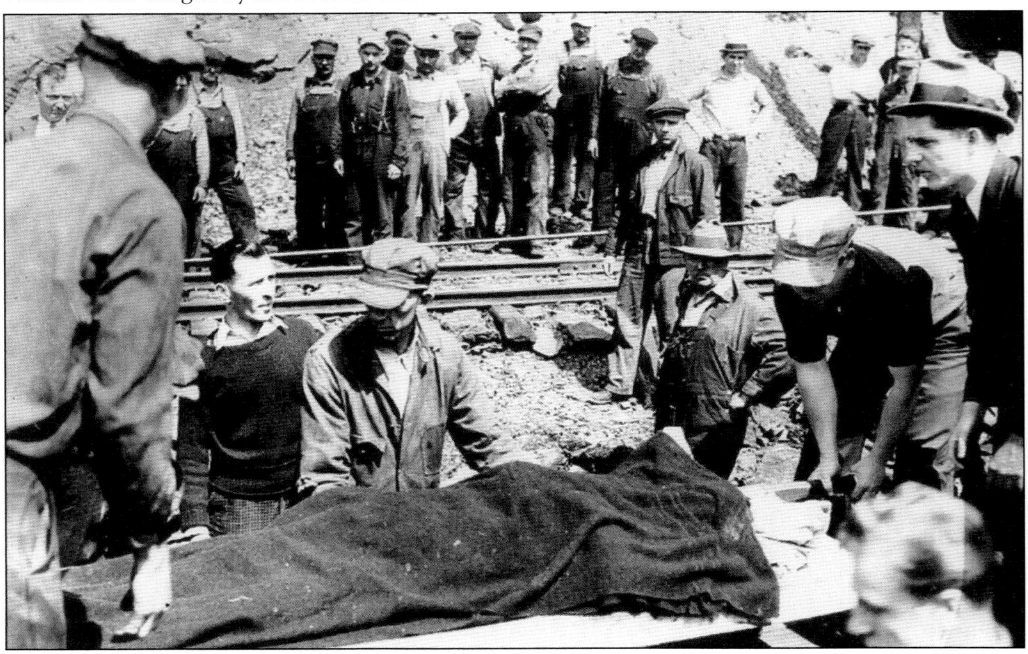

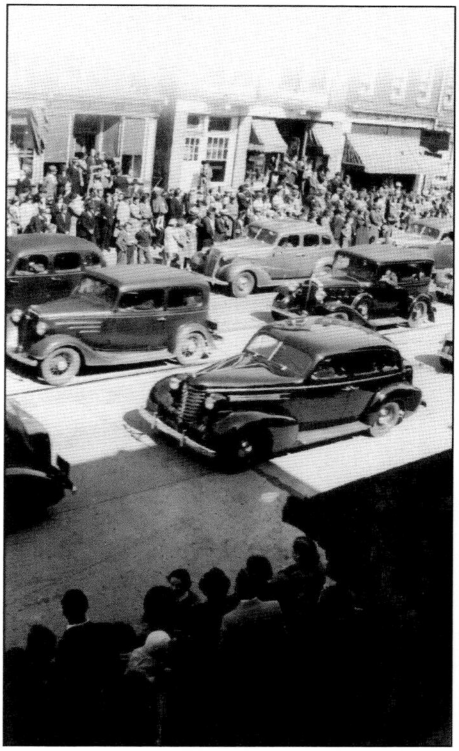

The streets were lined with the mourners for the two brothers and their brother-in-law who were killed by a gas explosion. A mass for the triple funeral was held at St. Nicholas Church on Morris Street, and a large motorcade of cars followed the hearses through the town to the cemetery.

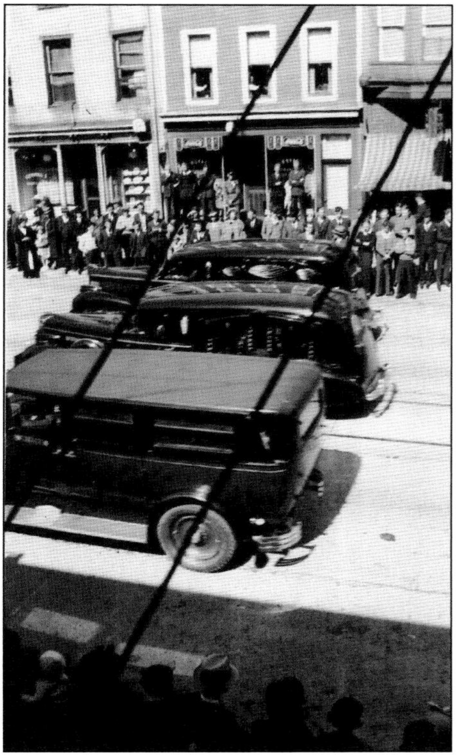

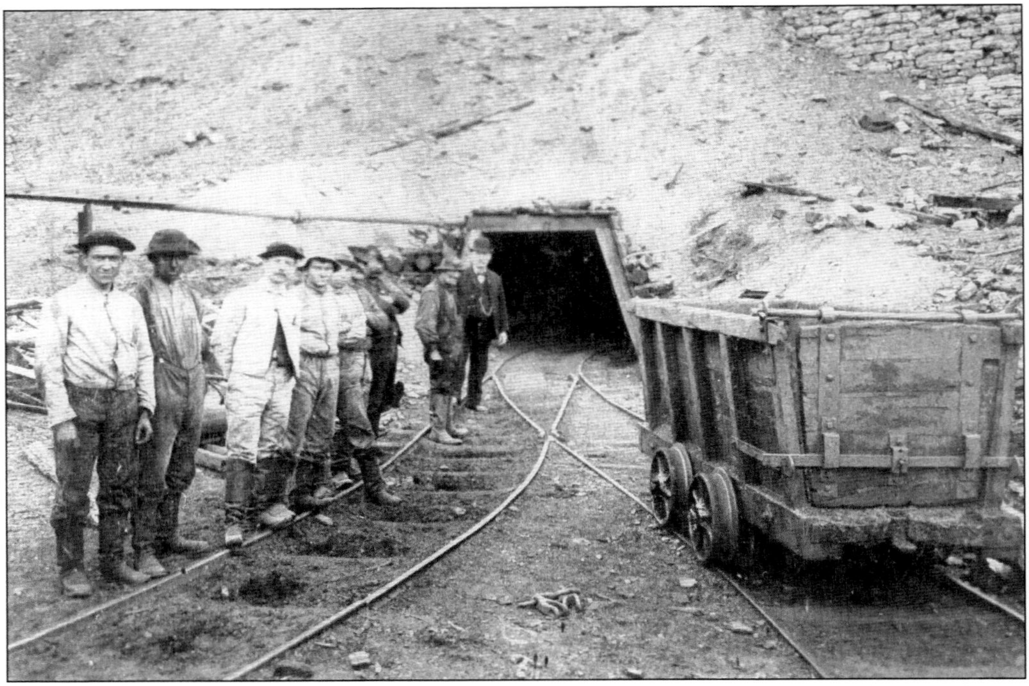

Miners and the mine boss stand outside the entrance to the drift at Eagle Colliery. The mine bosses were experienced Welsh miners. The Eagle Colliery was one of the largest and most profitable operations in Schuylkill County. The slope coal was carried in mine cars onto a horizontal roadway supported by a wooden trestle that led to the dumping platform at the top of the breaker.

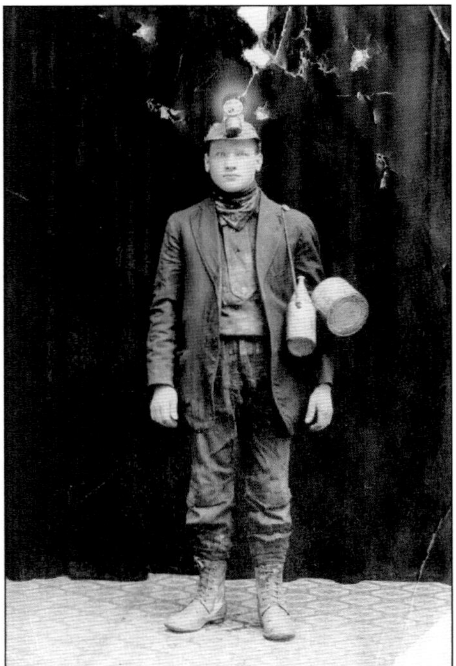

John Nanartavage emigrated from Lithuania in 1912 at the age of 18. He worked at various collieries as a miner and had a bootleg hold at Silver Creek and also operated a shoemaker shop from his residence. He died at age 47 from miner's asthma.

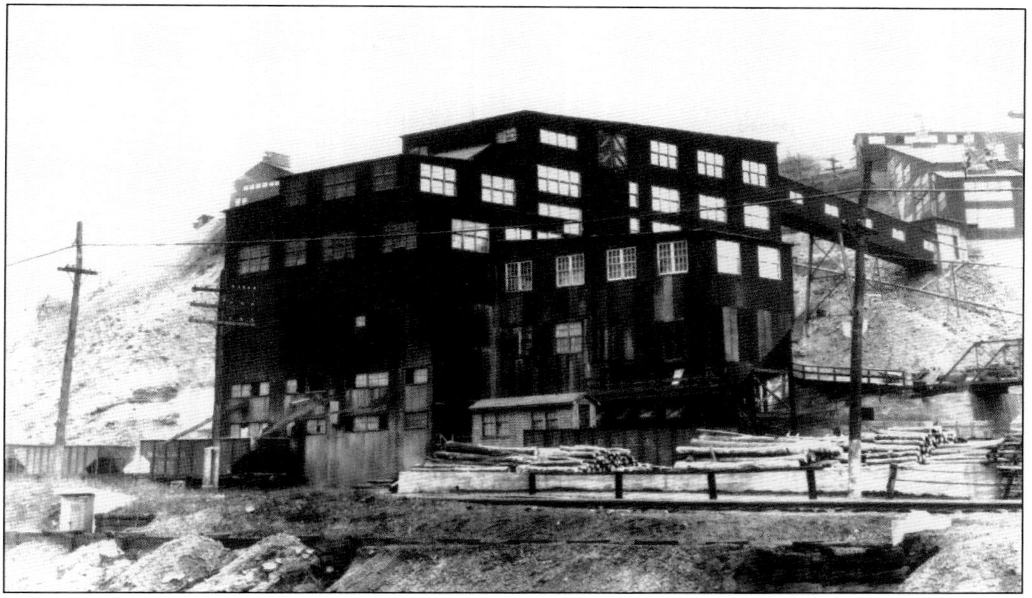

On September 12, 1957, the St. Clair Coal Company was denied renewal of the land lease where the colliery was located. After mining on this spot for over 100 years, the era came to an end despite pleas from the community, clergy, town officials, and the United Mine Workers of America. This rich anthracite coal area is now the Coal Creek Shopping Center on the north end of St. Clair.

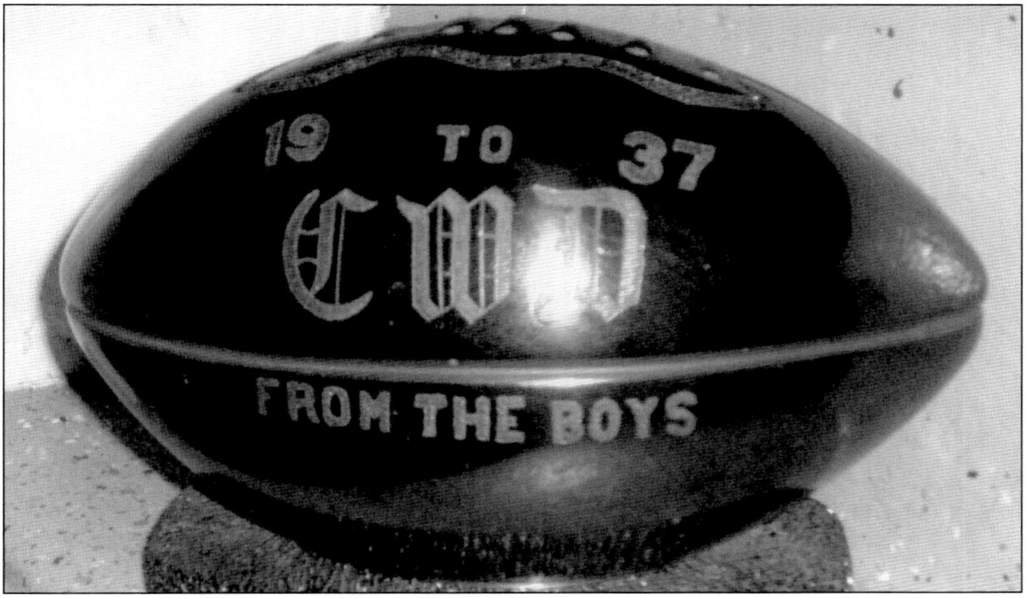

In 1937, Thomas Tobin required an operation at the Pottsville Hospital. The surgery was performed by Dr. Charles W. Delp. In appreciation for a successful surgery, Tobin asked a fellow miner, William Shappell of Arnots Addition, to carve a football from coal. Shappell was very talented in carving objects out of coal using the mining machinery. Work was done during the third shift so the foreman would not see him carving during work hours. The inscription reads, "1937 To CWD from the boys."

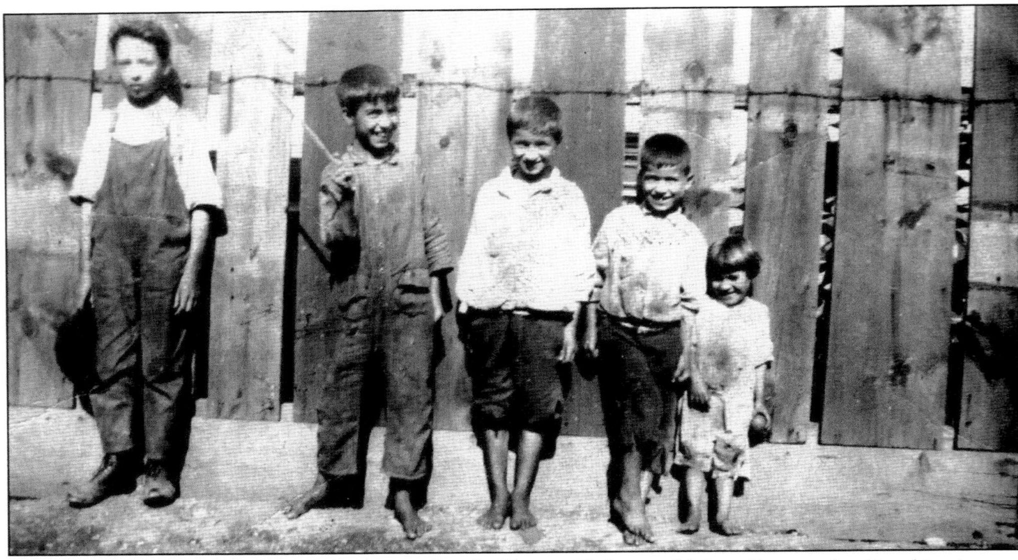

This photograph from the 1920s shows the children of John and Mary Sever who lived in Arnots Addition. John was an independent coal miner who sold the coal he mined to families and businesses in the area, making deliveries from his truck.

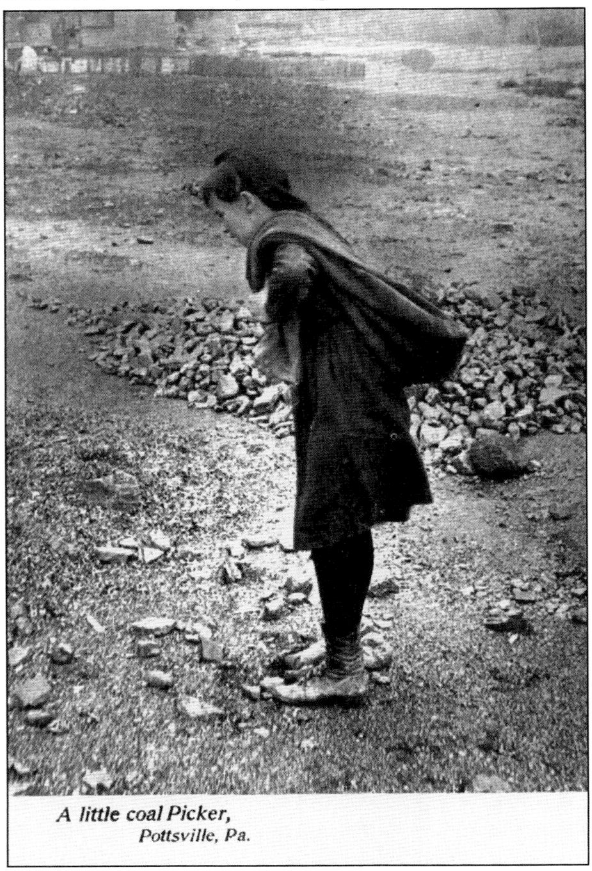

It was common for the children to pick coal from refuse piles or alongside the railroad tracks. Many old-timers remember waiting for one of the many coal trains that went through town to pass by so they could pick up any coal that fell off the cars.

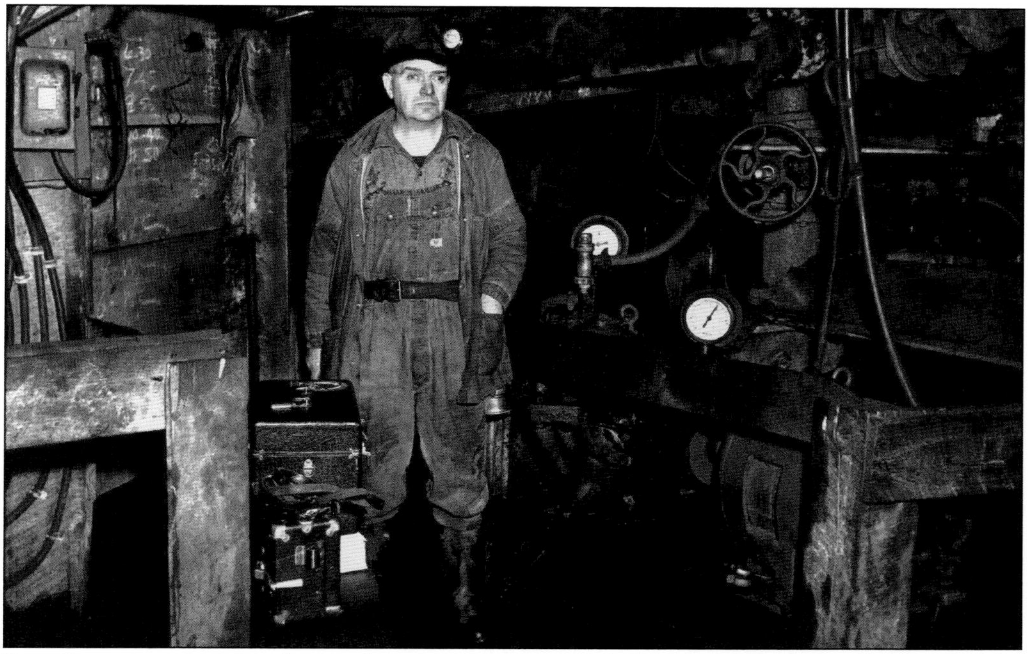

Evan Reese, miner, is standing in the pumping station in the 30 Slope mine. The pumping station at the 30 Slope was very important because any flooding would bring work in the mine to a halt. The miners and mechanics in and around St. Clair were leaders in pumping technology.

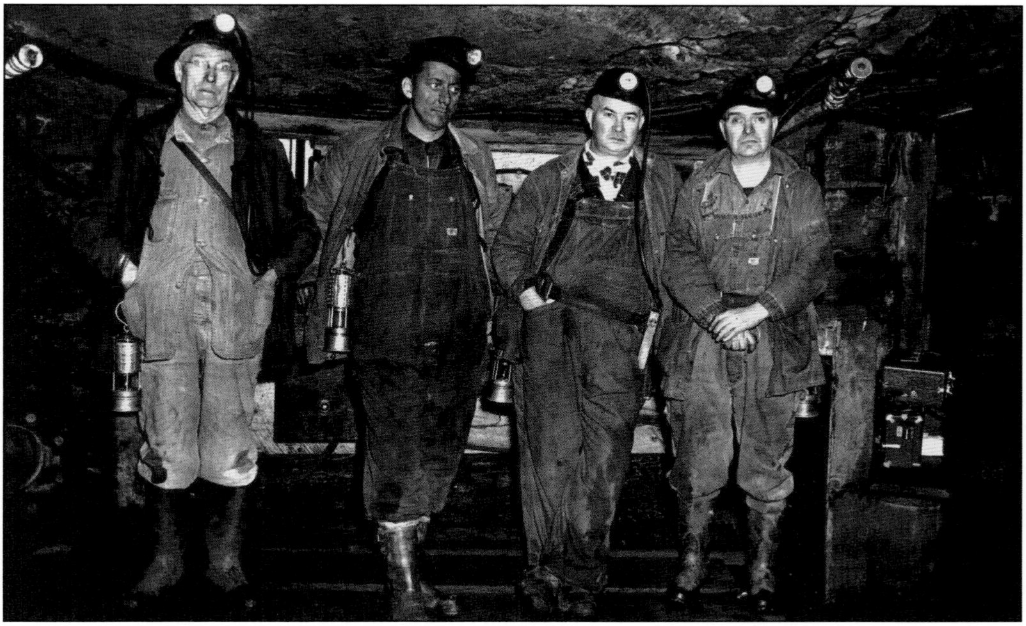

The Herbine Colliery was located in the north end of St. Clair. It was constructed by Frank Haas in 1826 as the Eagle Colliery and operated until 1832. William and Thomas Johns operated it as the Herbine Colliery until 1855. It was renamed the St. Clair Coal Company by lessees, William H. Taylor, and the Patterson family. The mine bosses in the picture are, from left to right, Mike Kanezo, Joe Lewis, unidentified, and Evan Reese.

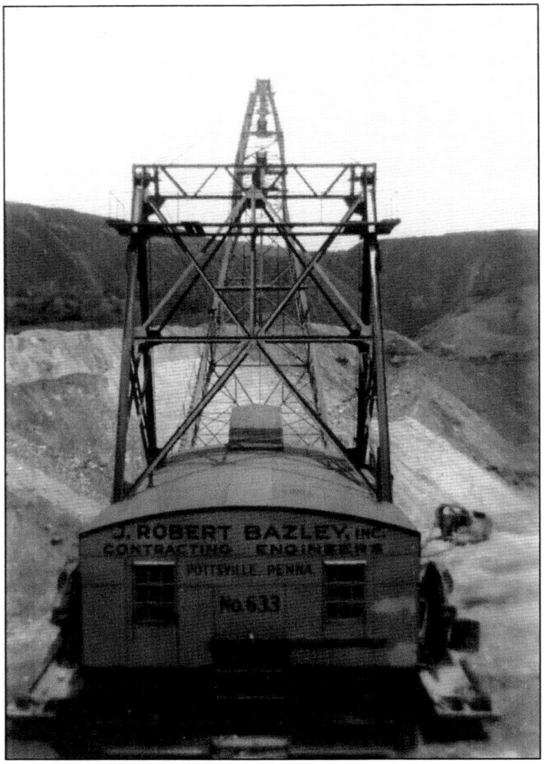

The Bucyrus Monighan walking dragline, with a 200-foot boom and an eight-cubic-yard bucket, commenced working about 1940 in the Pine Forest Colliery stripping on the east side of town. Much of the work done by the dragline was reclaiming coal left during the Civil War workings. The shovel was owned by J. Robert Bazley, who had the contract to supply coal to the St. Clair Colliery. This machine worked in the St. Clair area until about 1960 and was then sold to a stripping contractor where it worked near Eckley until about 2005.

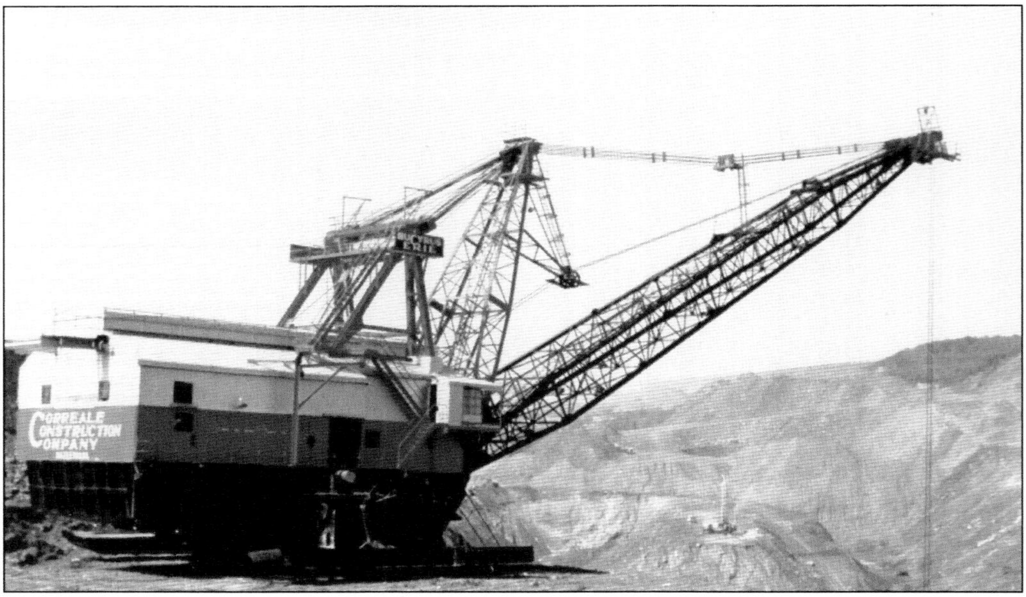

The largest walking dragline in 1944 was the Bucyrus Erie 1150B electric walking dragline, which was first assembled in this area at the Beechwood stripping project near Minersville. The dragline then worked at the Repplier Colliery before its 1962 move to the St. Clair Coal Company. The shovel had to cross several railroad tracks, a highway, and the Mill Creek into St. Clair. The highway was covered with a six-foot layer of dirt to cushion the shovel's 1,300 tons.

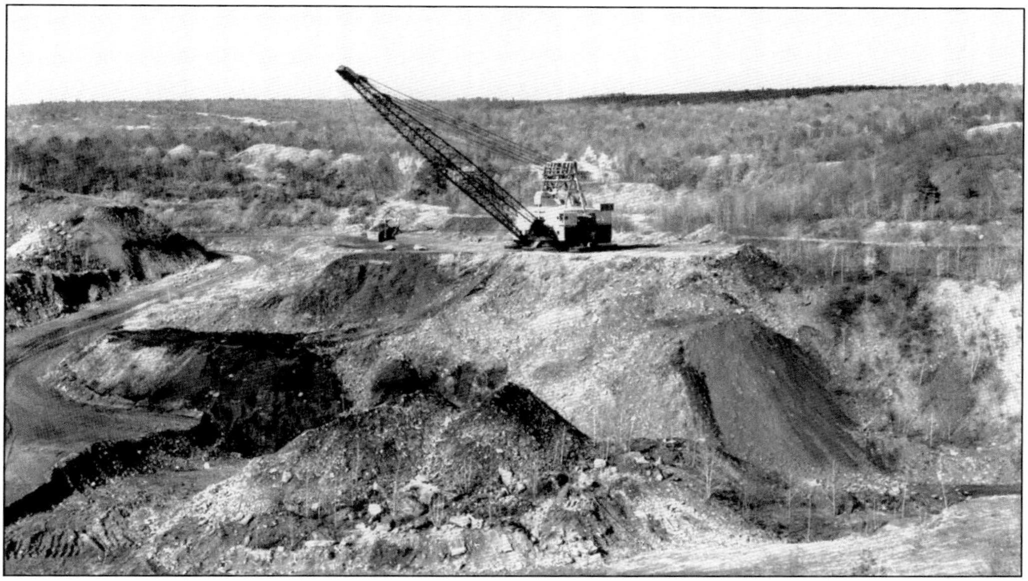

Marion 7800 electric walking dragline at Pine Forest Stripping just east of St. Clair was the first 7800 dragline assembled for Reading Anthracite Company during the summer and fall of 1961 for its Pine Forest stripping operation. The dragline has a 220-foot boom and a 35-cubic-yard bucket and cost approximately $1.75 million. This machine is still operating today at the Wadesville Stripping west of St. Clair.

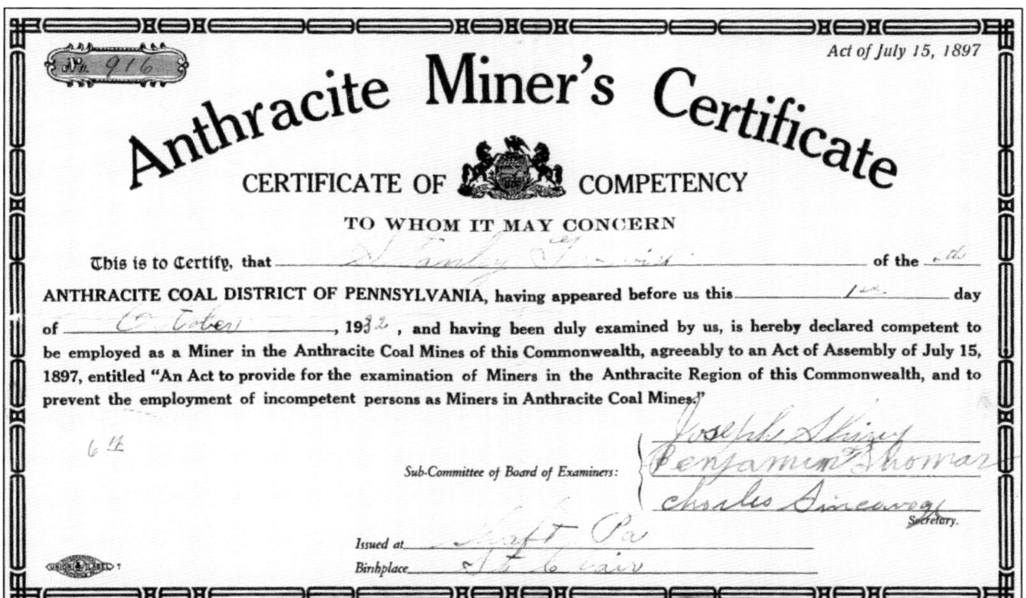

No. 916

Act of July 15, 1897

Anthracite Miner's Certificate

CERTIFICATE OF COMPETENCY

TO WHOM IT MAY CONCERN

This is to Certify, that [illegible] of the [illegible] ANTHRACITE COAL DISTRICT OF PENNSYLVANIA, having appeared before us this [illegible] day of October, 1932, and having been duly examined by us, is hereby declared competent to be employed as a Miner in the Anthracite Coal Mines of this Commonwealth, agreeably to an Act of Assembly of July 15, 1897, entitled "An Act to provide for the examination of Miners in the Anthracite Region of this Commonwealth, and to prevent the employment of incompetent persons as Miners in Anthracite Coal Mines."

Sub-Committee of Board of Examiners: Joseph [illegible], Benjamin Thomas, Charles [illegible], Secretary.

Issued at [illegible] Pa

Birthplace St. Clair

Miners were required to obtain certification to do the different jobs in the mine. This certificate is from Stanley Grabish from Arnots Addition. Laws established on July 15, 1887, stated workers must start in the mines as a helper, and after several years of experience and an extensive test, they could become certified as a miner.

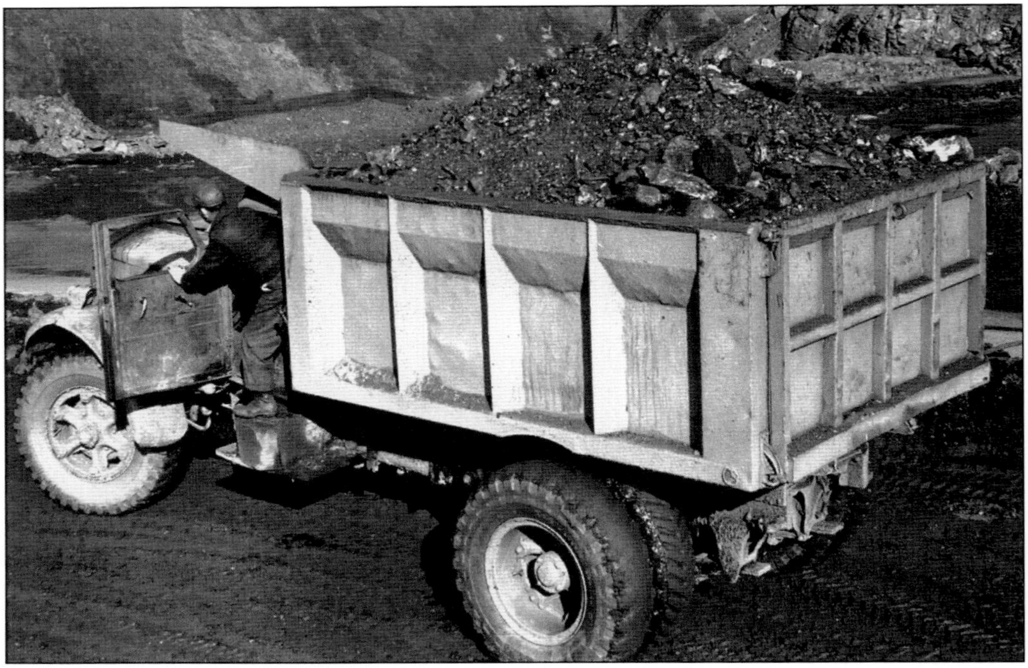

By the mid-1900s, another method of coal mining became popular. Strip-mining was done from the surface as opposed to underground mining. Huge power shovels and draglines are used to remove earth and rock, the overburden, from above the coal seam. Smaller shovels load the coal directly into trucks. Cletus Tobin is ready to drive this load of coal to the breaker to be washed and sorted by size.

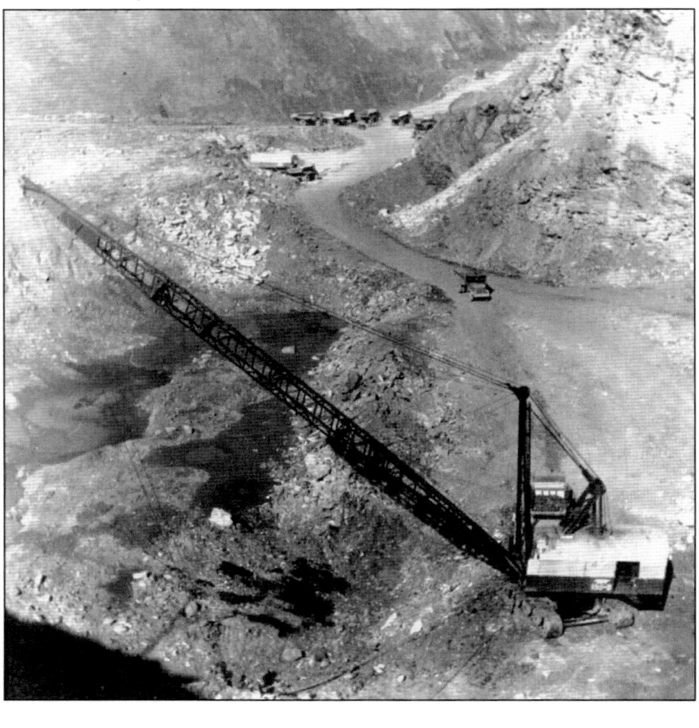

Here a Bucyrus Erie crawler dragline removes overburden from a coal seam near St. Clair. These shovels were either diesel-electric or fully electric powered and were somewhat limited in bucket capacity, boom length, and digging depth.

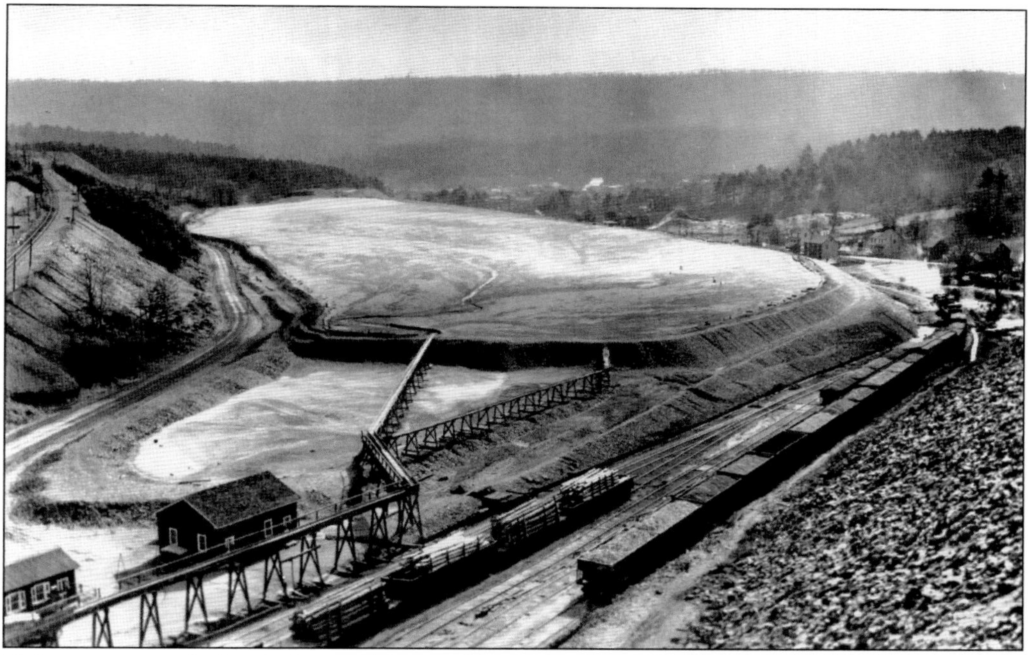

Culm is composed of rock slate and fine coal from processing at the breaker. Culm was hauled in mine cars by mules or sometimes it was pulled up a hill slope by wire rope and a winding engine and dumped down a hillside. After washing was introduced at the Silver Creek Colliery, much of the culm was deposited in huge settling basins to prevent clogging of streams below the colliery.

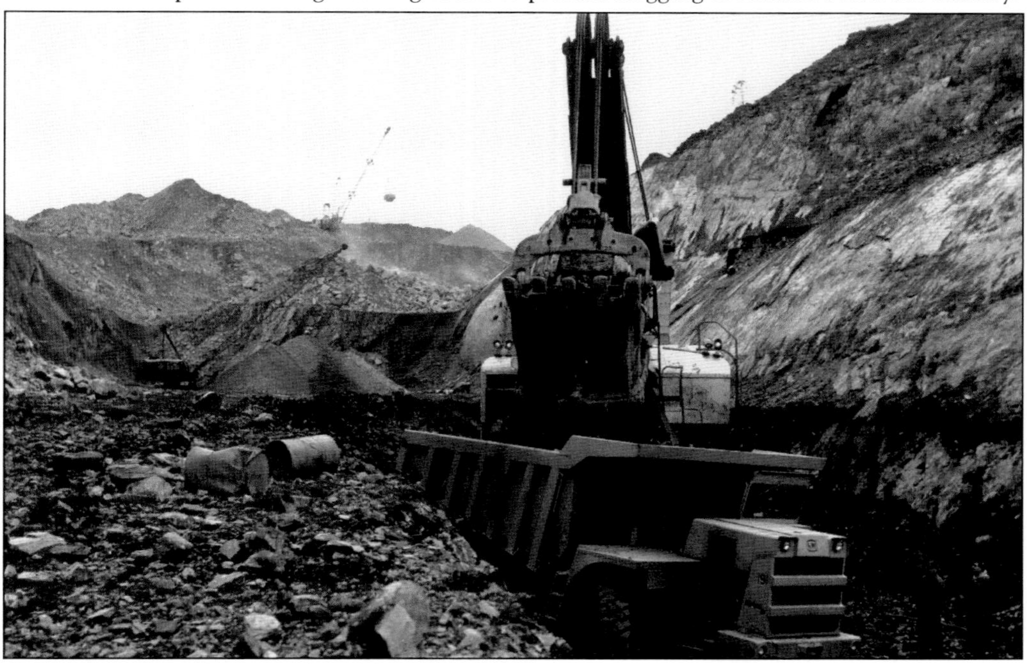

A crawler-mounted mining shovel loads a waiting truck with overburden to uncover a coal seam near St. Clair. In some cases this type of mining shovel was also used to remove the exposed coal that was loaded into large trucks to be taken to the breaker for processing.

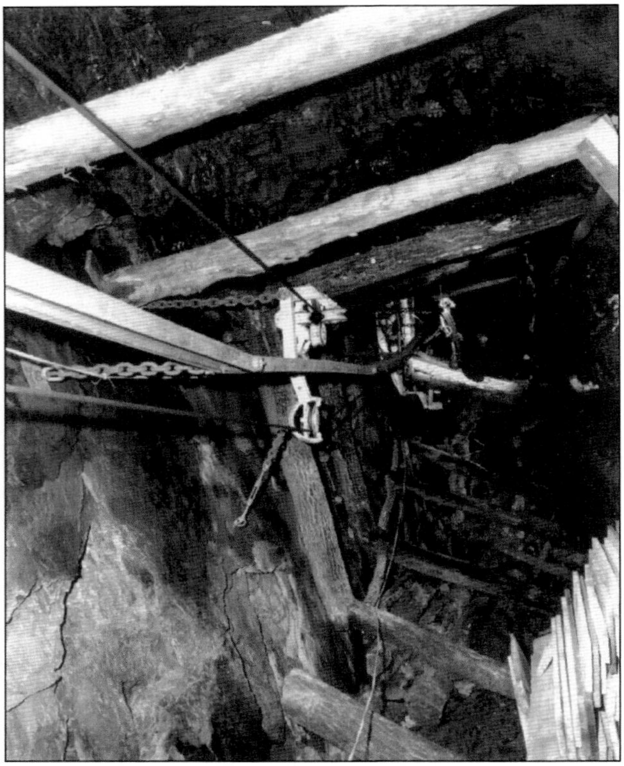

Opened by an independent miner in 1968, the 30 Slope monorail only operated for several years. The underground monorail, the first of its kind, hauled coal to the bottom of the slope where it was then taken to the surface in a gunboat.

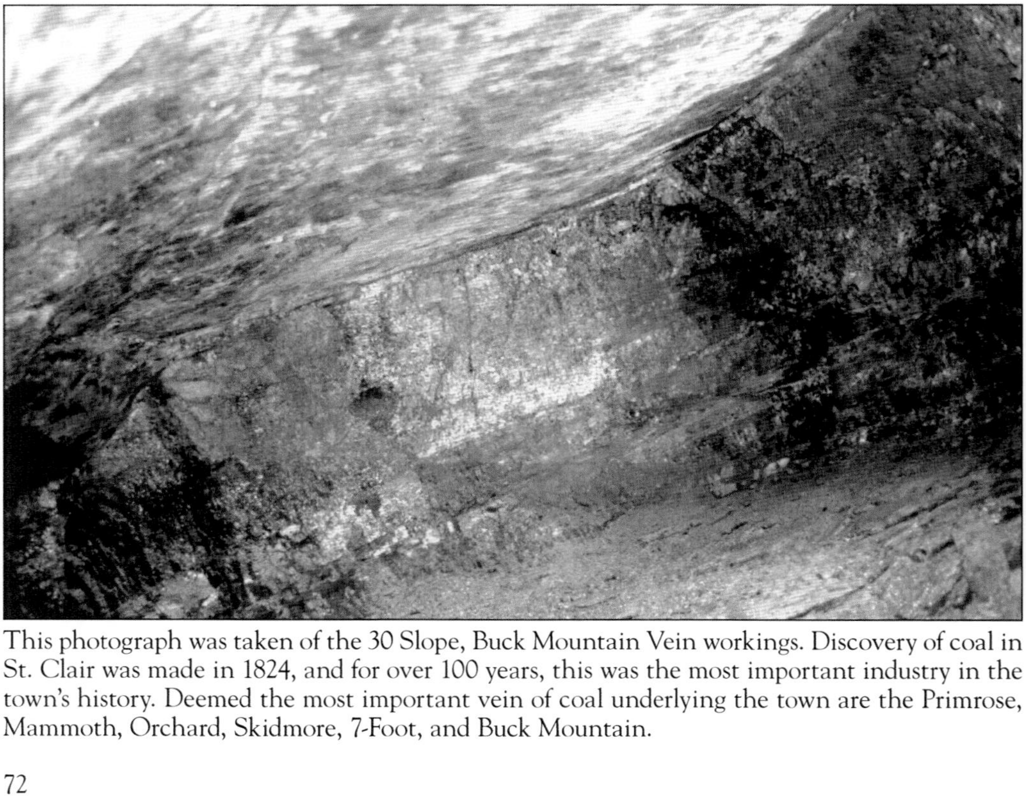

This photograph was taken of the 30 Slope, Buck Mountain Vein workings. Discovery of coal in St. Clair was made in 1824, and for over 100 years, this was the most important industry in the town's history. Deemed the most important vein of coal underlying the town are the Primrose, Mammoth, Orchard, Skidmore, 7-Foot, and Buck Mountain.

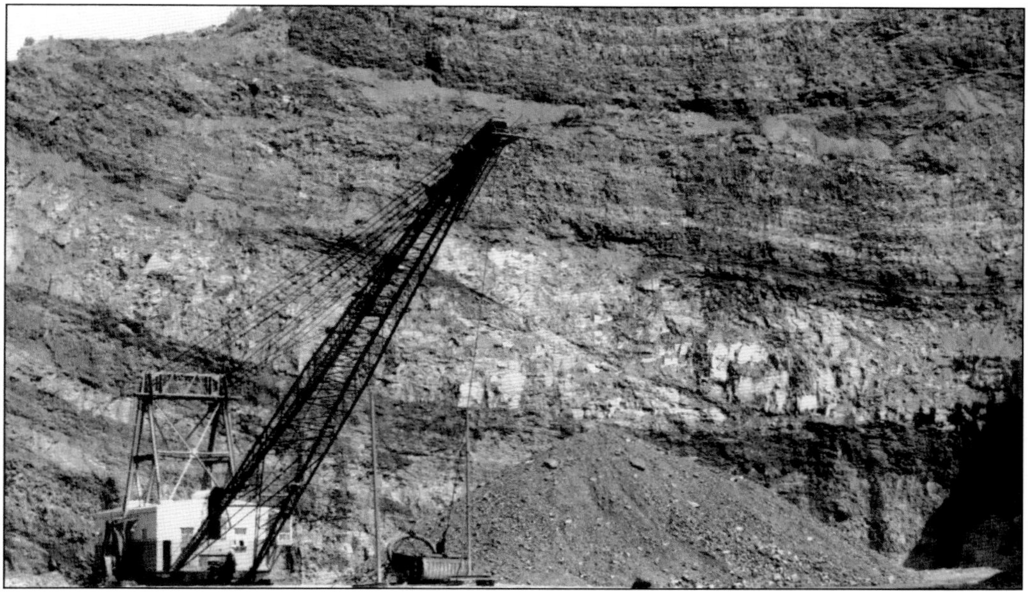

Another machine working in the St. Clair area was the Marion 7400 electric walking dragline, which had a 160-foot boom and 14-cubic-yard bucket. The above photograph shows the 7400 dragline at the bottom of the pit at Wadesville Stripping on September 15, 1974. The large pile of coal seen to the right of the shovel is from the Mammoth Vein that waits to be hauled by huge trucks to the breaker for processing.

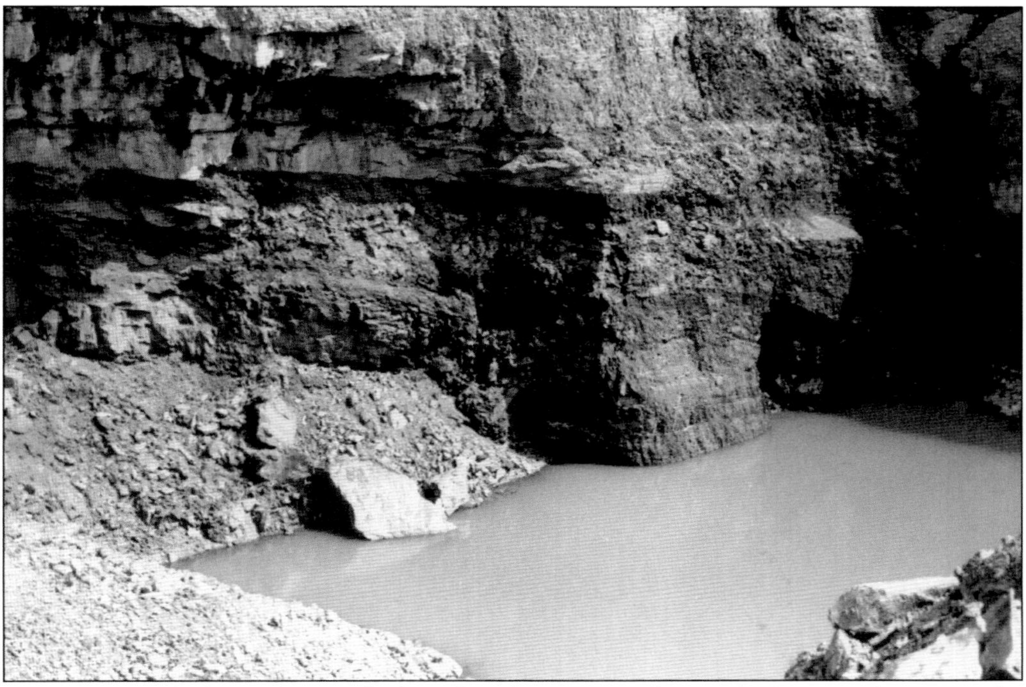

This photograph shows the east high wall with strata overlaying the Mammoth Vein at the bottom of the Wadesville Stripping. The Mammoth Vein is partly visible at the bottom of the photograph as water from old mine workings fills the pit.

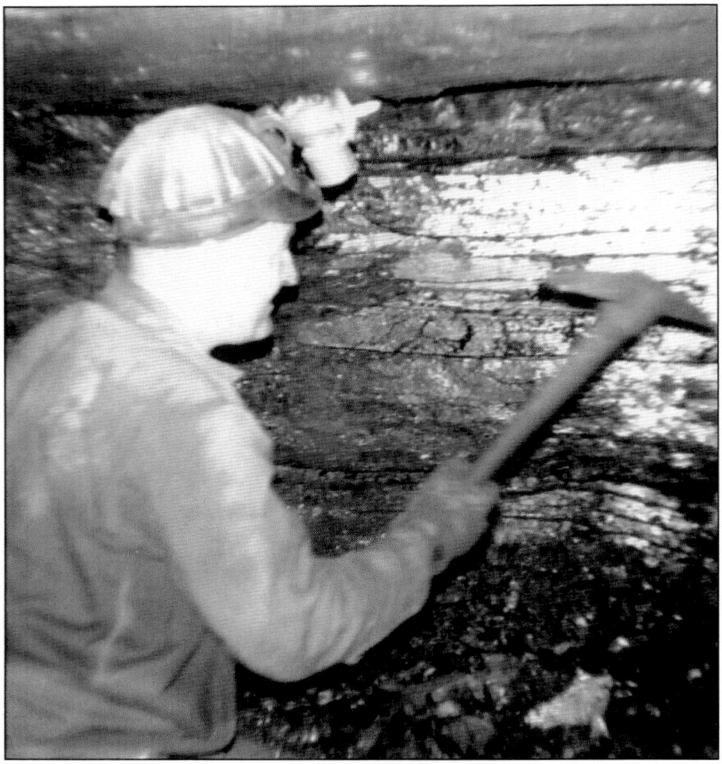

Steve Metroka, an independent coal miner (sometimes called bootlegger), operated the mine of the former Hooker Colliery. The Hooker Colliery closed in 1918, but the site was bootlegged up until the 1960s. The proximity of the thin coal seams to the surface provided a major temptation to unemployed miners. The coal seams were not substantial enough to be worked profitably by the coal companies, but for a father and a few friends willing to sink a hole and operate with primitive equipment, it represented bread on the table.

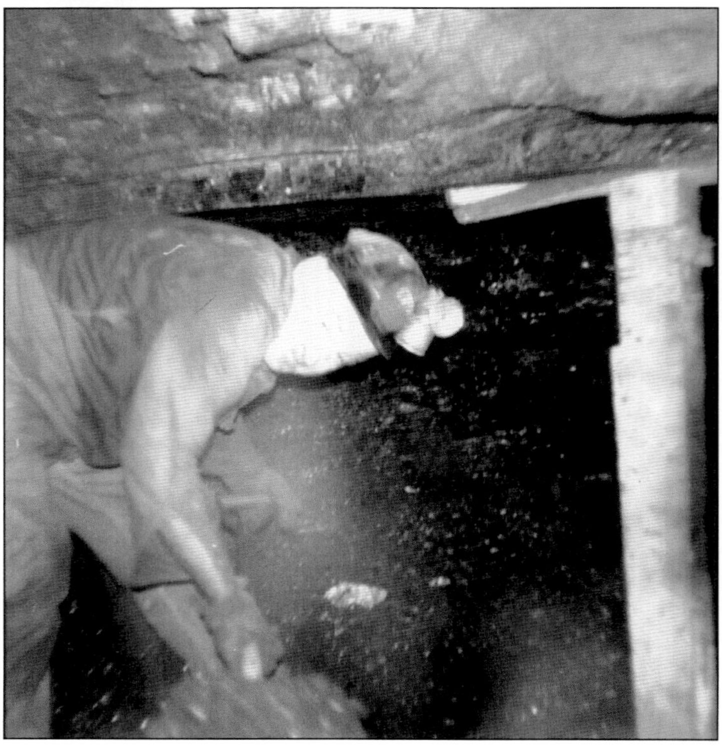

Five

EDUCATION

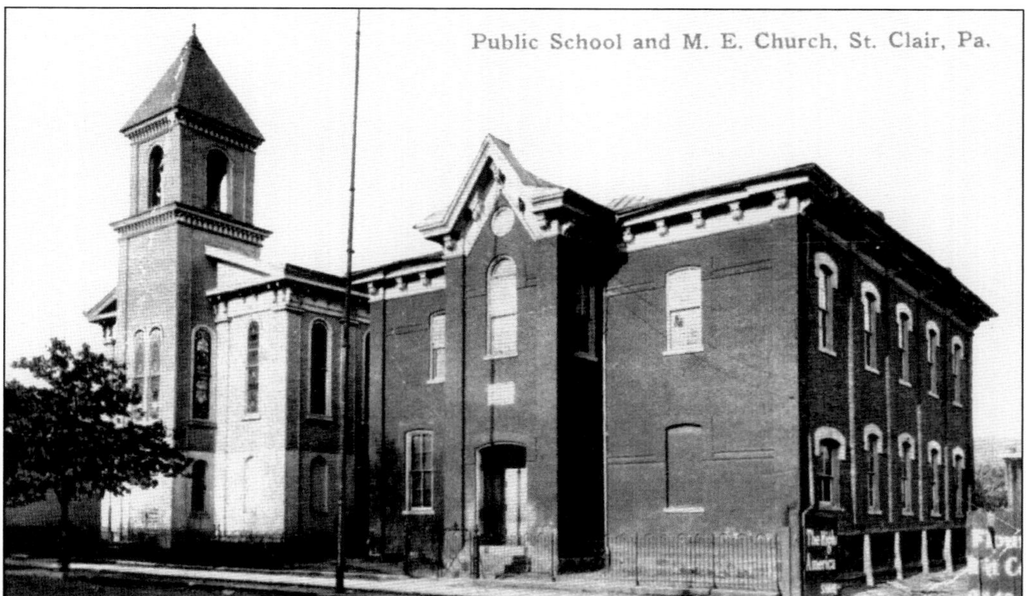

Private schools were first established in town around 1834 by several of the founding families. Public schools began in 1838 with a teacher named Benjamin Jackson from Catawissa. A building in the borough cemetery was used as the first school and continued there until the building on Front Street was built in 1846. This school was known as the Front Street School or Creek School.

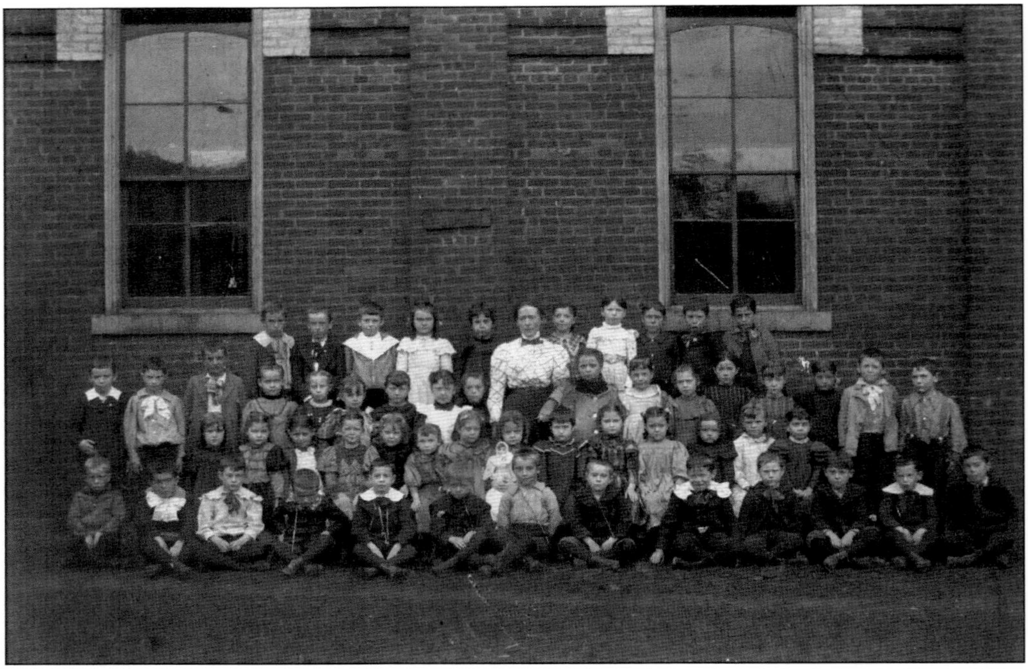

The Creek School House was constructed in 1846 and was located on North Front Street. The rear of the building bordered the Mill Creek, so the school was often referred to as the Creek School. This building provided the children with a 200-square-foot playground. In 1892, the school was rebuilt to accommodate the growing number of students in town.

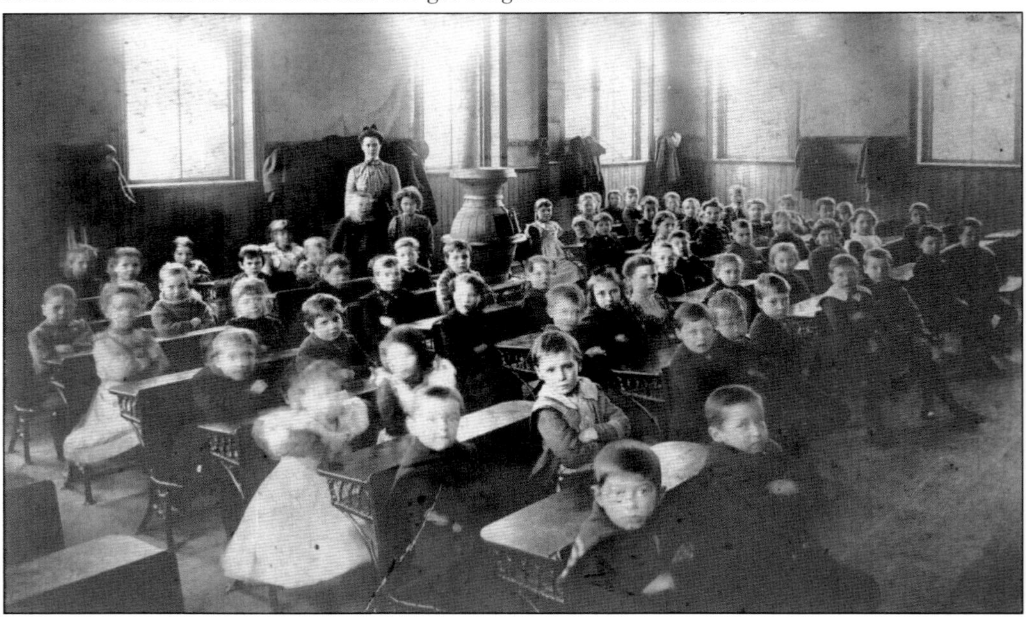

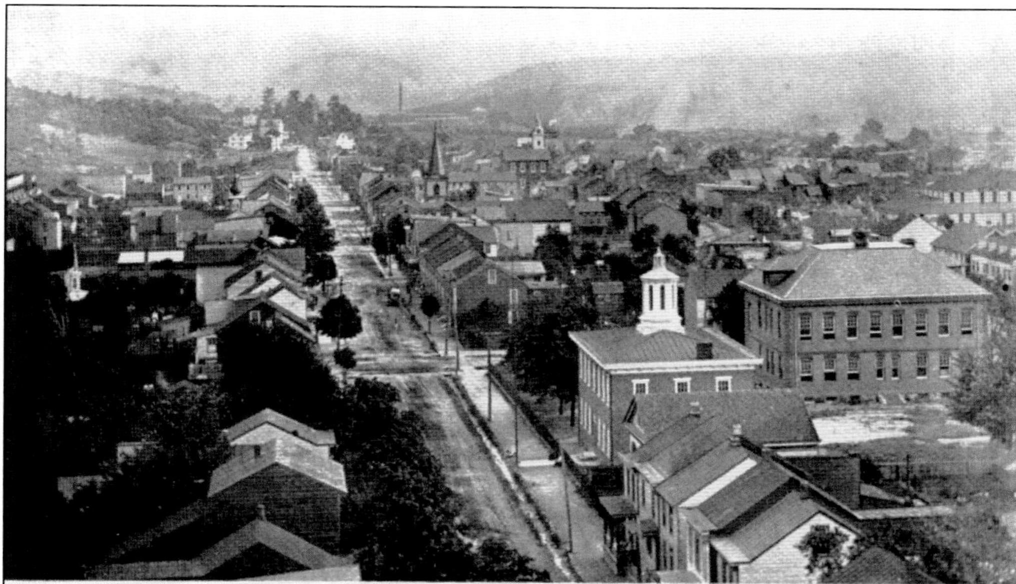

South on Nichols Street, St. Clair, Pa.

The Nichols Street School building was built in 1862 and was located on the west side of North Nichols Street. The building was also called the Brick School. This school contained four classrooms with a total capacity of 320 pupils. The bell from this building is now at the St. Clair football stadium.

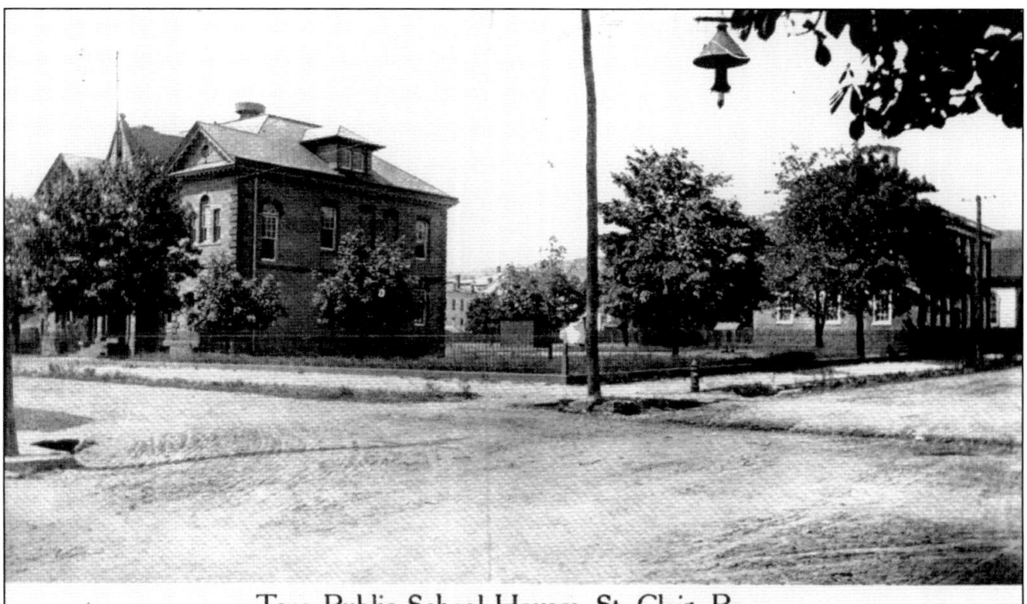

Two Public School Houses, St. Clair, Pa.

This c. 1910 photograph shows the Carroll Street High School in front and Nichols Street School behind it on the right.

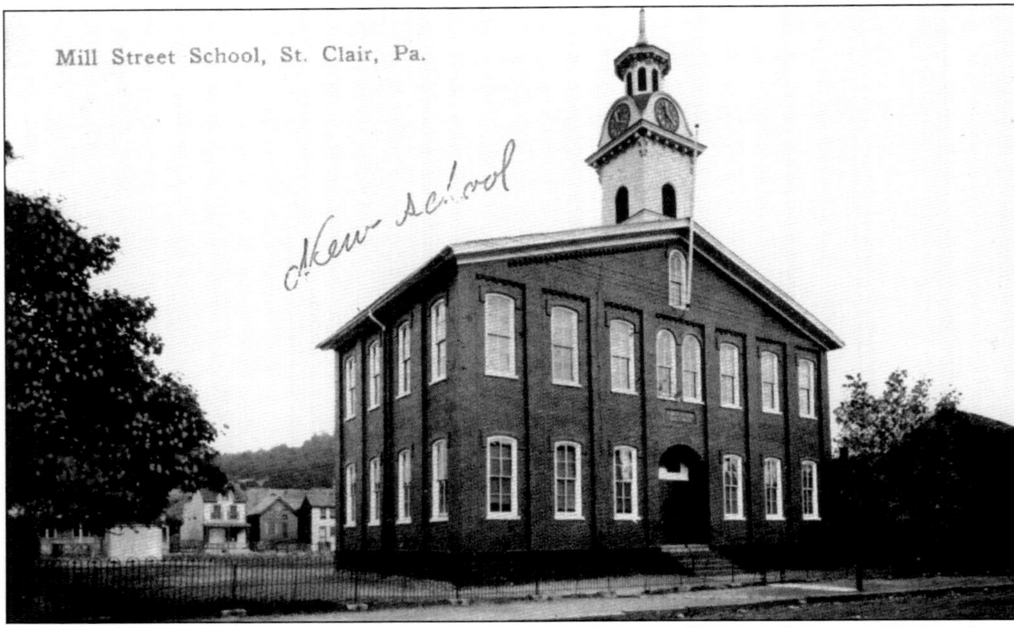

In 1873, the Town Clock Elementary School was built on Mill Street between Railroad and Patterson Streets. On many old pictures the clocks on top of the school could be seen peering out for everyone to see. By the late 1930s, the again growing population outgrew the Carroll Street High School, and the Town Clock School was torn down. A new high school was erected in 1938.

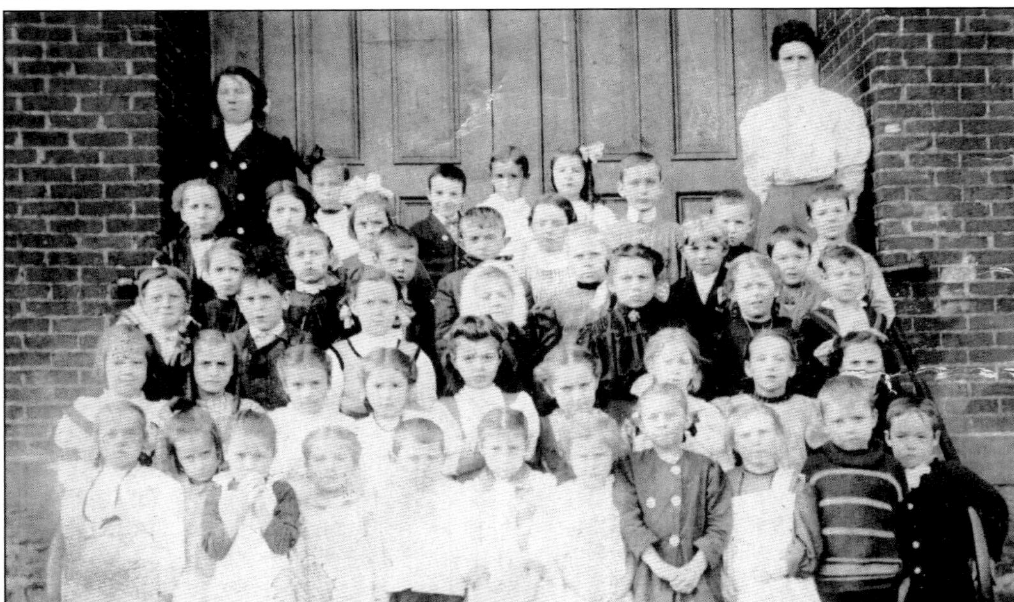

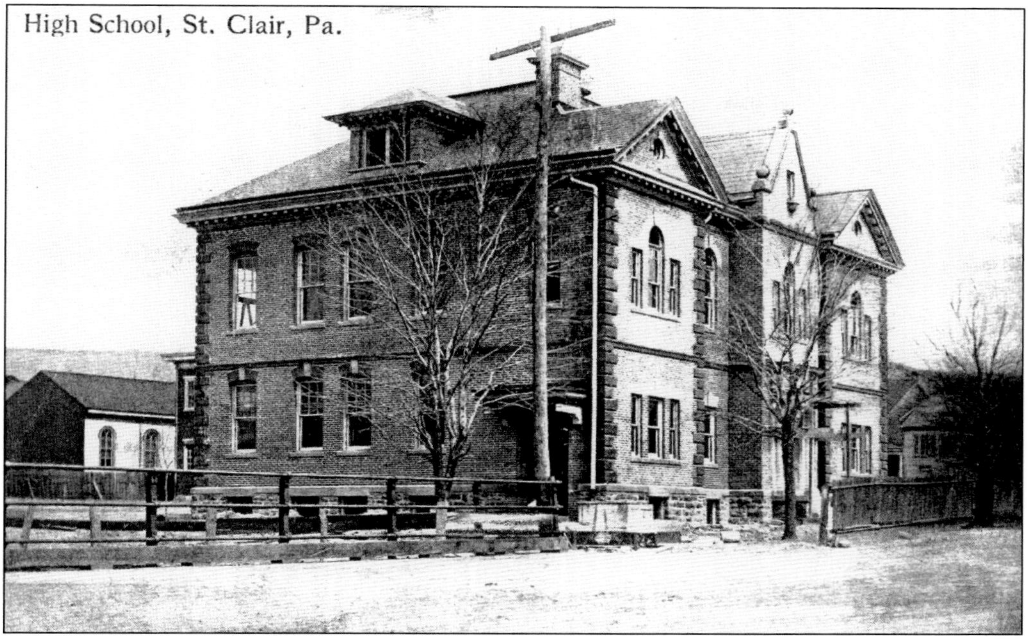

The Carroll Street School, located at the corner of Mill and Carroll Streets, became the new high school in 1909. In 1922, an addition was completed that included classrooms and an auditorium. It was further enlarged in 1927. This high school became an elementary school in 1938, with the completion of a new high school on South Mill Street. The Carroll Street High School housed elementary students until 1986.

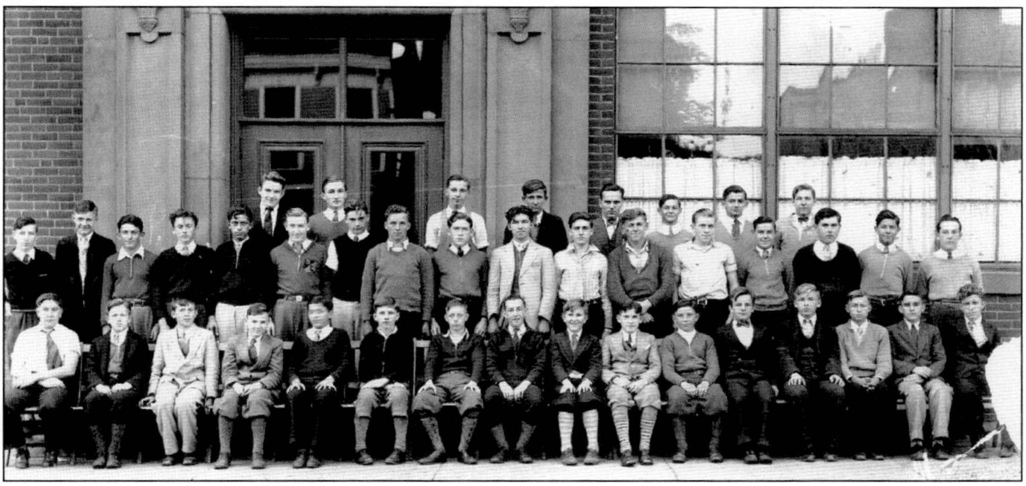

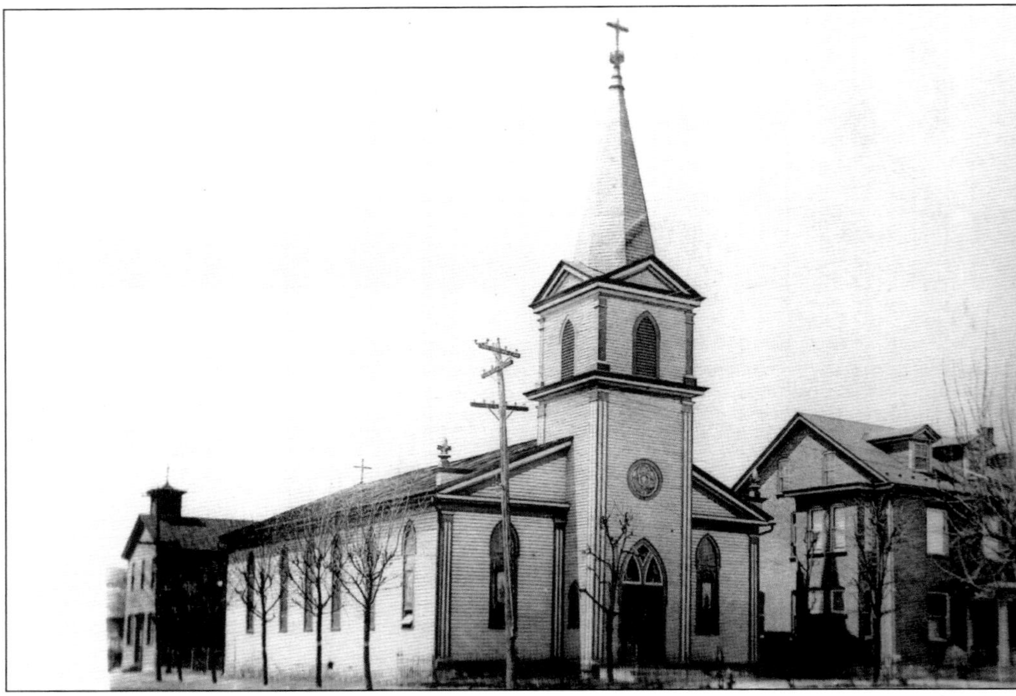

In 1855, the parishioners of St. Boniface German Catholic Church opened a grade school on West Lawton Street behind their church. It was the first parochial in town and continued operation until the 1950s. This *c.* 1911 picture is an early photograph of the school when it still had the wooden siding. This siding was replaced with brick in 1928.

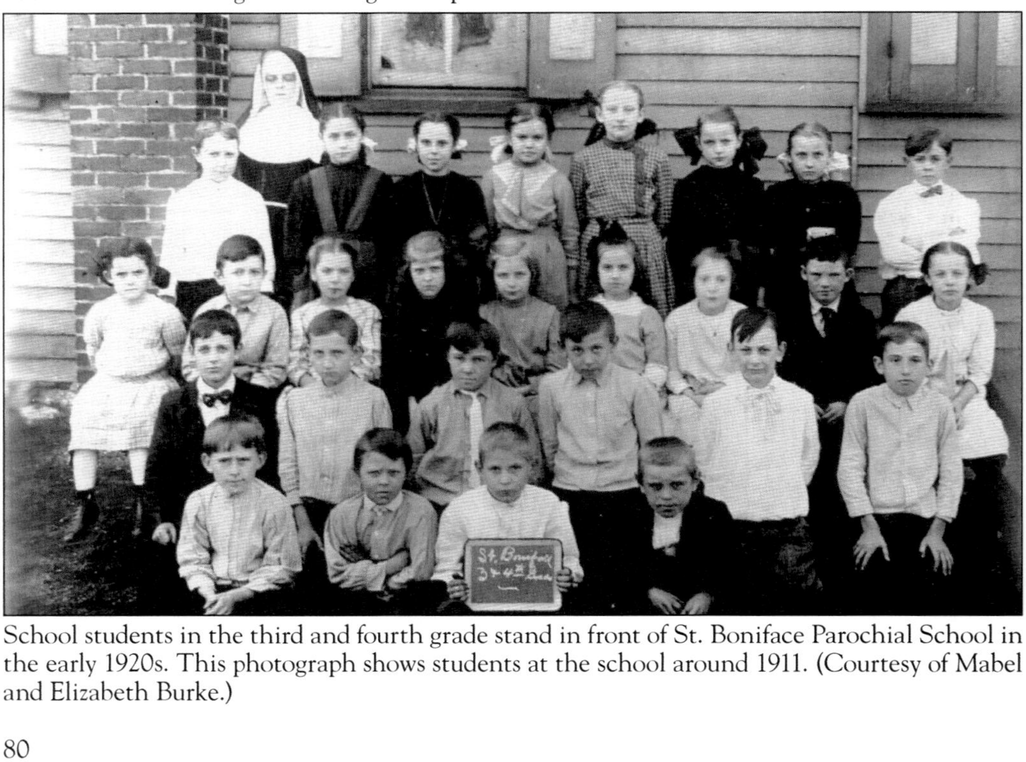

School students in the third and fourth grade stand in front of St. Boniface Parochial School in the early 1920s. This photograph shows students at the school around 1911. (Courtesy of Mabel and Elizabeth Burke.)

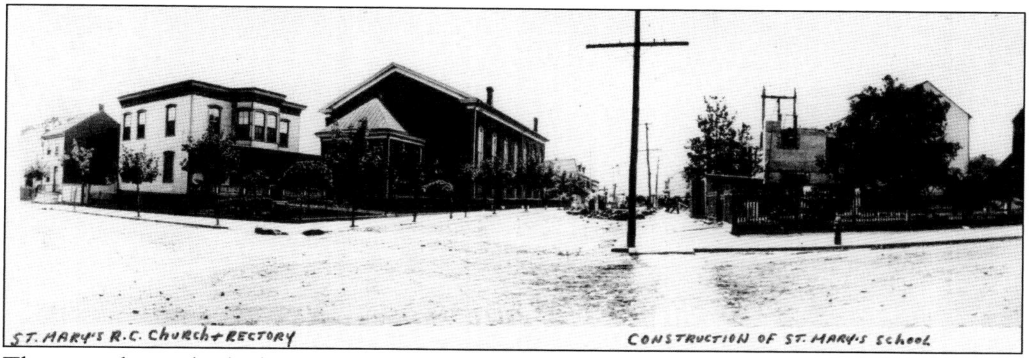

The second parochial school in town was erected by St. Mary's Roman Catholic Church in 1914. It was constructed on West Hancock Street across from the church and rectory.

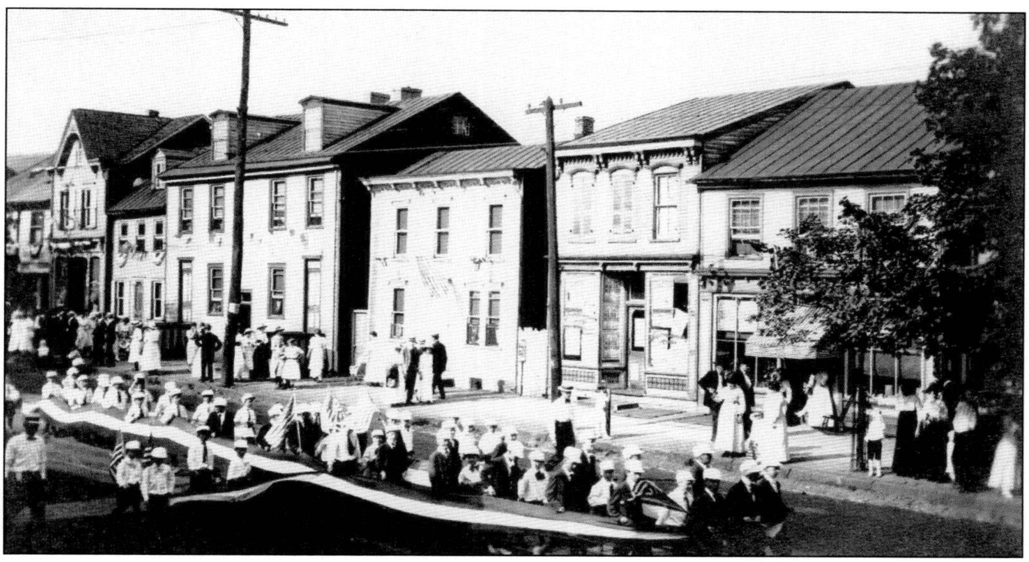

Another notable parade in town was conducted for the opening of St. Mary's parochial school in 1914. Floats and banners as well as a U.S. flag from a frigate line the streets for this celebration. The flag from this parade was saved in the rectory and is still used by the St. Clair Community and Historical Society in parades today.

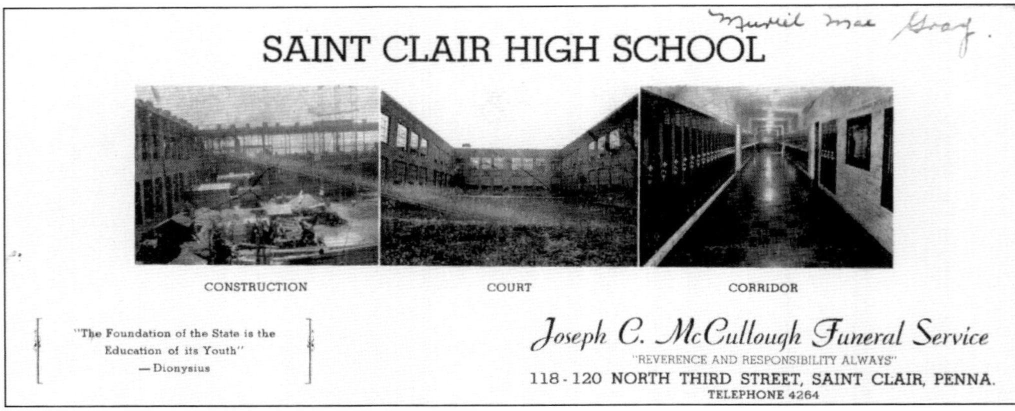

Shown is an advertising blotter showing the construction of the last high school built in St. Clair. Built in 1938, this school building served successfully until the graduating class of 1989 and now serves as an elementary school.

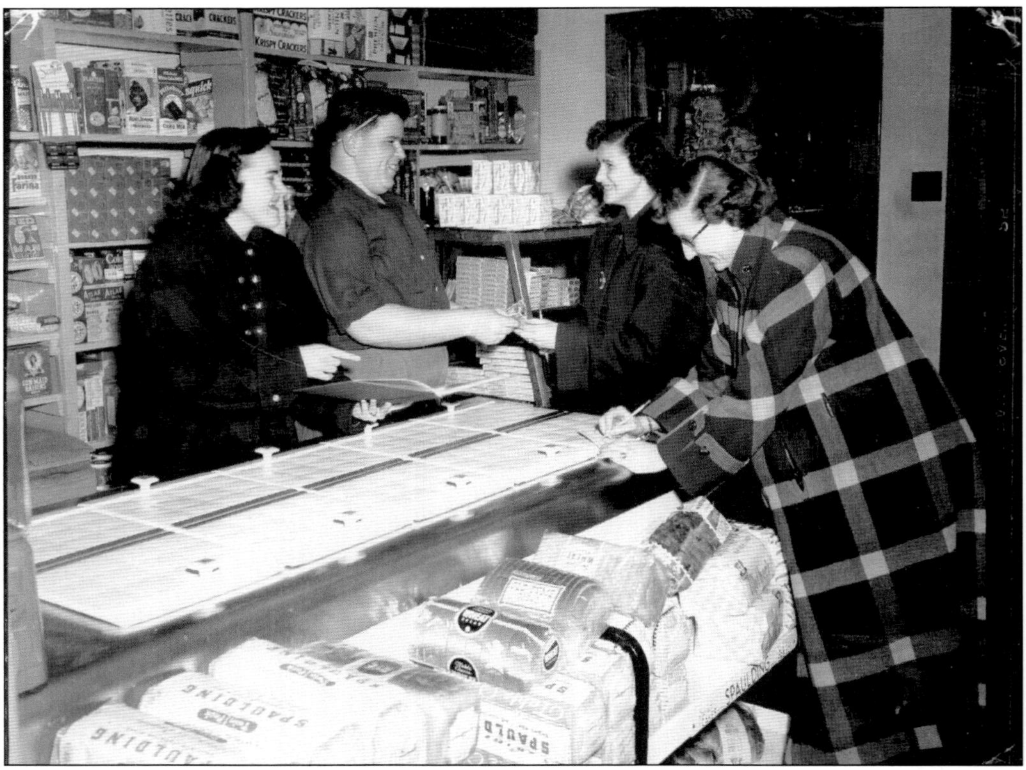

A popular mom-and-pop grocery store located on Nichols Street directly across from the high school was McMullins Market. It was always busy before classes, after classes, and during lunch breaks. Jean Kellagher and Rosalie Potts from the class of 1951 stop in to solicit advertising for the school yearbook, the *Clarian*. (Courtesy of Bill and Jean Connors.)

All the surrounding areas of St. Clair had their own elementary schools. Students here were from the one-room schoolhouse in East Mines, just southwest of town. The picture was taken around 1935. (Courtesy of Mrs. James Rosenburger.)

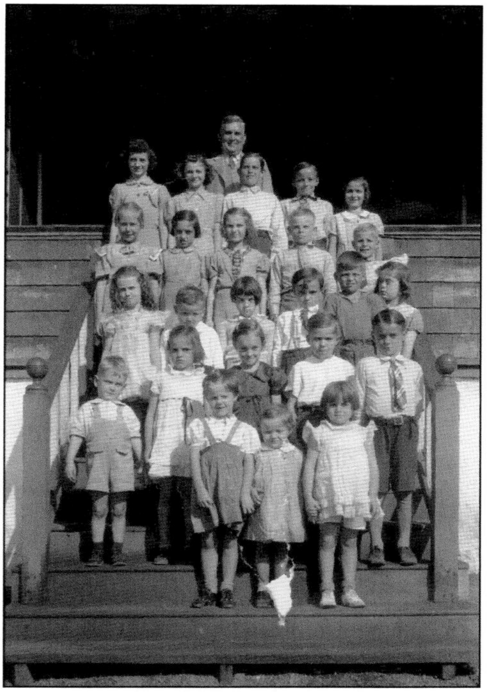

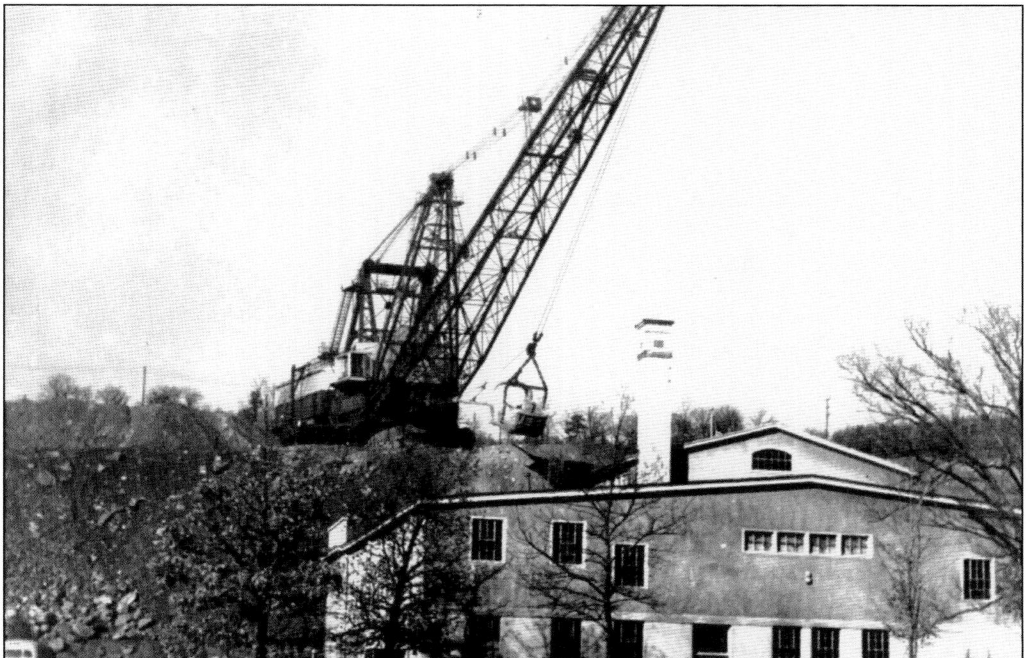

The working dragline at Mount Laffee was quite a distraction for the schoolchildren at the Mount Laffee schoolhouse. Former students remember watching the shovel working instead of paying attention to the teacher. This school was ahead of its time with a huge gymnasium and indoor pool. (Courtesy of Robert Scherr.)

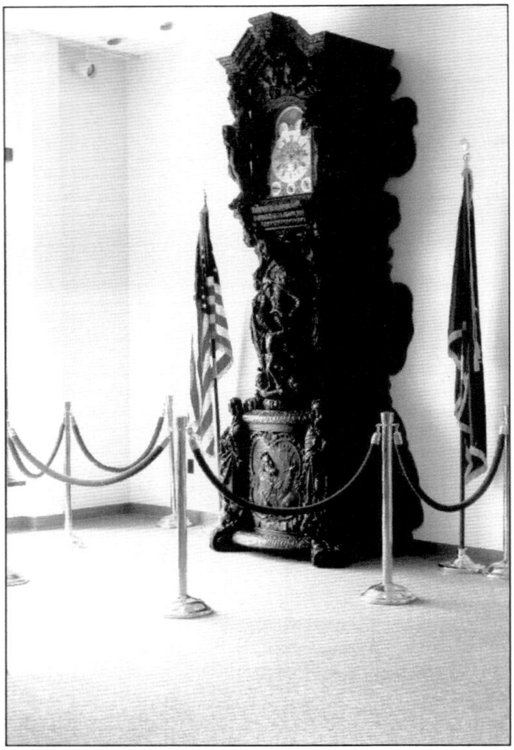

This clock was imported to the country by William H. Taylor, owner of the St. Clair Coal Company, who purchased it directly from the estate of the Earl of Pembroke. It was exhibited at the Chicago World's Columbian Exposition in 1893. This clock was originally made for William Herbert, Earl of Pembroke, in honor of his wife, the Lady Margaret. Work began on the clock in 1718 and continued for half a century. In the late 1920s, Mrs. William H. Taylor, a great patron of the schools of St. Clair, presented the clock to the school. The clock is still on display in the school library. (Photograph by John Zamecnik.)

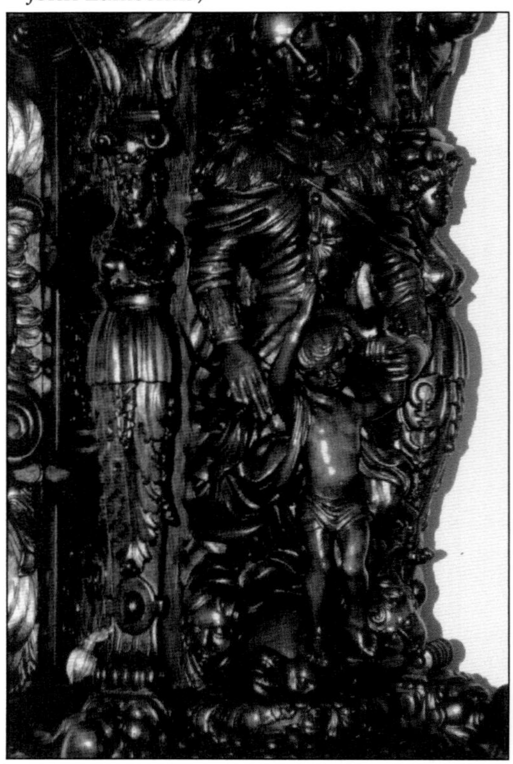

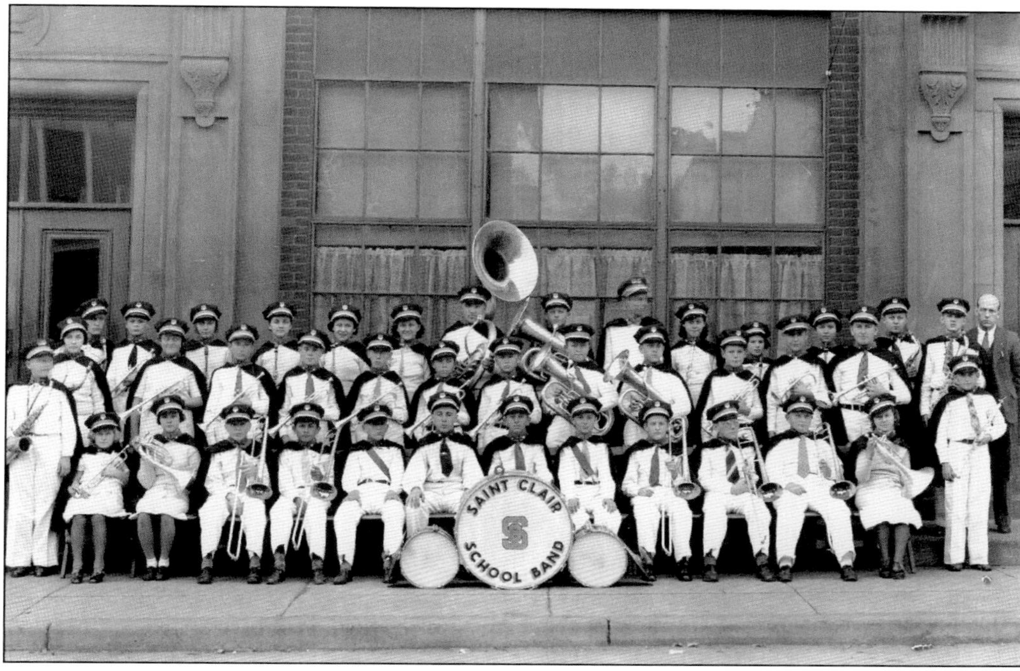

Members of the St. Clair High School band of 1937 pose for their photograph in front of the Carroll Street High School.

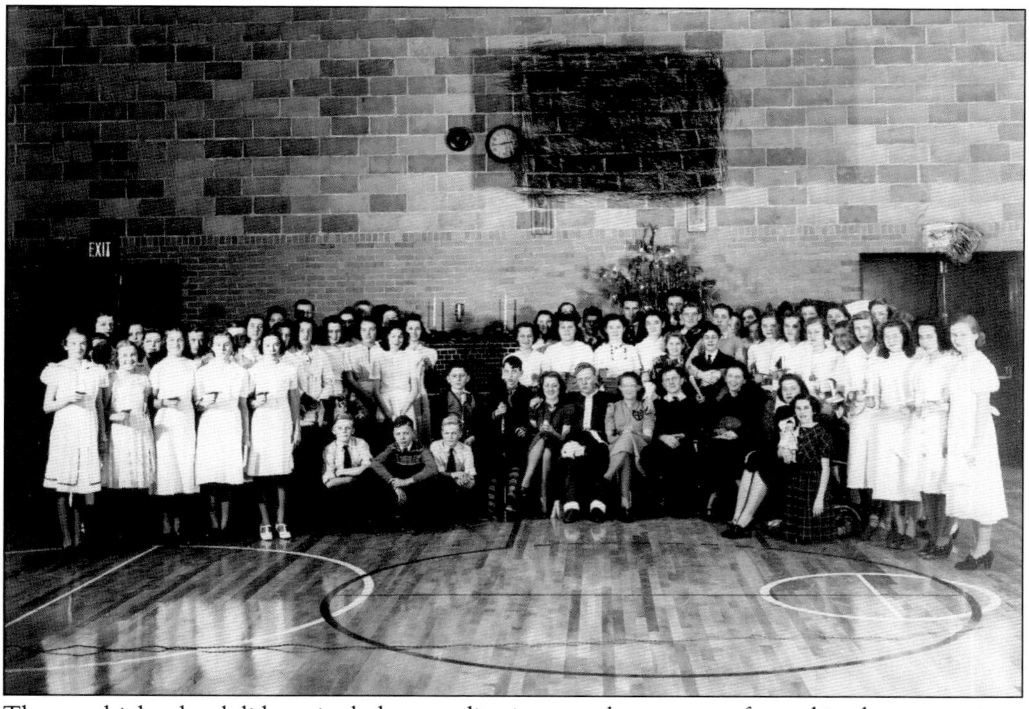

The new high school did not include an auditorium, so plays were performed in the gymnasium, such as this one at Christmastime in 1939. The black area above the actors was the basketball backboard that was edited out.

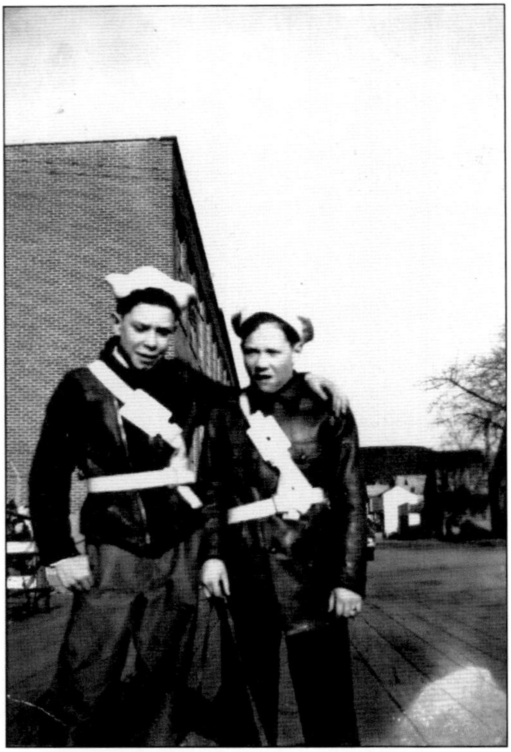

Safety patrols consisted of students from the uppermost grades in the elementary school who assisted younger children crossing the streets. Bill Connors and Jack Miller were members of the St. Mary's Parochial School Safety Patrol; notice their sashes and caps. The public school had its own safety patrol with officer "Cap" Morrow as an advisor. (Courtesy of Bill and Jean Connors.)

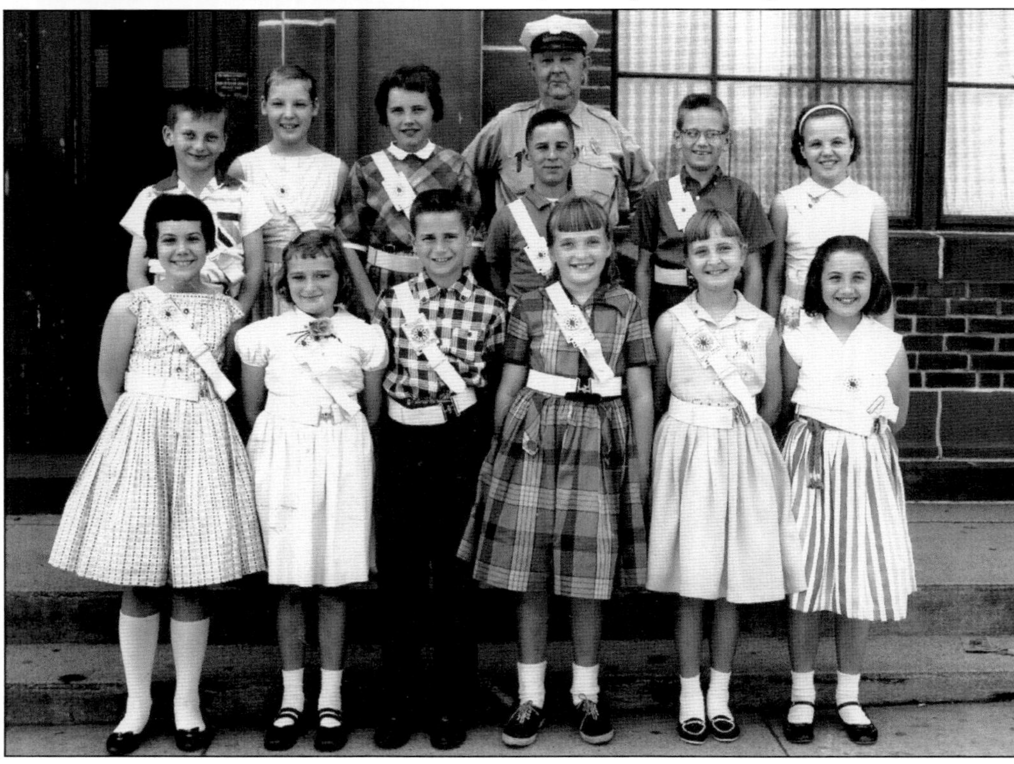

Six

SPORTS

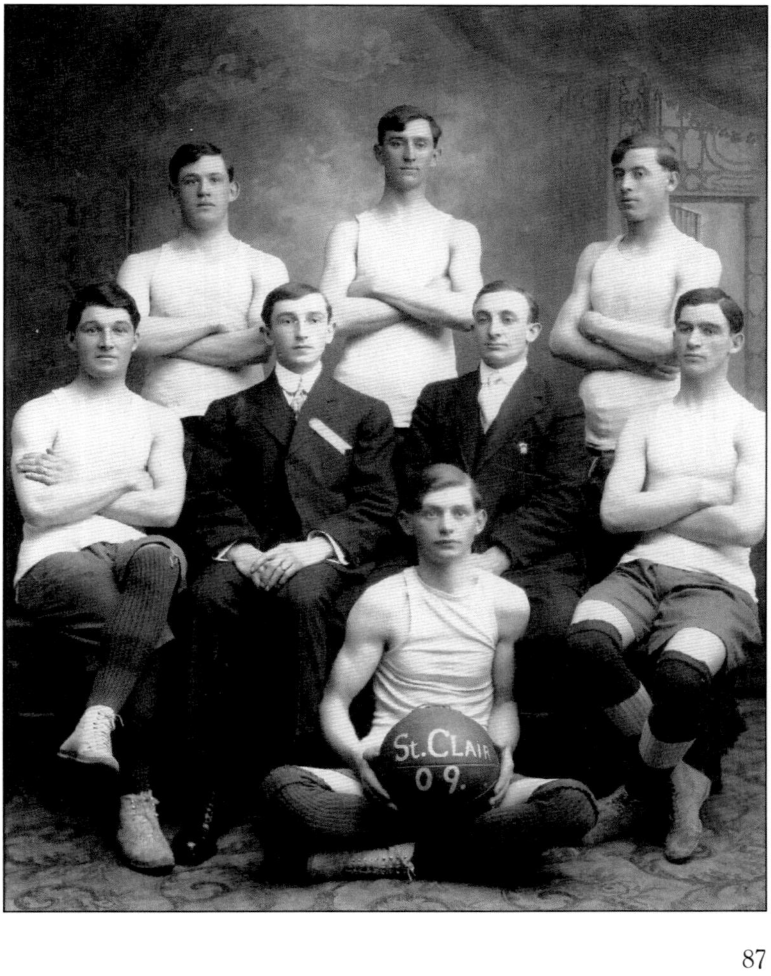

This 1910–1911 championship team was formed by Henry E. Snayberger, a prominent shoe factory owner in Schuylkill Haven. The first professional basketball teams were formed nationally around 1898 with teams in St. Clair following shortly thereafter. Snayberger organized the first basketball team in 1900 and continued through 1915. In 1908, admission to a game was 15¢, and it went up to a quarter the following year. Teams were paid $25 to $40 per game, while the crack teams could get up to $50 per game.

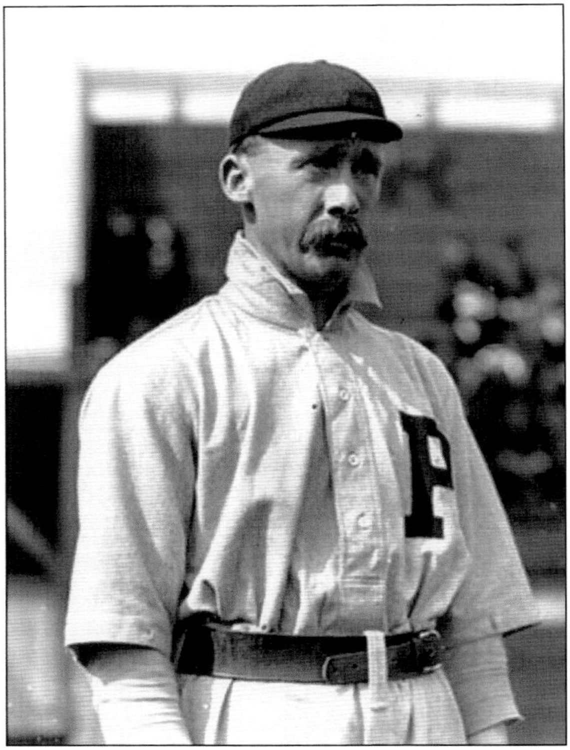

John Franklin Titus was born on February 21, 1876. Before his career in baseball, he was a coal miner, served in the army during the Spanish-American War, and played basketball for the St. Clair Athletics. He went professional in 1903 and played with the Philadelphia Phillies until 1912 when he was traded to the Boston Braves and played until 1915, when he retired at the age of 38.

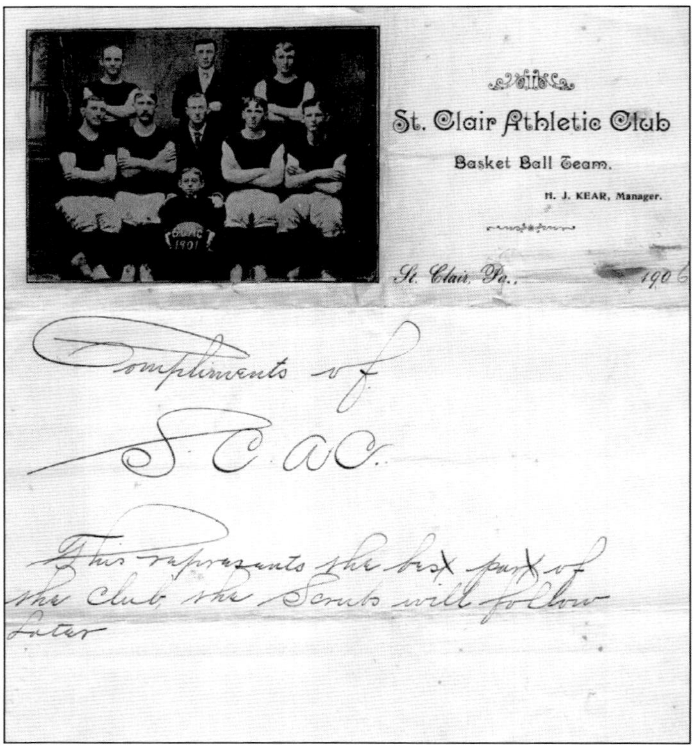

St. Clair Athletic Club
Basket Ball Team.
H. J. KEAR, Manager.

St. Clair, Pa., 190

Compliments of
S.C.A.C.

This represents the best part of the Club, the Scrubs will follow Later

St. Clair basketball teams flourished in the first few years of the 20th century and upheld a claim to a national championship—not interscholastic, but professional. The team of 1901 met all the best teams in the game at that time and won by such one-sided scores it gained recognition as a national champion. On the team was Jack Titus, who afterward became a great baseball star for Pottsville and the Philadelphia Phillies.

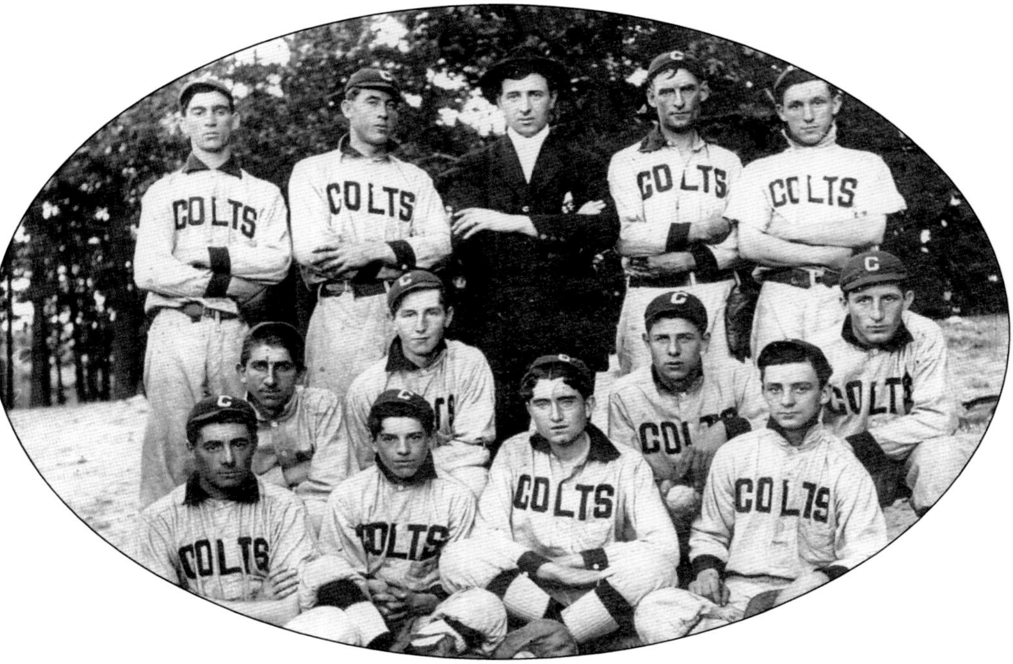

As baseball grew in popularity during the 19th century throughout the country, teams were forming in St. Clair. One such group was named the St. Clair Colts. This picture shows 12 players, with names like Goody, Dumpy, Mix, Chippy, and Patsy, and their manager posing for their picture around 1910. Richard Gray was an all-around athlete who played with the championship Snayberger basketball team and the Colts.

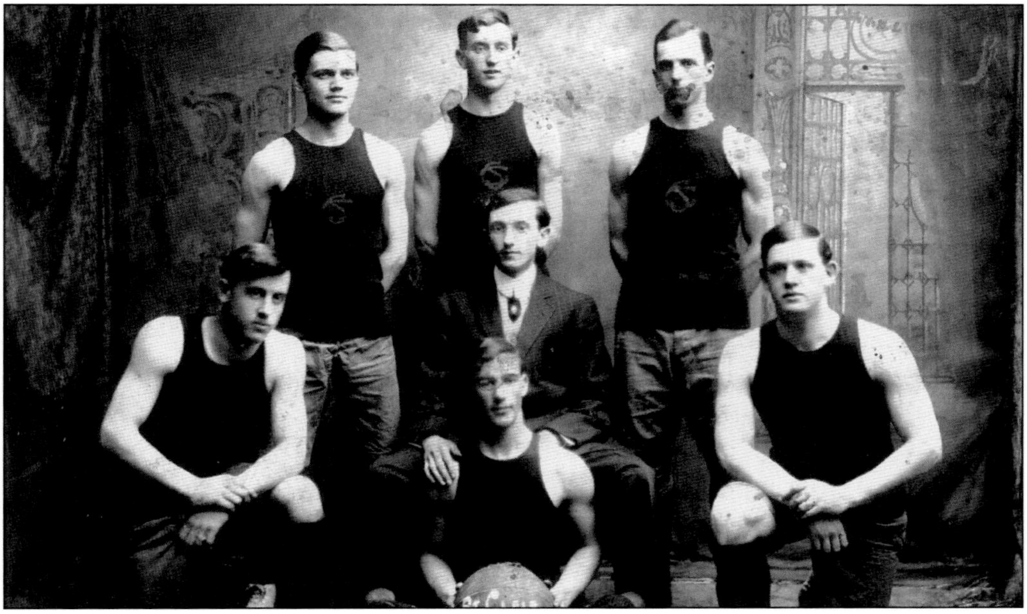

The first professional basketball teams were formed nationally around 1898 with teams in St. Clair following shortly thereafter. The game consisted of five players and often used wooden fruit baskets for the hoops. This photograph shows the 1910–1911 championship team.

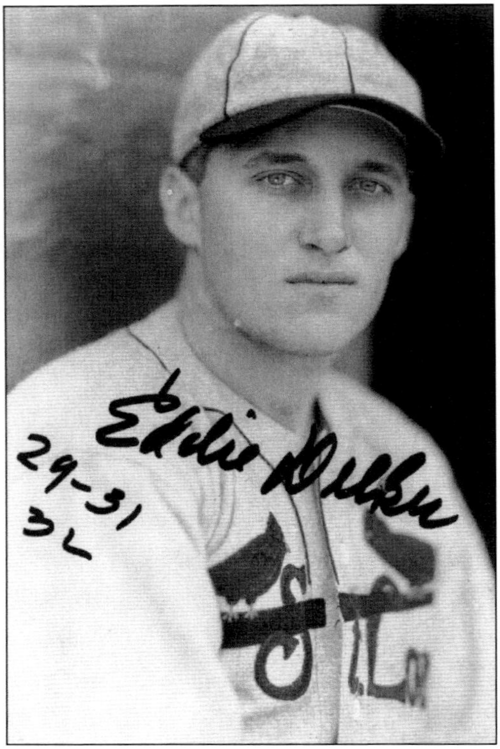

Eddie Delker was born on Tuesday, April 17, 1906. Delker was 23 years old when he broke into the big leagues in 1927, playing for a team in Topeka. In 1932–1933, Delker played in the infield of the Philadelphia Nationals, and ended his career in 1934 with the St. Louis Cardinals. After retiring from baseball, he became a well-known collector of mining memorabilia, even re-creating a coal mine entrance in his home.

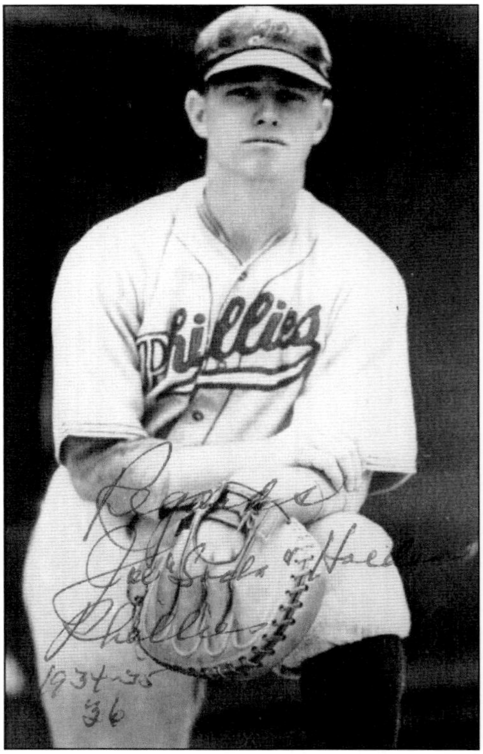

The name of Joseph "Socks" Holden has been synonymous with baseball for 45 years. While attending Duke University on a baseball scholarship, the St. Clair native dropped out to begin his baseball career as a catcher with the Philadelphia Phillies. Holden played for various leagues throughout the years and ended his baseball career as a scout for eastern Pennsylvania. He held this position for 17 years before resigning to take over the insurance business of his deceased father.

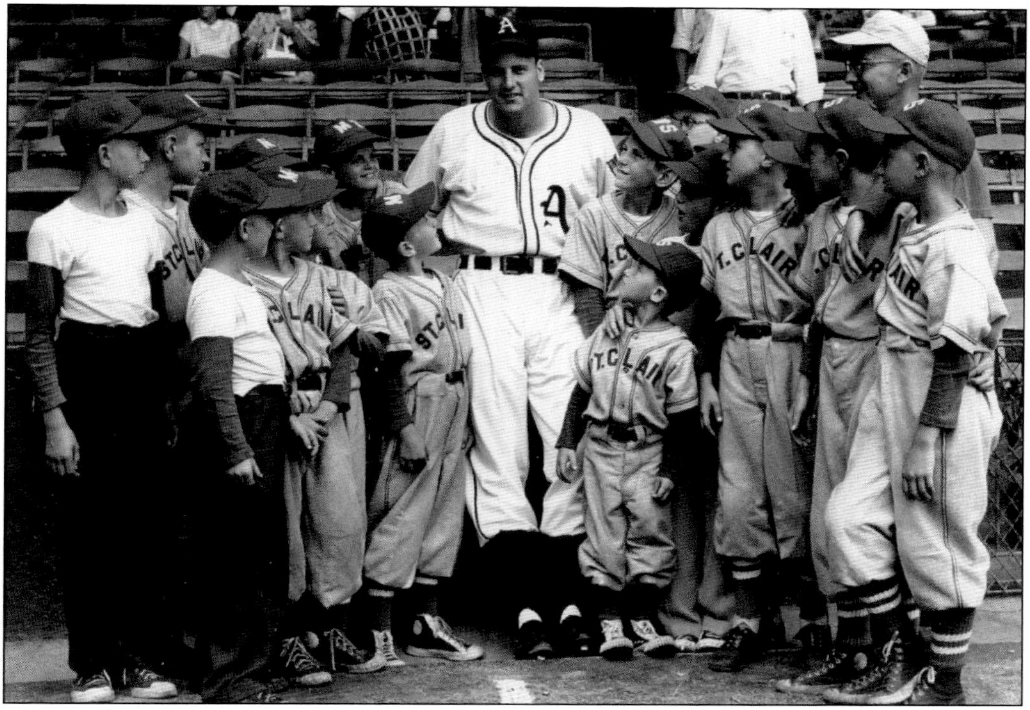

In 1939, the Little League was born in Williamsport. With a love of sports, it did not take long for St. Clair to form its own teams. Teams were sponsored by local organizations, businesses, and fire companies. In 1950, the All-Stars, led by their coach Milton Hercha, took a road trip to Shibe Park, later known as Connie Mack Stadium, in Philadelphia for a professional game between the Philadelphia Athletics and New York Yankees. The boys had the opportunity to get pictures taken with their heroes, Gus Zernial, outfielder for the Philadelphia Athletics, and Phil Rizzto, shortstop for the New York Yankees.

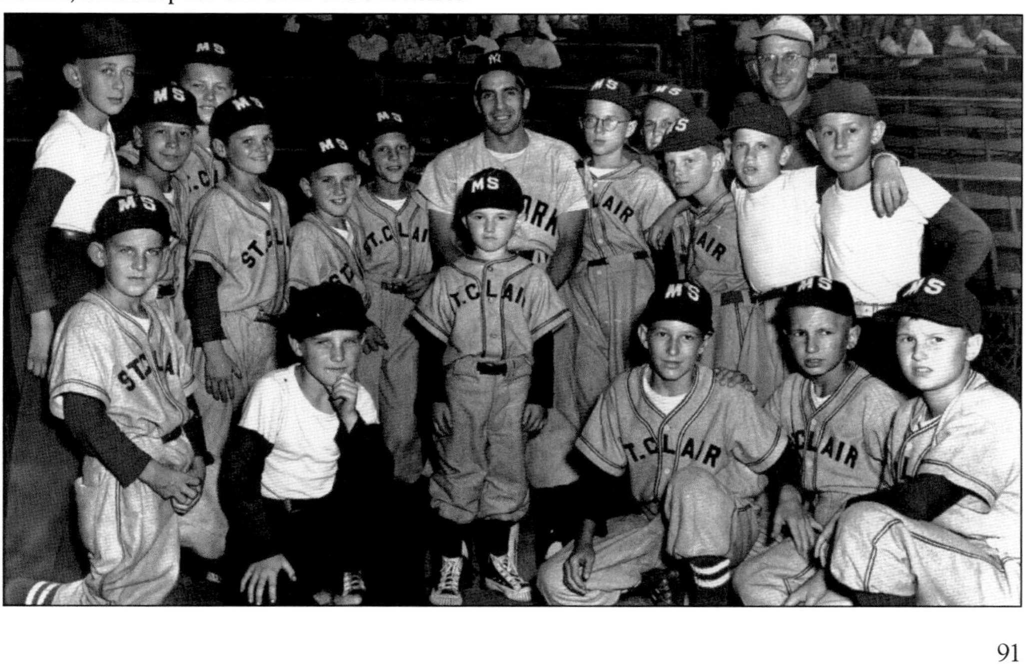

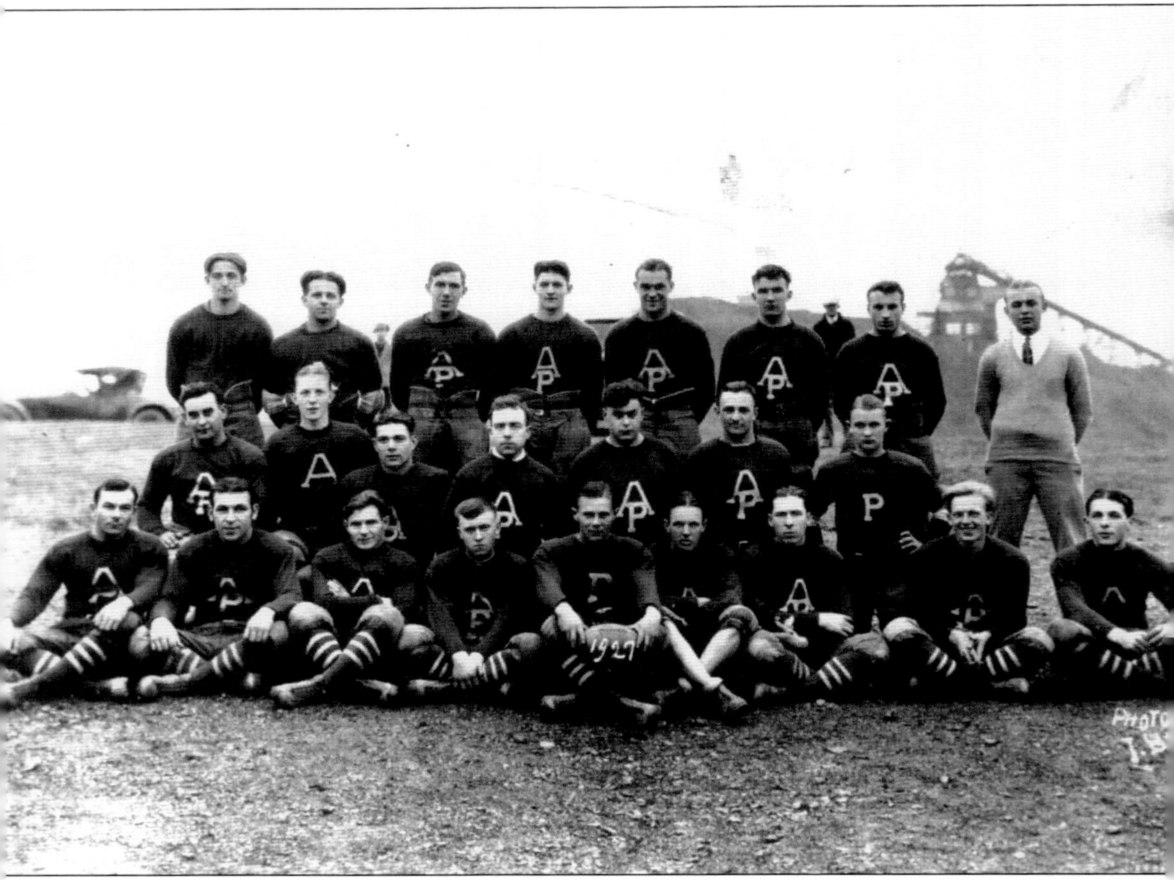

Football players in Arnots Addition formed a team called the Panthers. Members of the team are pictured with the coal colliery standing behind them.

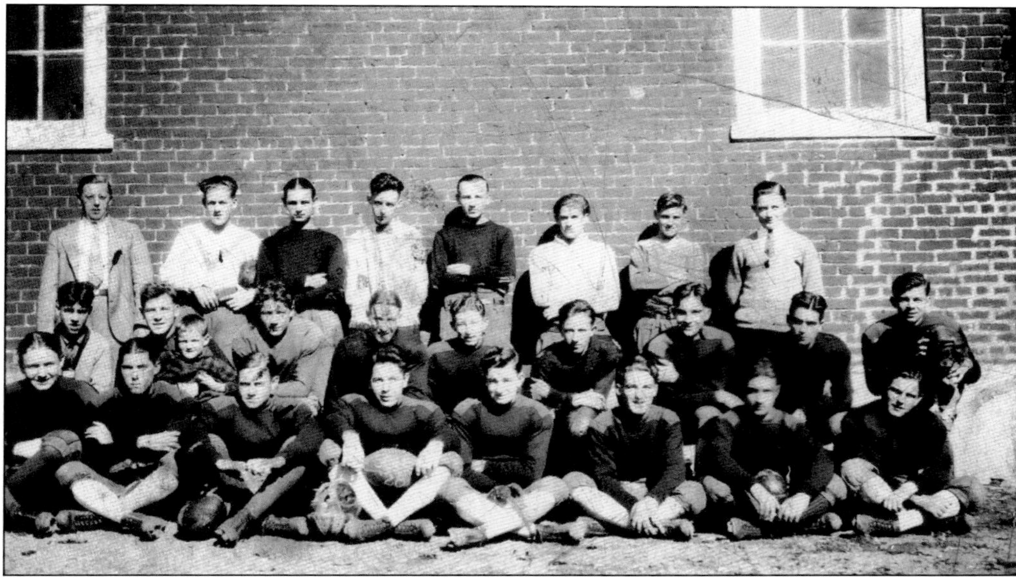

Early high school football players often played against some tough competition and had little safety equipment and very little rules. Several members of this 1928 team recalled some schools pulling muscular miners out of the mines to compete against them. These men were friends of the Pottsville players who made up the professional team the Pottsville Maroons.

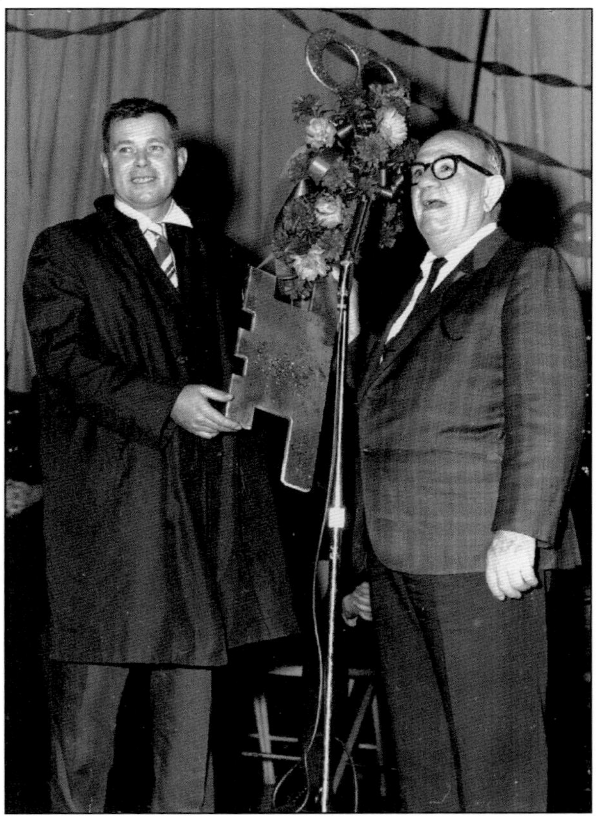

Coach William Wolff coached football and basketball at the St. Clair High School from 1954 to 1970. He led the 1969–1970 basketball team to a state championship. He left St. Clair shortly after to coach for a school in Danville.

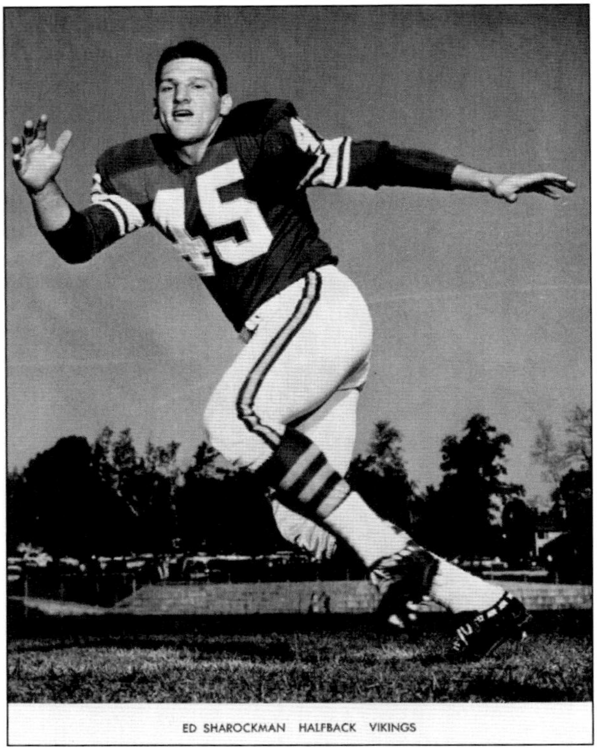

A 1957 St. Clair high school graduate, Ed Sharockman was an integral part of all three sports that won their division championships. On a full football scholarship, Sharockman graduated from the University of Pittsburgh where he starred as quarterback. In 1961, he was drafted by the Minnesota Vikings of the National Football League and played for 12 years. He started in Super Bowl IV on January 11, 1970, Kansas City Chiefs versus Minnesota Vikings.

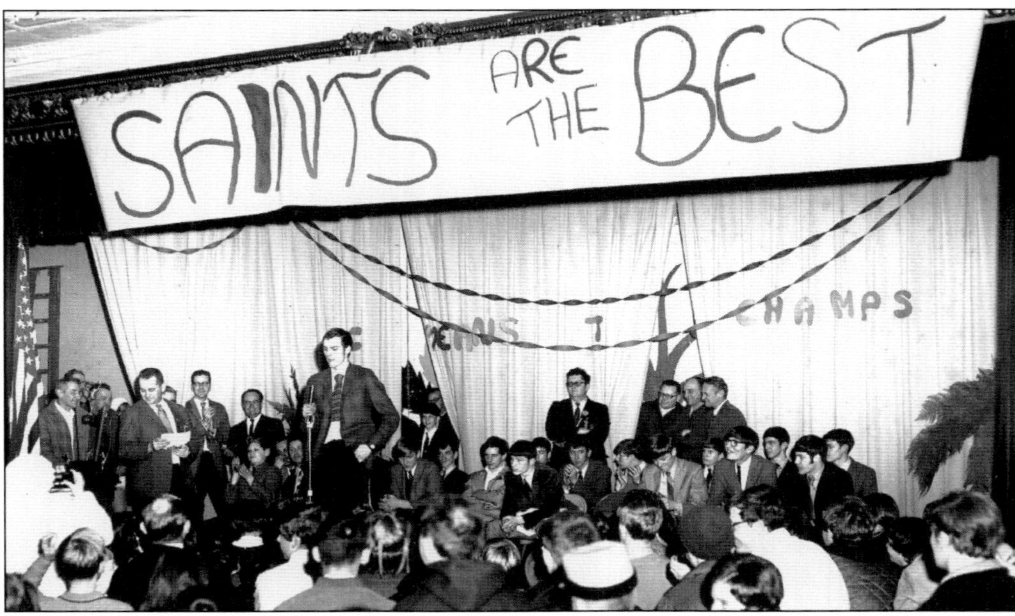

The St. Clair boys' basketball team won the 1970 Class 3 state championship. Not only was it a first for any boys' team in St. Clair, but in 38 years, no other boys' team in Schuylkill County obtained the title. This was partially achieved by chemistry between the players who played together since fifth grade, the fact that each player had a double-digit game average, and the enormous encouragement from the school and community.

Seven

Religious Diversity

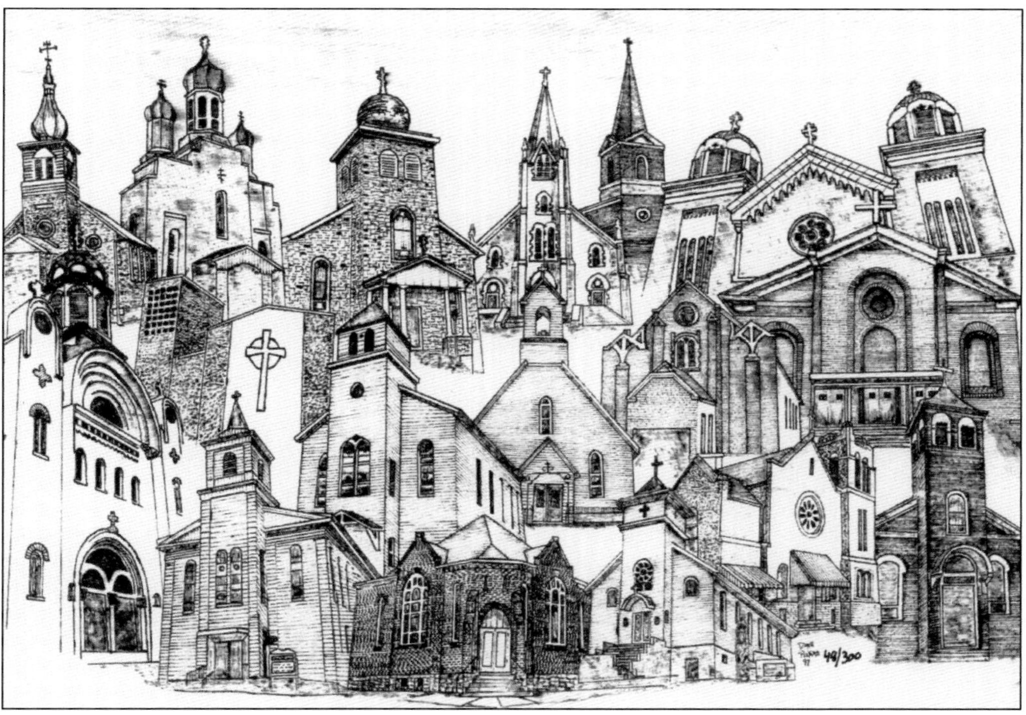

The 17 churches of this small community attest to the residents' strong religious faith and diversity of ethnic background. The churches are St. John's Slovak Lutheran, Bethlehem Baptist, First Presbyterian, First Primitive Methodist, Holy Apostles Episcopal, Holy Trinity Ukrainian, Immaculate Conception Roman Catholic, St. Boniface Roman Catholic, St. Casmir's Lithuanian Catholic, St. Clair-Wade Methodist Church, St. John's United Church of Christ, St. Mary's Byzantine Catholic, St. Mary's Orthodox, St. Mary's Roman Catholic, St. Michael's Russian Orthodox, St. Nicholas Ukrainian, and St. Peter and Paul Roman Catholic. (Drawing by Dave Pukas.)

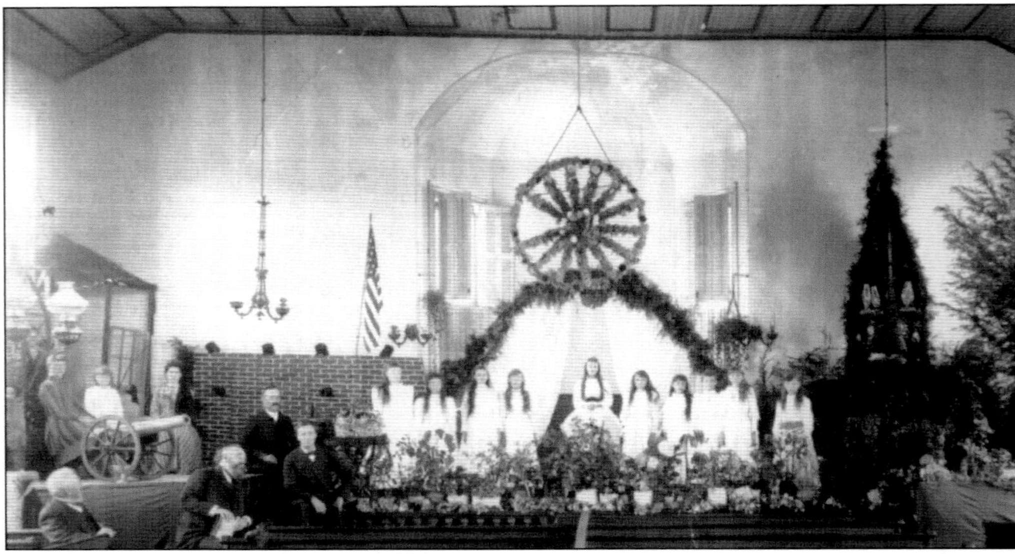

The First Primitive Methodist Church of St. Clair is the oldest Primitive Methodist church in America with a continuous history. The picture is from the late 1890s; notice the cannon and Civil War veteran on the left side of the photograph.

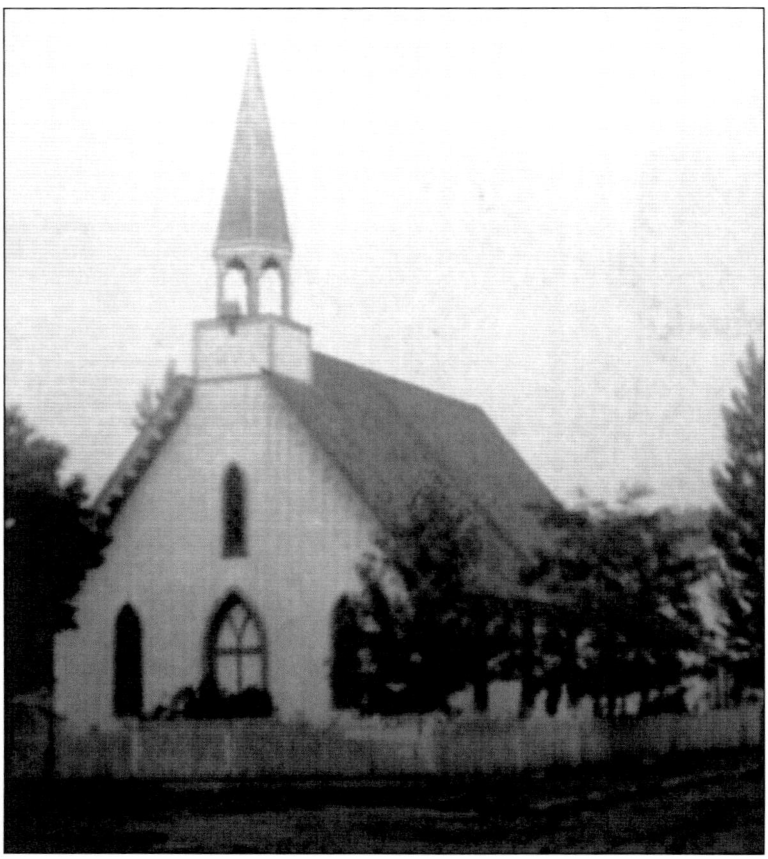

The first vestry was organized on October 8, 1847, in the home of Charles Lawton. The cornerstone was laid in 1854, and the church formally opened for public worship on February 10, 1856. The steeple looks different today due to a lightning strike and fire.

The United Methodist Church in Wadesville was the oldest church in the village. It was organized as a branch of the Methodist Episcopal Church of St. Clair in 1867. Once located in the part of Wadesville called Georgetown, the entire church was moved to Wadesville in 1949 to expand mining in Georgetown. In August 2000, the congregation joined the Methodist Episcopal Church of St. Clair to form the St. Clair-Wade United Methodist Church, and the Wadesville church was torn down. (Courtesy of Rosemary McCoach.)

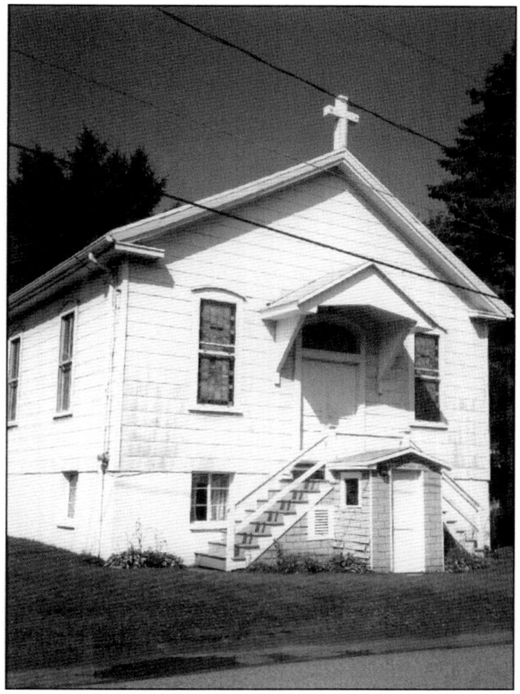

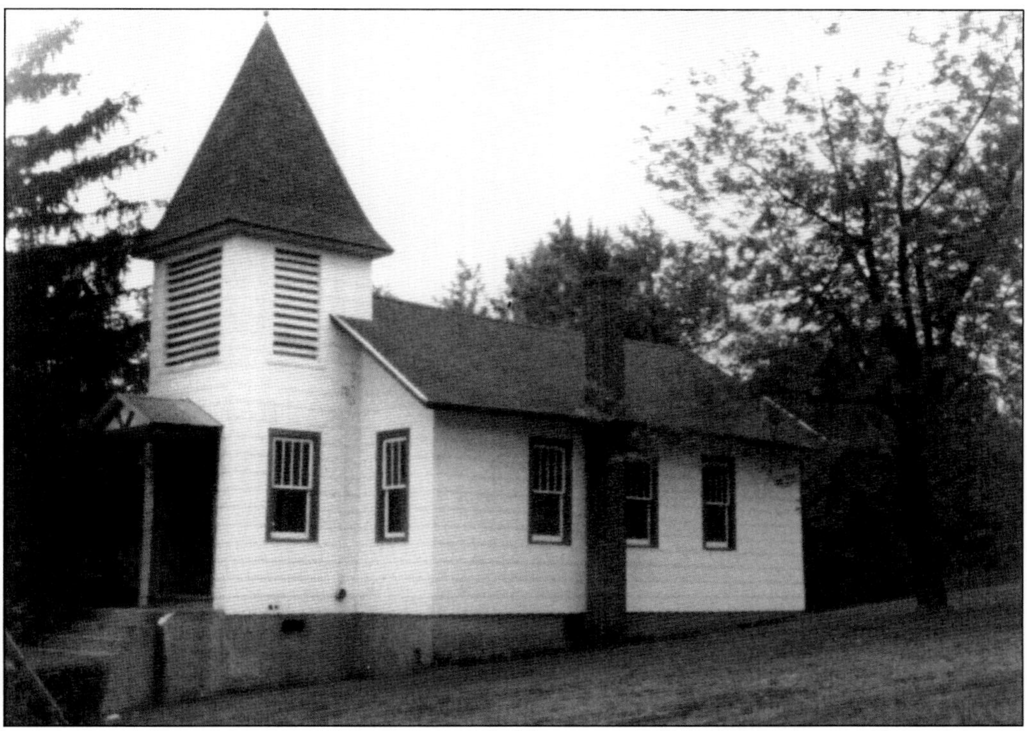

The Seventh Day Adventist Church of Wadesville was organized in 1904. In 1915, a church was erected next to the schoolhouse with an active membership until the year 2000, when the church was torn down to allow for coal-mining operations. (Courtesy of Rosemary McCoach.)

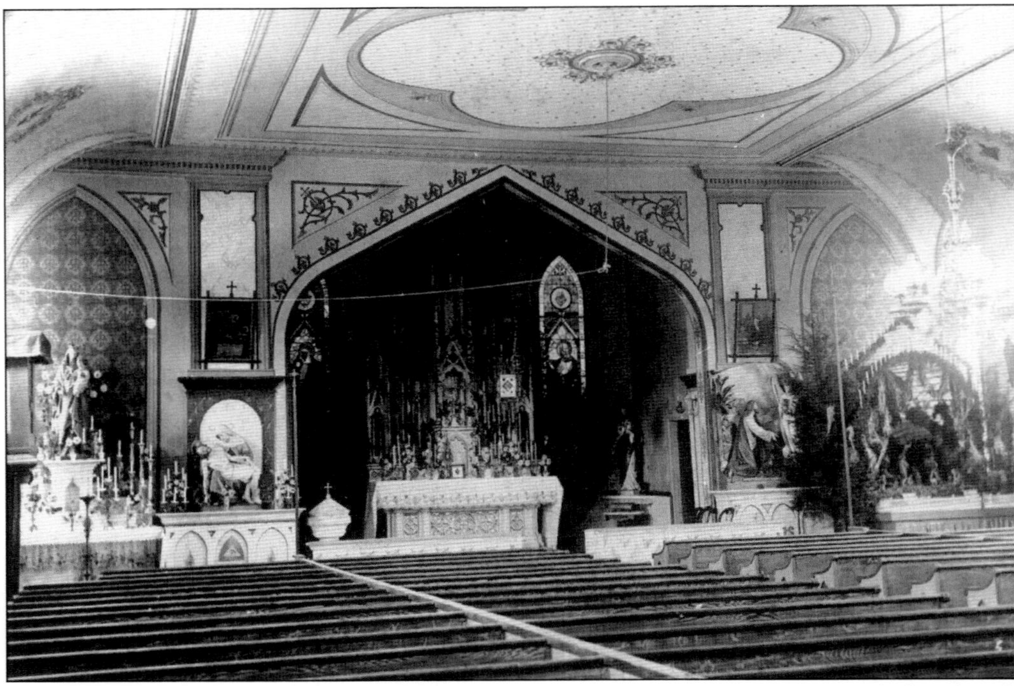

This photograph from 1885–1890 shows the inside of the St. Boniface German Catholic Church. In 1852, Bishop John Neumann gave the German Catholics of St. Clair permission to build a church. The church was built by Jacob Metz, who was assisted by members of the congregation; the building was completed in 1853. When the church closed on July 13, 2008, it was the oldest Catholic church in St. Clair. (Courtesy of Robert Scherr.)

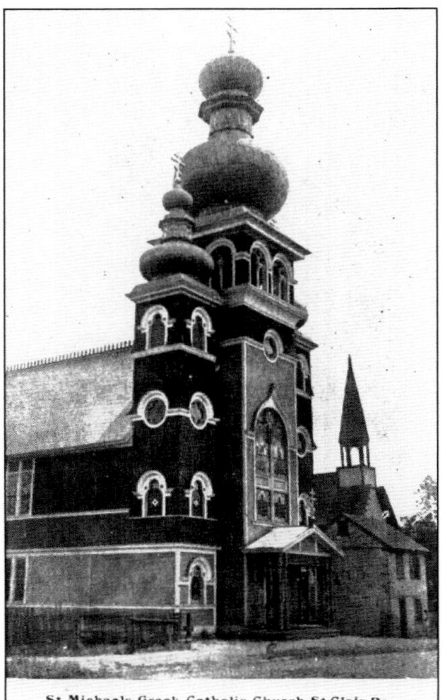

St Michaels Greek Catholic Church St Clair Pa.

Shown is an early picture of St. Michael's the Archangel, the first Greek Catholic Church in St. Clair, founded in 1897. The congregation was organized by immigrants from Carpatho, Russia, Czechoslovakia, and Galacia. The church building on North Nichols Street was completed in 1932.

The men of St. Peter and Paul's Roman Catholic Church continued to carry on many of the customs followed in their native land of Poland. At Easter, a replica of the tomb of Jesus was constructed in the front of the church by a side altar. Members of a group called the Polish Soldiers took turns standing guard at the tomb from Good Friday until Easter Sunday morning.

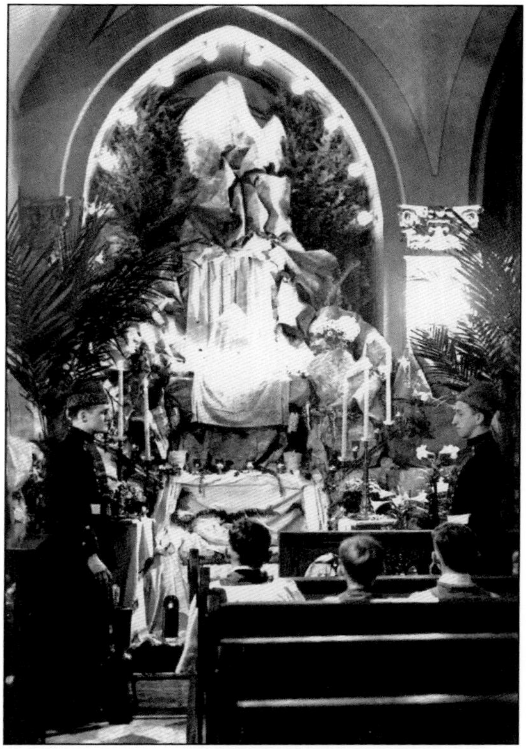

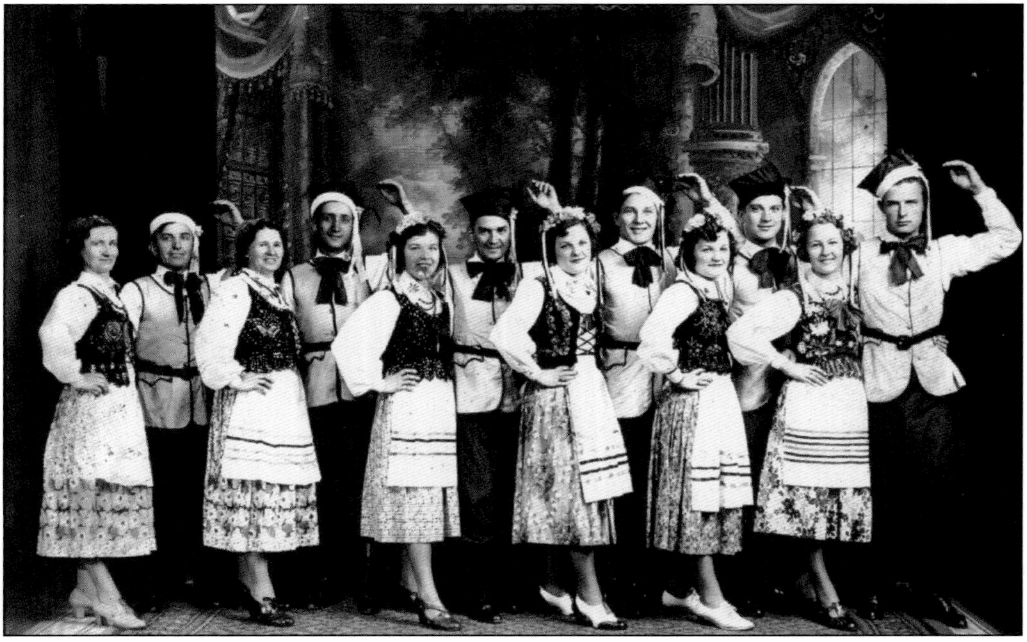

The Polish dance group known as Krakowiac was formed by members of St. Peter and Paul's Roman Catholic Church. They performed authentic dances of their native country, Poland, at social events held in the basement hall of the church. As their reputation grew, they were asked to perform throughout Schuylkill County and other surrounding counties.

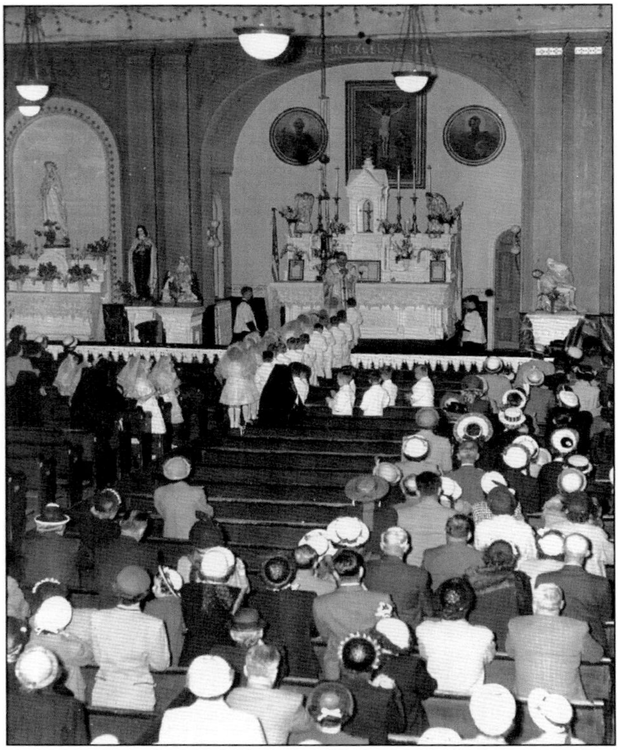

On May 1, 1864, the first mass was celebrated in this new classical Roman–designed church with rounded arch windows, Roman-style altars, and a floor plan based on the basilica plan. The new parish was called the Church of St. Mary the Immaculate Mother of God, which was later changed to St. Mary's Roman Catholic Church.

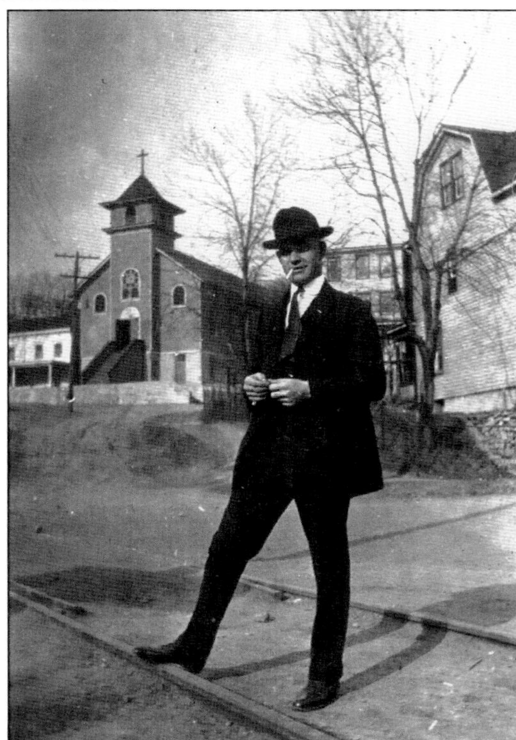

For years, the Lithuanian Catholics of St. Clair held services in various buildings and churches of different denominations. In September 1916, a piece of land was purchased on South Nichols Street and construction began on the present Lithuanian church. It was completed on October 22, 1917, and officially named St. Casmir's Church. This photograph was taken a few years after the church was finished and shows the remaining rails from the edge of the White Bridge. This large bridge that crossed several streets connected the Hooker Colliery with the rail yards in Mill Creek. A photograph of the White Bridge has never been discovered.

In 1903, the Catholic Slovak people in St. Clair started a movement to have their own church erected. Land known as Dormer's Farm was purchased for this purpose. In 1913, the parish had grown so rapidly that a new church had to be built. It was erected on the site of the old picnic grounds next to the old church. This photograph shows the new church on Diener's Hill around 1913, before the homes across the street were built. (Courtesy of Robert Scherr.)

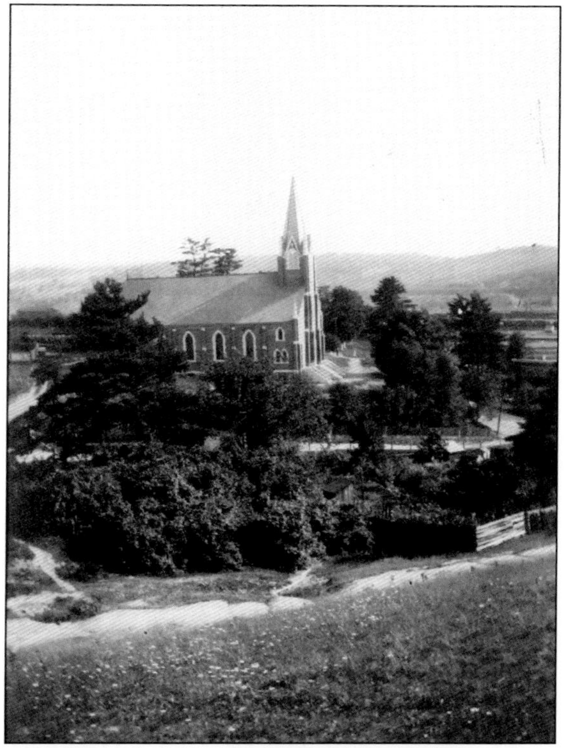

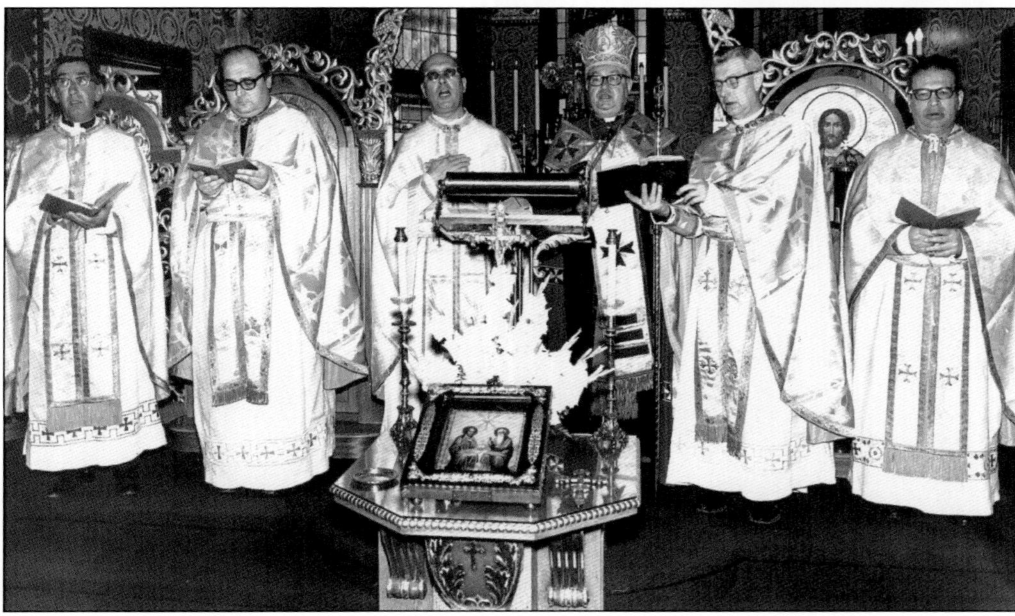

The founders of the Holy Trinity Ukrainian Catholic Church emigrated from the Ukraine and part of the Austrian-Hungarian Empire. In 1922, a lot with an existing framed house on North Mill Street was purchased, and the building moved to the rear of the lot to be used as a temporary chapel and rectory. A new church was completed in 1923. This church was closed in 2008. (Courtesy of Robert Scherr.)

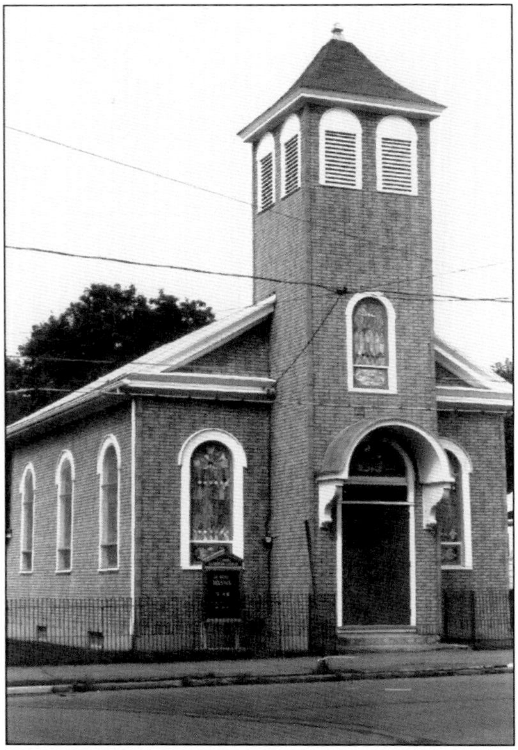

St. John the Evangelist Lutheran Catholic Church was built in 1873 by German Lutherans who left the joint Reformed Lutheran congregation after a long battle over whether German or English should be used in worship services. (Photograph by John Zamecnik.)

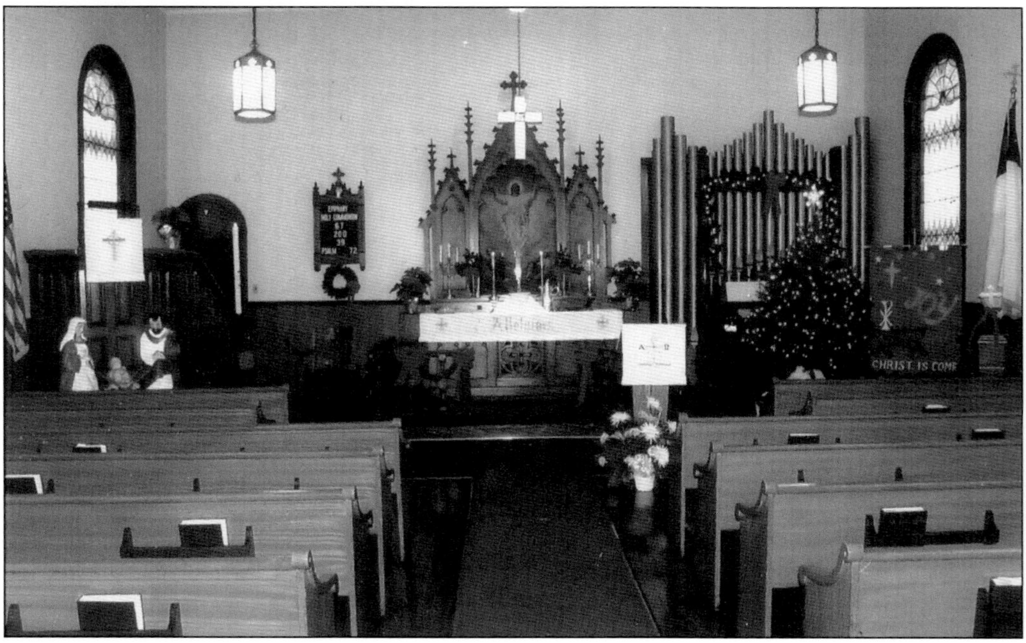

Due to a decline in membership, the St. John the Evangelist Lutheran Catholic Church closed and was sold. Extensive renovations were made to the building, including removing the organ, pews, stained-glass window over the door, new siding, and restrooms. The building was then made available for use as the St. Clair Community and Historical Society. (Photograph by John Zamecnik.)

Eight

Native Sons

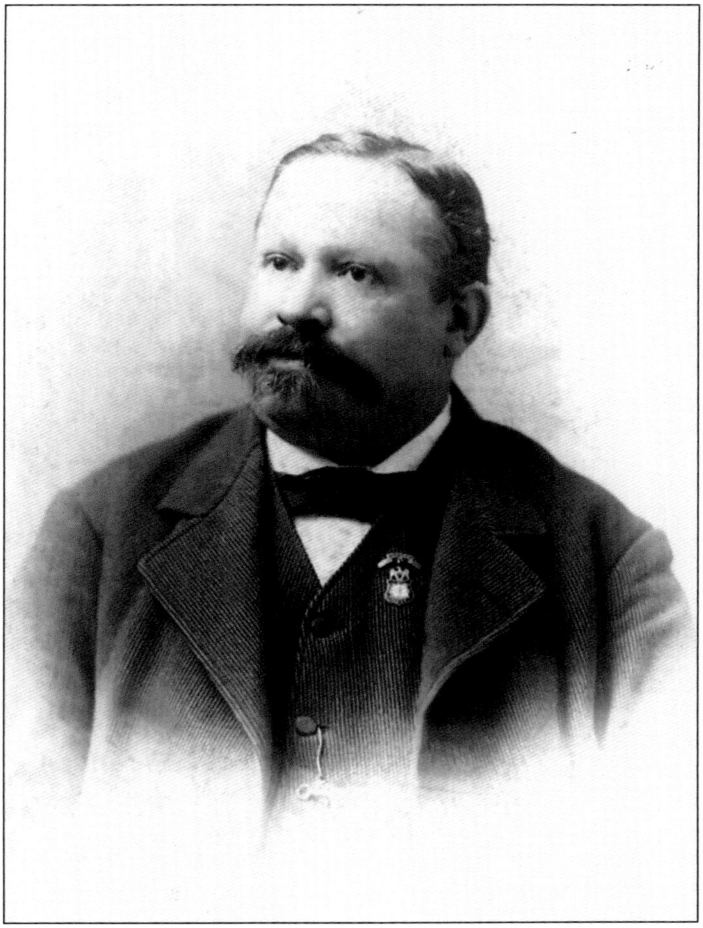

Seth Orme was born in Oldham, England, on November 8, 1847, and came to this country in 1855. Orme worked in the mines until the age of 14 when a mining accident prevented his further work in the mines. Orme, a shoemaker, went on to serve as councilman, school director, president of both bodies, and the postmaster of St. Clair from 1881 to 1894. In 1894, he was nominated as one of the Republican candidates for the legislature. He served in the last term of the legislature until his death in 1898.

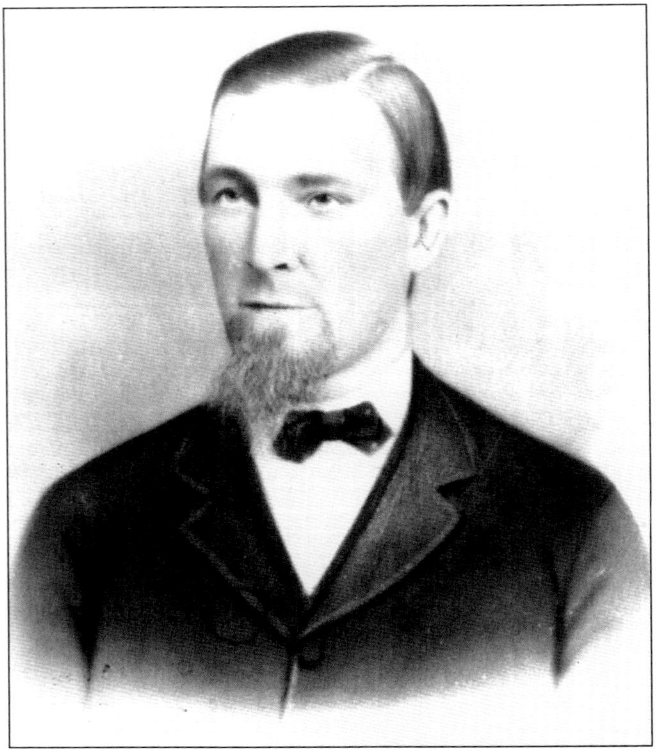

Walker's Hall on the corner of Third and Carroll Streets became the birthplace of the Workingmen's Benevolent Association (WBA). Around 1868, John Siney helped organize and was elected president of the union that grew to 20,000 members nationwide. As president, he worked to enact the first mine safety laws and minimum wage agreements through collective bargaining. Siney organized and became president of the first national miners union, Miners National Association, which became the origin of the United Mine Workers Union.

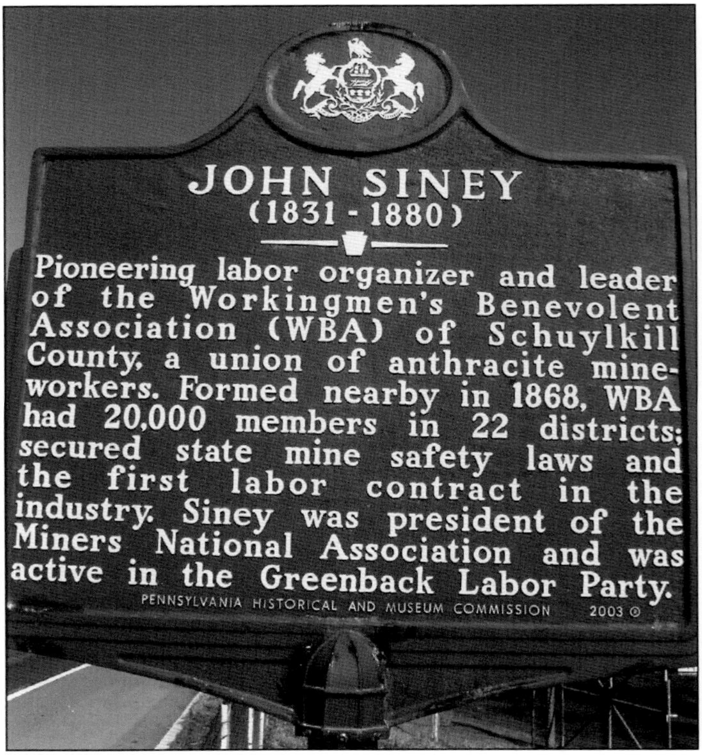

A historical marker honoring John Siney was unveiled by Catherine Holden, Siney's granddaughter. The major participants were U.S. representative Timothy Holden and Margaret Hess, both great-grandchildren of Siney; James Hess; and Edward Yankovich, District II president of the United Mine Workers Union. Yankovich pointed to Walker's Hall and dramatically stated, "in that building, the United Mine Workers recognize its origins."

Vice Adm. Joel Thompson Boone was born in St. Clair on August 29, 1889. He was awarded the Congressional Medal of Honor for his bravery in France during World War I on July 19, 1918. He was physician to presidents Warren Harding, Calvin Coolidge, and Herbert Hoover. Boone served as the Navy Medical Corps representative at the Japanese surrender aboard the USS *Missouri* in 1945. He was the first to set foot on Japanese soil at the end of World War II and to oversee the release of sick, starving, and mistreated prisoners.

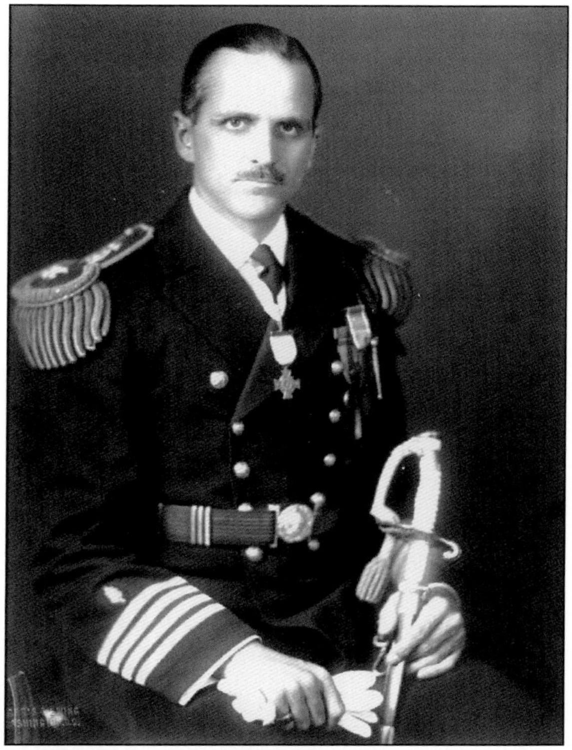

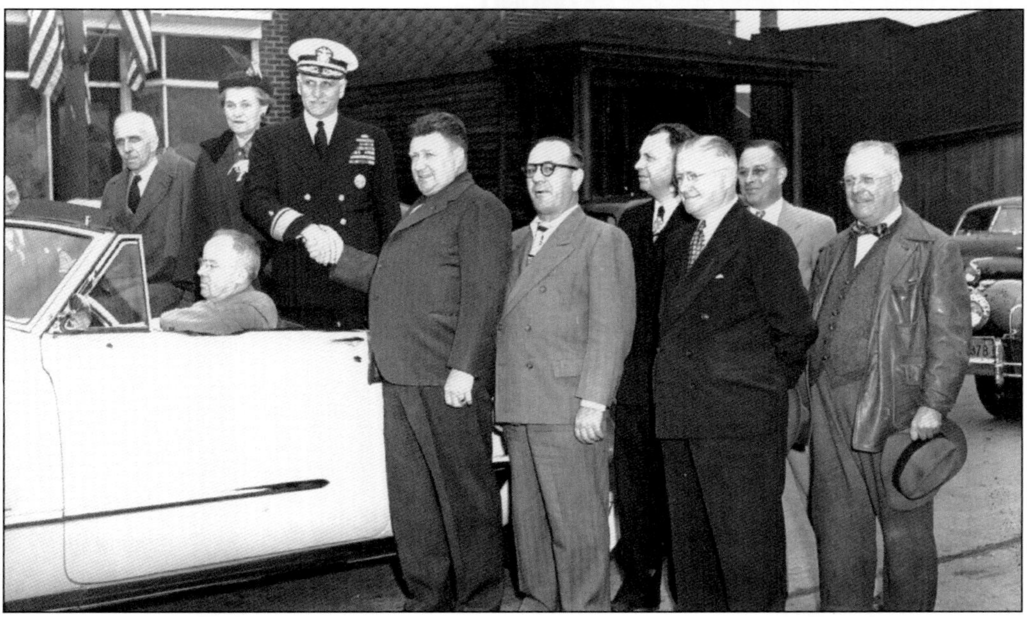

St. Clair mayor Bill Brady welcomes Admiral Boone to the town in 1949. Other St. Clair dignitaries in the picture are, from left to right, council president Joseph Long, St. Clair school superintendent Charles R. Birch, postmaster James Monahan, teacher Alfred Roberts, and Harold Smythe of the St. Clair Coal Company. At Admiral Boone's left are his brother, E. Herbert Boone, and Admiral Boone's wife, Helen.

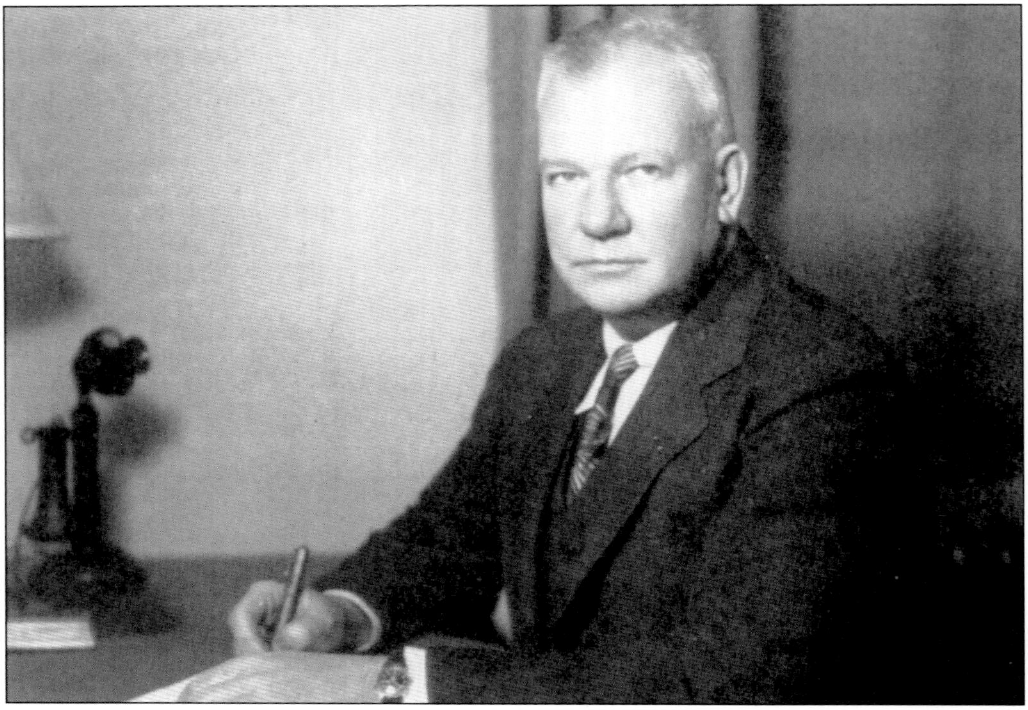

Born in Shamokin but raised in St. Clair, Dr. Claude S. Beck graduated from St. Clair High School in 1911. He earned a doctorate of medicine degree from Johns Hopkins University in 1921. Beck, a heart surgeon, was the first doctor to perform open-heart surgery and recognized that what was called the "worming heart" was really a heart out of sync. In 1947, he invented the defibrillator and made his mark in medical history.

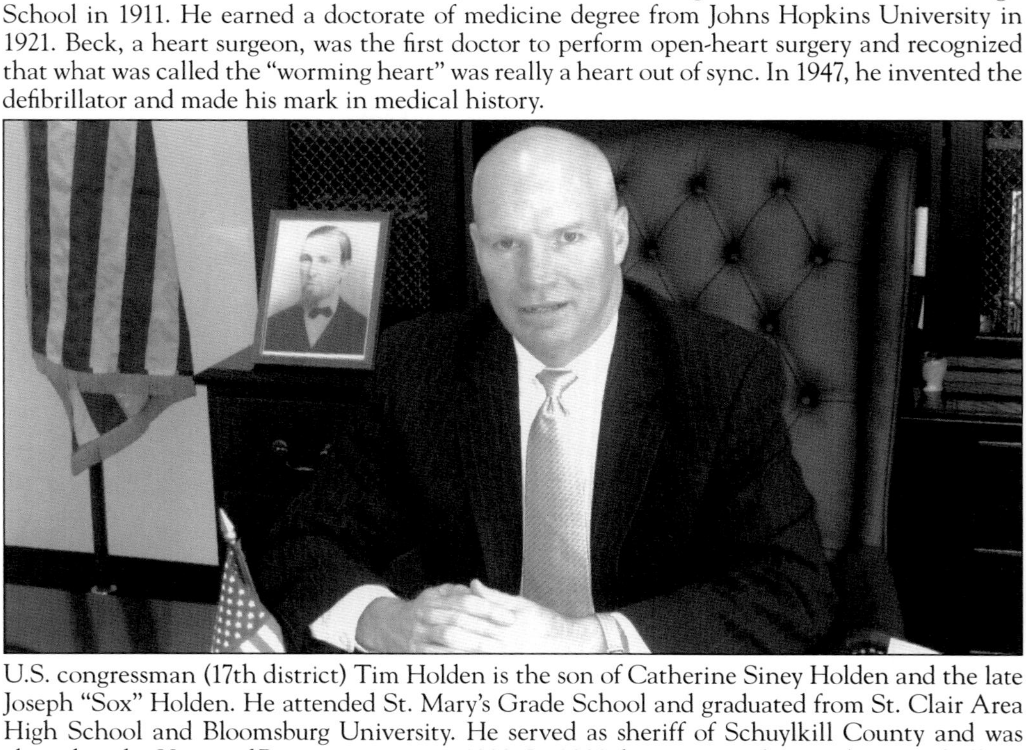

U.S. congressman (17th district) Tim Holden is the son of Catherine Siney Holden and the late Joseph "Sox" Holden. He attended St. Mary's Grade School and graduated from St. Clair Area High School and Bloomsburg University. He served as sheriff of Schuylkill County and was elected to the House of Representatives in 1992. In 2009, he is serving his ninth term of office.

Nine

MILITARY

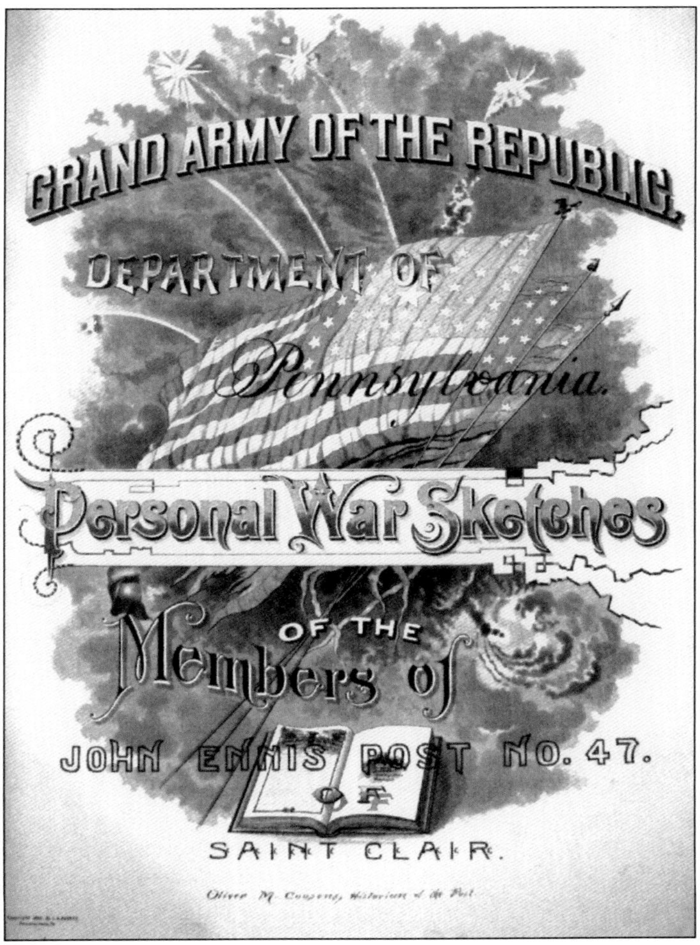

GAR was a military/civic organization formed by Union veterans of the Civil War. In St. Clair, the veterans formed the John Ennis Post No. 47 and put together a book of their war memories. This book was recently found in a wall of the elementary school during renovations.

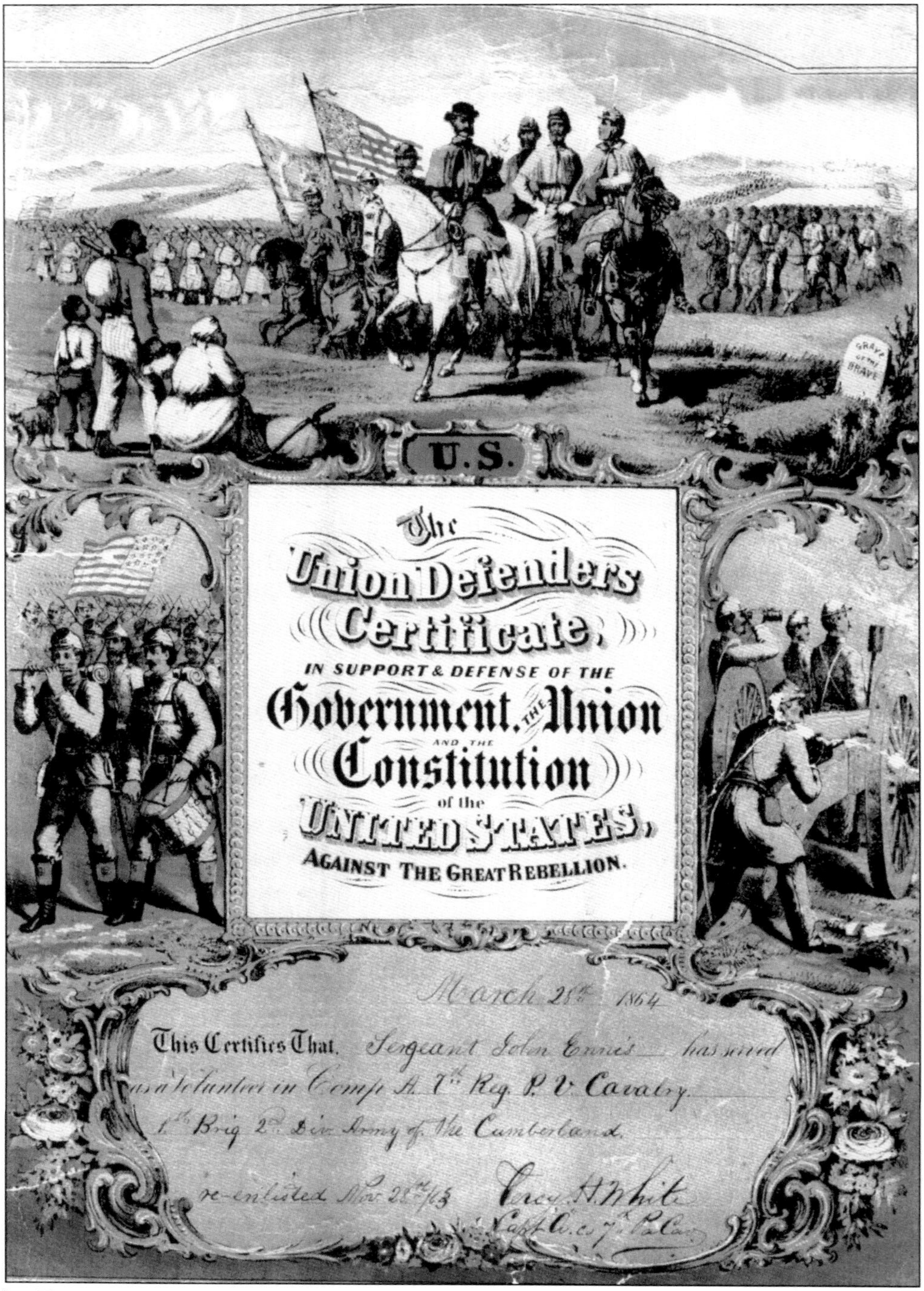
U.S.

The Union Defenders Certificate,

IN SUPPORT & DEFENSE OF THE

Government, the Union and the Constitution of the United States,

AGAINST THE GREAT REBELLION.

March 28th 1864

This Certifies That, Sergeant John Ennis has served as a volunteer in Comp. A. 7th Reg. P. V. Cavalry

1st Brig 2nd Div. Army of the Cumberland.

re-enlisted Nov. 28th/63

Percy H. White
Capt Co. 7th Pa Cav

John Ennis, a sergeant in Company A of the Pennsylvania 7th Cavalry during the Civil War, served as color bearer of the regiment. Ennis was mortally shot as he carried the flag across a field without any cover and charged the enemy's fort in Selma, Alabama, on April 2, 1865. His comrades paid homage to this brave sergeant by naming the GAR Post No. 44 of St. Clair in his honor.

Soldier Theodore D. Thorn was a St. Clair native who served with the U.S. Army in the Medical Corps during the Great War, later known as World War I.

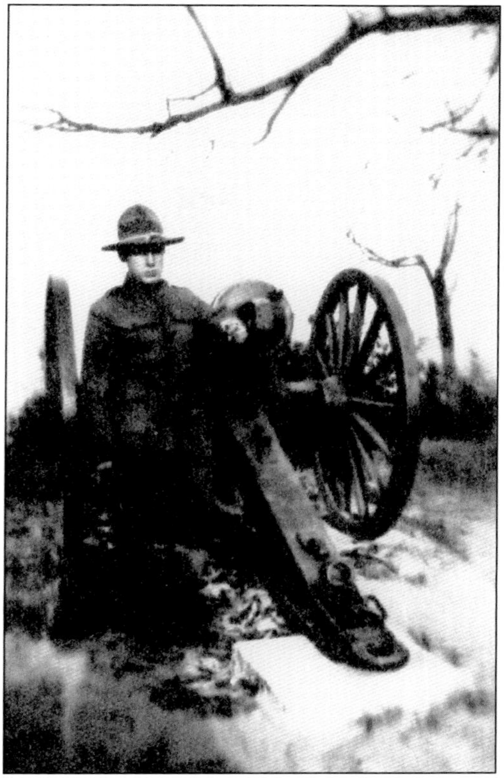

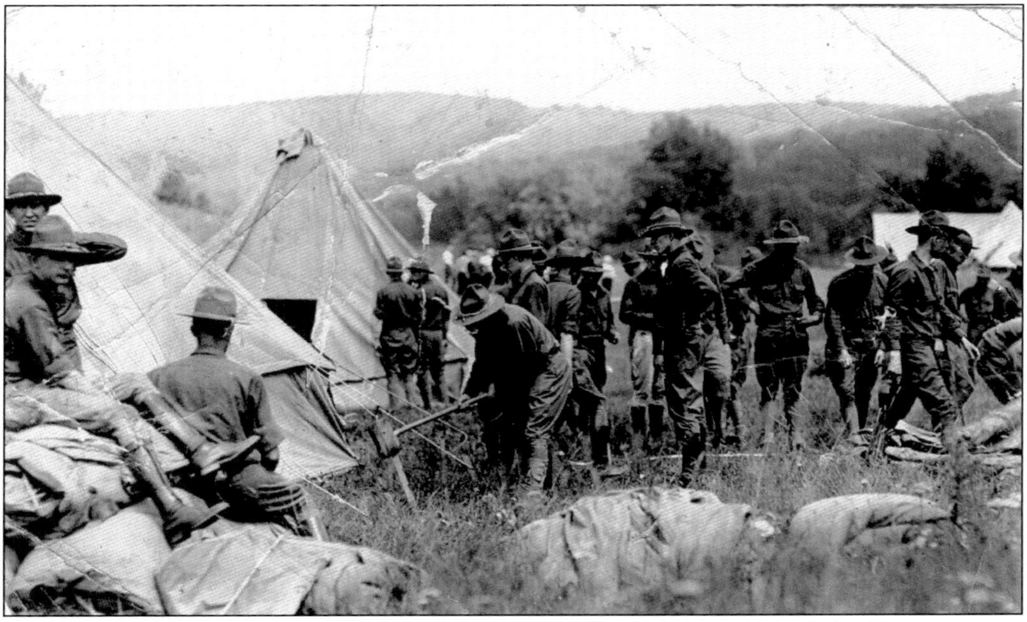

Training camps sprang up across the nation as the United States entered the European war in 1917 after being neutral for the first two years of the conflict. Men from St. Clair trained at this camp.

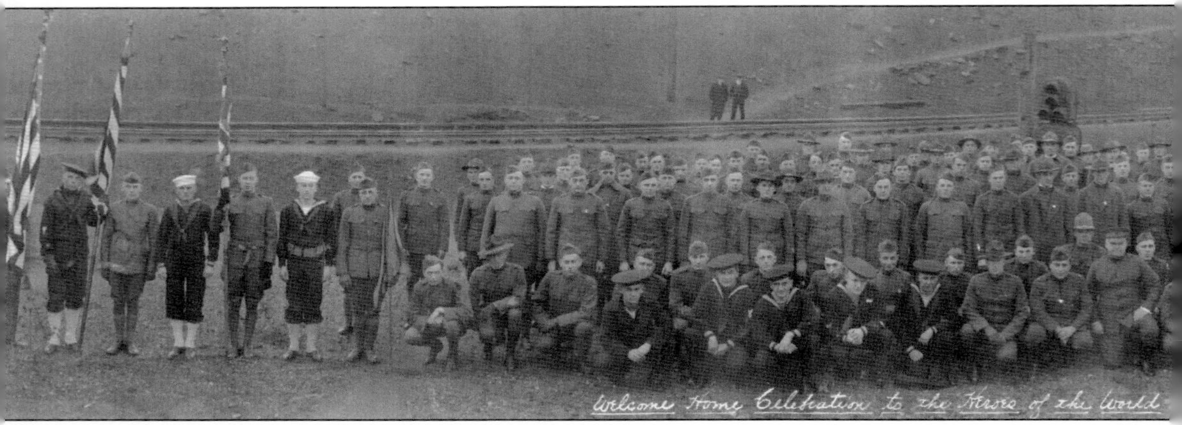

St. Clair demonstrated its gratitude to the World War I veterans of the area by holding a parade in their honor. Some 410 men and 4 Red Cross nurses from this area served in the war; 18 did not return home. There were 237 veterans who marched in the 1919 welcome home parade. The

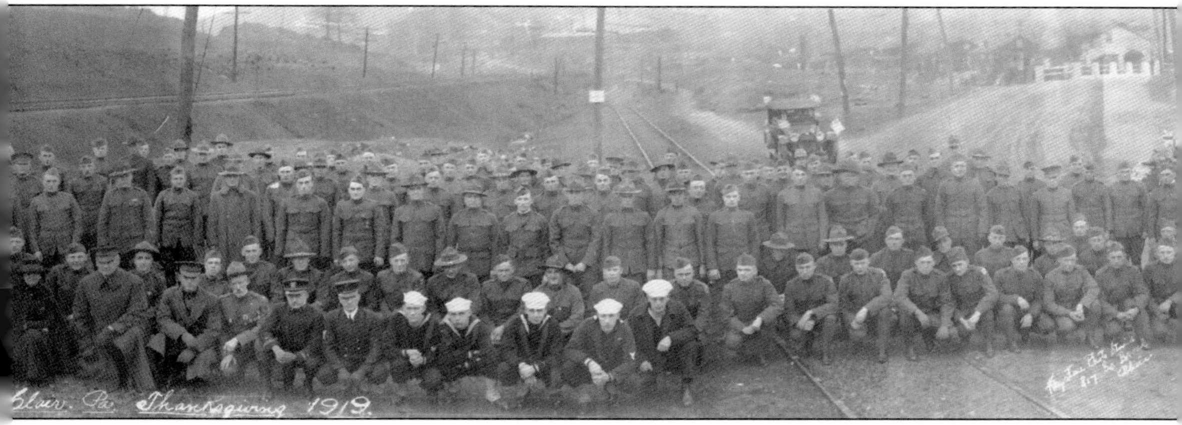

large number of volunteers in relation to the small population to the St. Clair area prompted the *Pottsville Journal* to state that St. Clair holds the record for the largest number of men in World War I from the state of Pennsylvania.

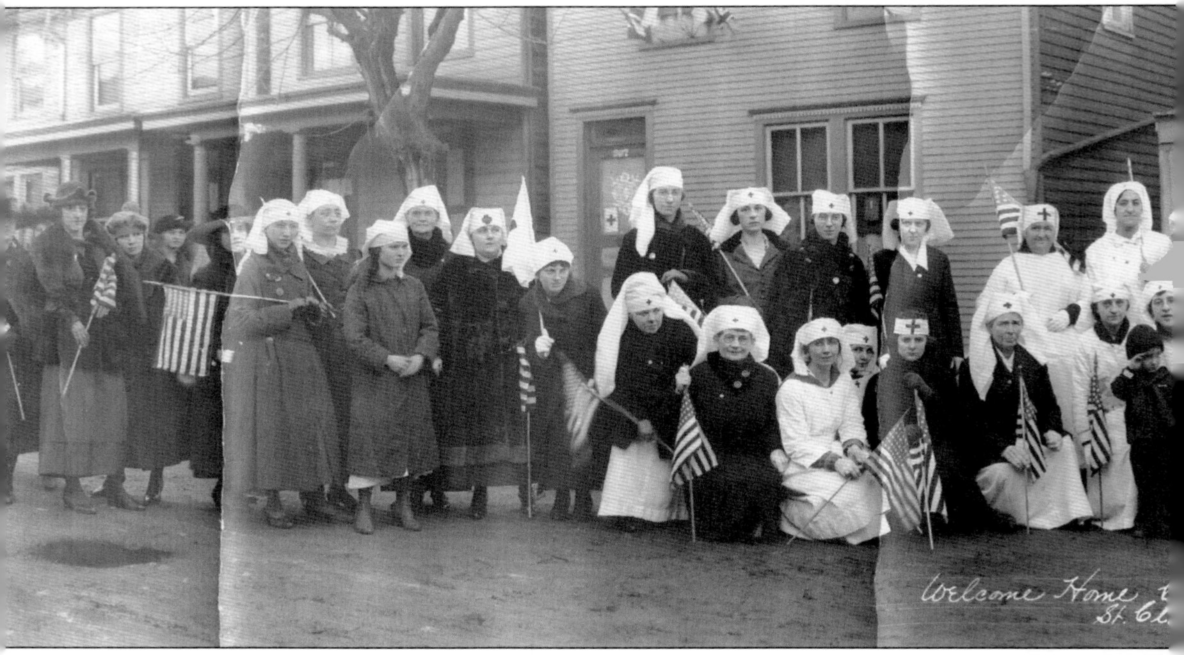

Red Cross volunteers decorated a float with a solid field of American flags that was in the 1919 Thanksgiving welcome home parade. Four St. Clair Red Cross volunteers served in World War I. Volunteers at home met at headquarters at the Lyric Theatre (Ritz Theatre). The Red

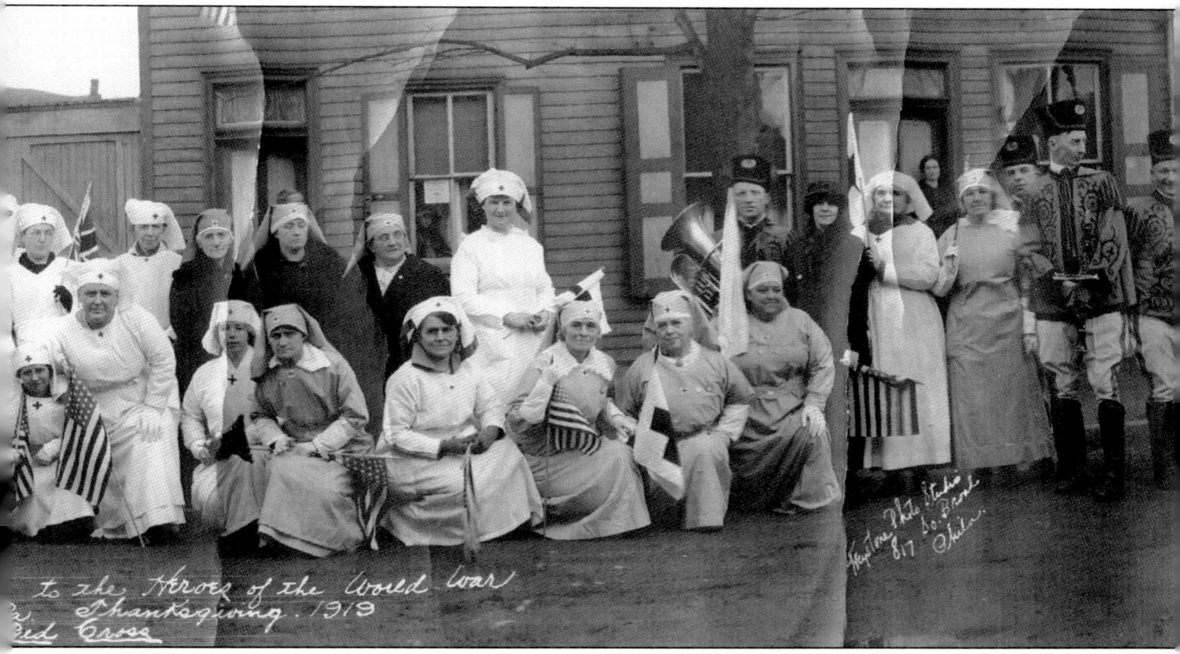

Cross, along with the Knights of Columbus, YMCA, and Salvation Army, shipped 263 sweaters, 275 service kits, and a Christmas box to the servicemen.

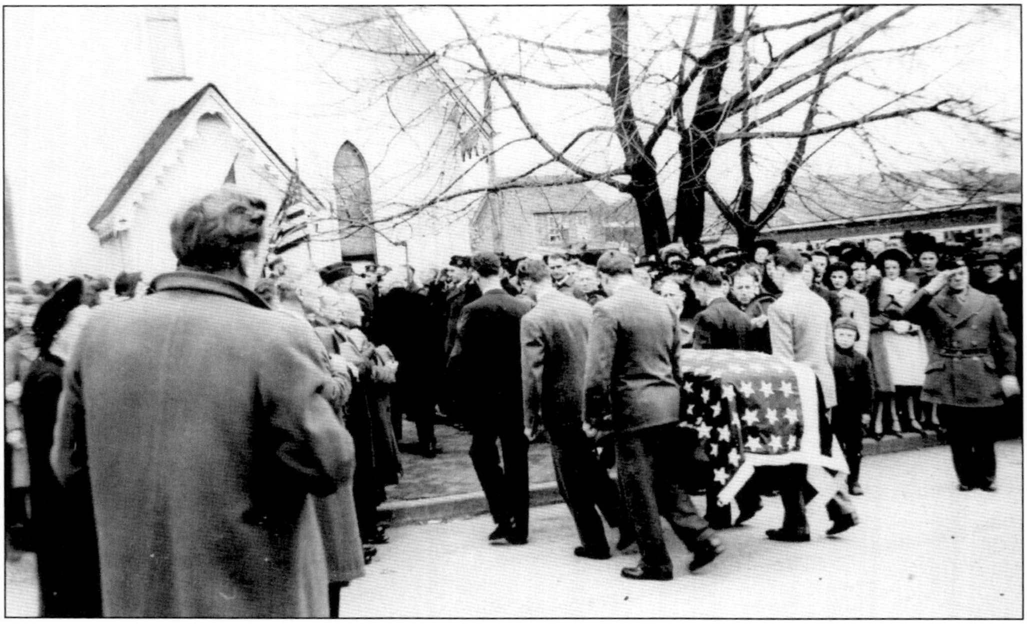

Pallbearers carried the flag-draped casket of flight officer Robert B. Goodman from his aunt and uncle's home at 329 South Mill Street. Officer Goodman was the first St. Clair man to pay the supreme sacrifice for his country. Legionnaires from Port Carbon, St. Clair, and surrounding communities formed a guard of honor for the community's first military funeral of World War II.

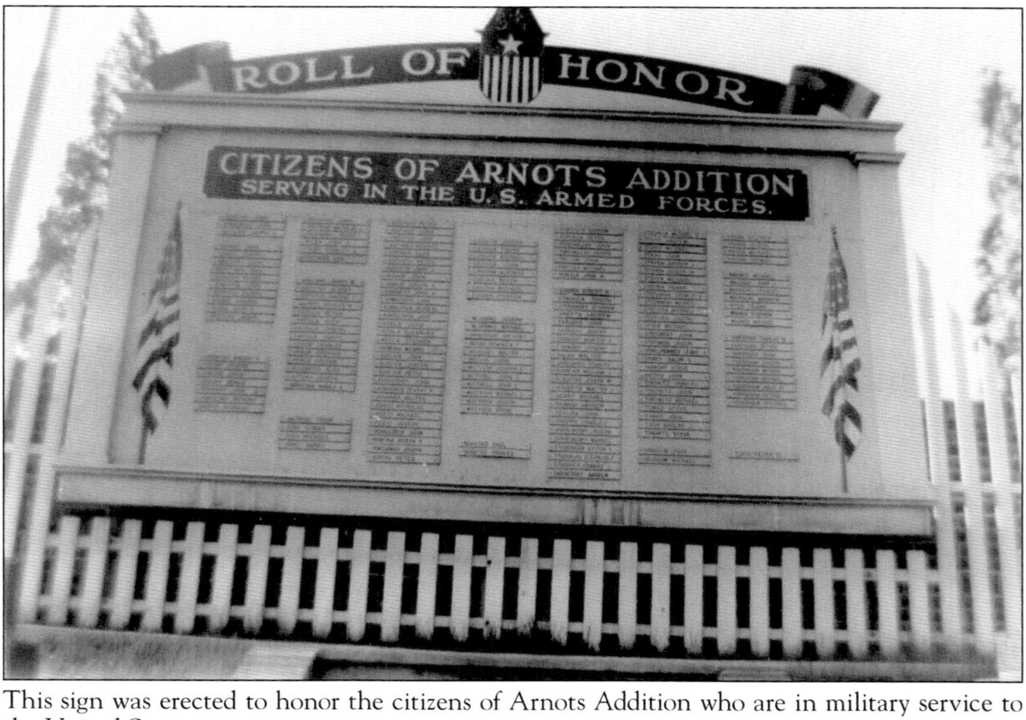

This sign was erected to honor the citizens of Arnots Addition who are in military service to the United States.

Bob Plummer was a staff sergeant in the 264th Regiment, 66th Division. His unit had been ordered to Cherbourg, France, and was aboard the troop ship *Leopoldville* when it was hit by a torpedo on December 24, 1944, at 5:50 p.m. The Belgian crew abandoned ship and had taken a few lifeboats, leaving the Americans on the sinking ship. After some time, the British HMS *Brilliant* pulled along the crippled *Leopoldville*, and Plummer was able to jump to safety. He attributes his survival to his tendency for seasickness. This sinking was classified and survivors sworn to secrecy until 1996, when the government released the details to the public.

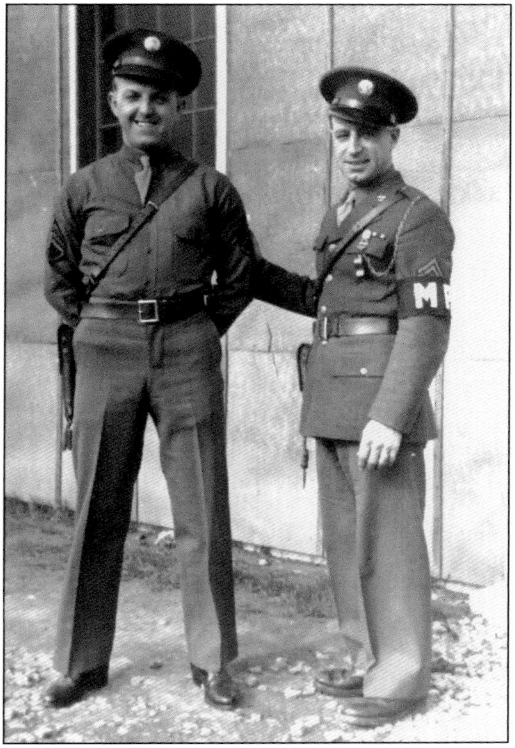

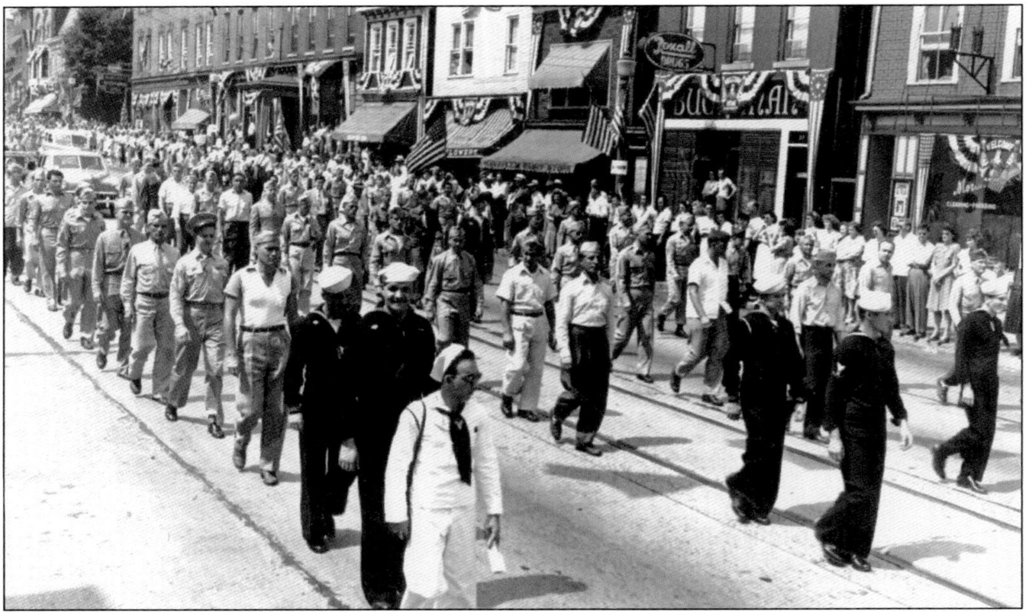

A homecoming parade was held on July 4, 1946, for the men and women who answered the call to war during World War II. There were more than 1,500 men and women from St. Clair and surrounding areas. The supreme sacrifice was made by 47 local residents. The town football stadium, Veterans Memorial Stadium, and the Veterans Memorial Ambulance Building were dedicated to those who served during World War II.

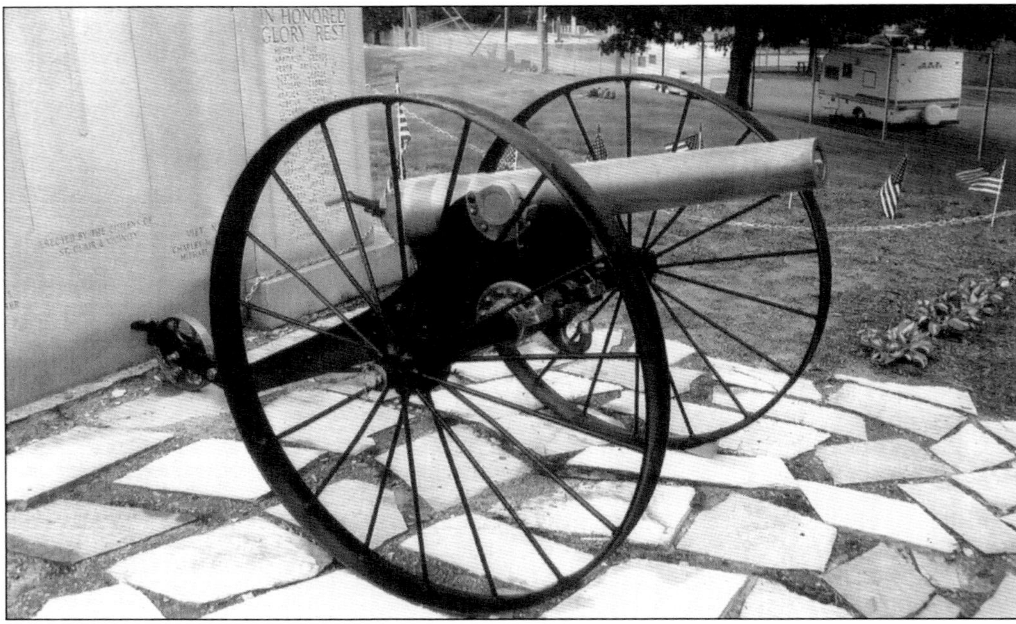

For many years, a pair of cannons sat on the island in front of the old American Legion next to the war memorials before later being moved to the Veterans Memorial Football field. They were not given much notice and painted over several times. Around 2000, it was decided to restore the cannons. The long and painstaking restoration was completed by Edward J. Pollack, who discovered them to be historical treasures, two 1875 U.S. Navy gunboat howitzers.

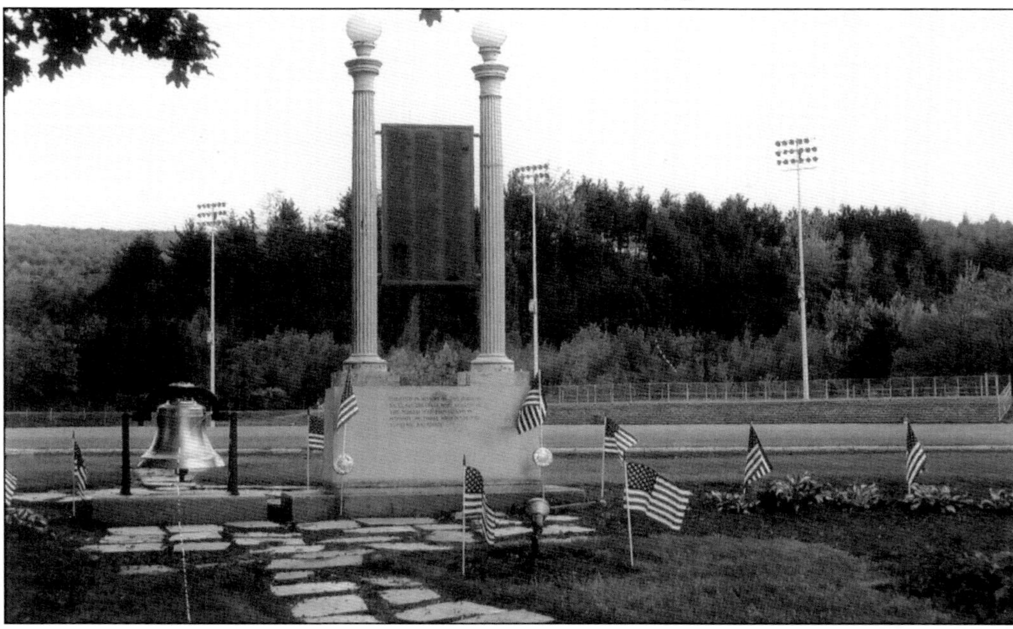

This monument was erected to honor those from St. Clair who served in World War I. It was once located at the island but moved with the cannons and World War II Memorial to the Veterans Memorial Stadium in the 1950s. This bell was cast by the Joseph Berhard Foundry of Philadelphia, which also cast the second Liberty Bell.

Ten

Around the Town

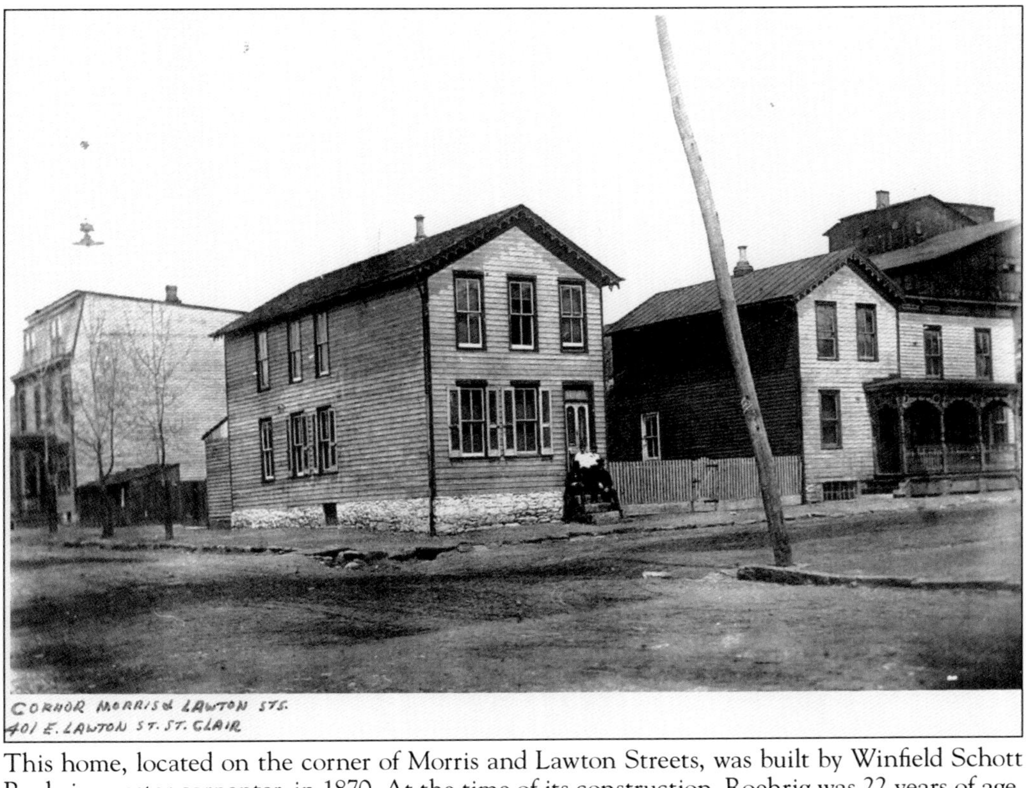

This home, located on the corner of Morris and Lawton Streets, was built by Winfield Schott Roehrig, master carpenter, in 1870. At the time of its construction, Roehrig was 22 years of age. The Hooker Colliery can be seen in the background. The home has been in the Scherr family since 1904.

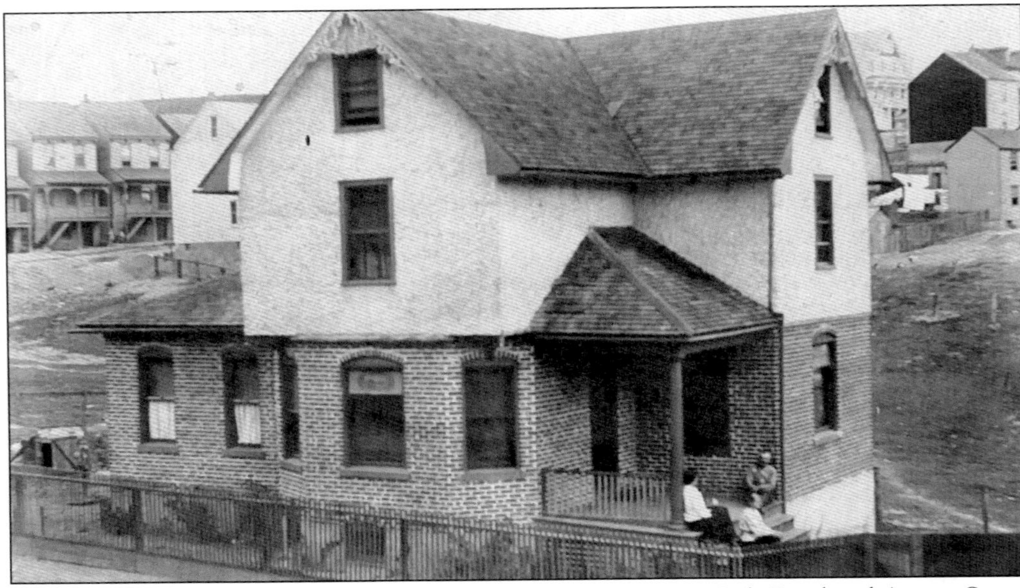

This Sears mail-order house, home No. 24, was built in 1908 on Wade Road and Arnots Street in New Castle Township by Squire William Gittins, a Civil War veteran. During 1908, homes were springing up in Arnots Addition in record numbers, doubling in one year. Between 1908 and 1940, Sears was the place to find everything to furnish the American home but also the home itself. Often the entire mail-order house (in the form of labeled timbers) came via freight train. Some home owners chose to purchase the mail-order house plans and use local materials to their construct homes. This is now home to John and Rosemary McCoach.

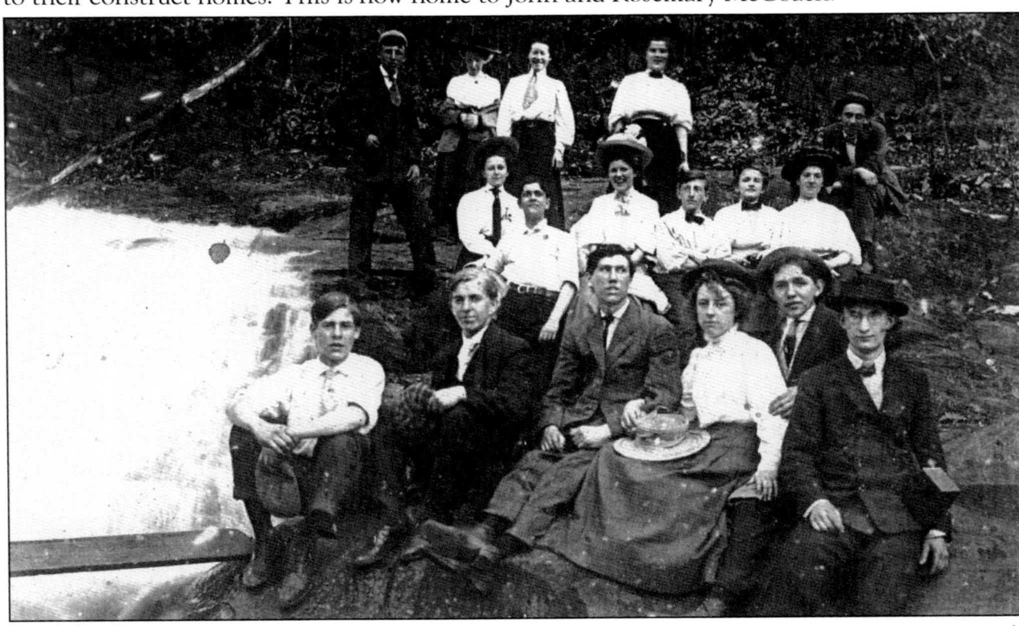

For over 100 years, a popular place for a picnic or hike has been Wolf Creek. In 1852, an early newspaper in Schuylkill County, the *Miner's Journal*, published the legend of Wolf Creek. The legend states, "the shady banks in days of yore were haunted by a fearful Ghoul; who had a fancy for prowling in the shape of a huge Wolf, and carrying off all the young Papooses."

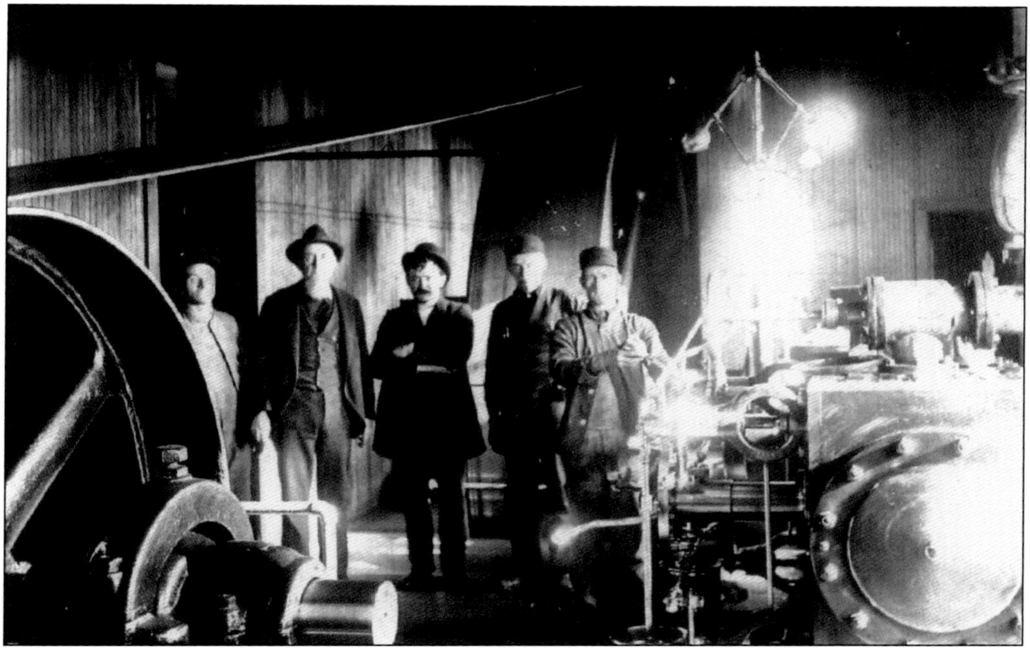

The St. Clair Electric Light Department was organized in 1892, and light service was turned on for the first time on December 24, 1892. This early system supplied electricity to the town proper, East Mines, and Upper Mill Creek.

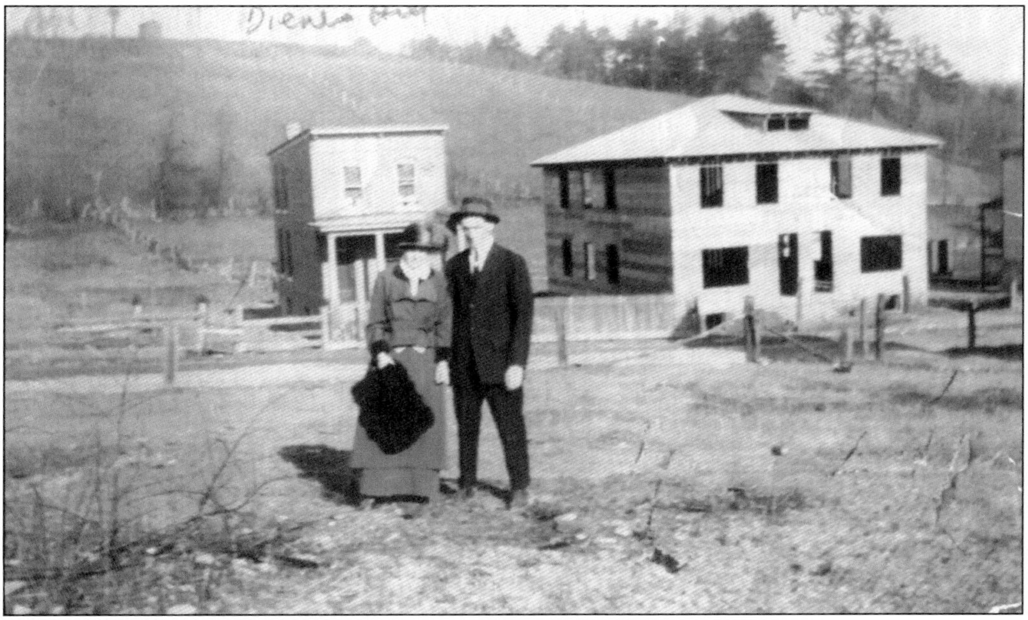

The southeastern hill surrounding St. Clair, like the town itself, was named after an early landowner and farmer, Charles Diener. Diener's farmhouse was built around 1865 and is still in existence today. In 1915, when this picture was taken by the Silcox family, the township area experienced such growth that there were talks in the town of annexing Diener's Hill to St. Clair. (Courtesy of David Silcox.)

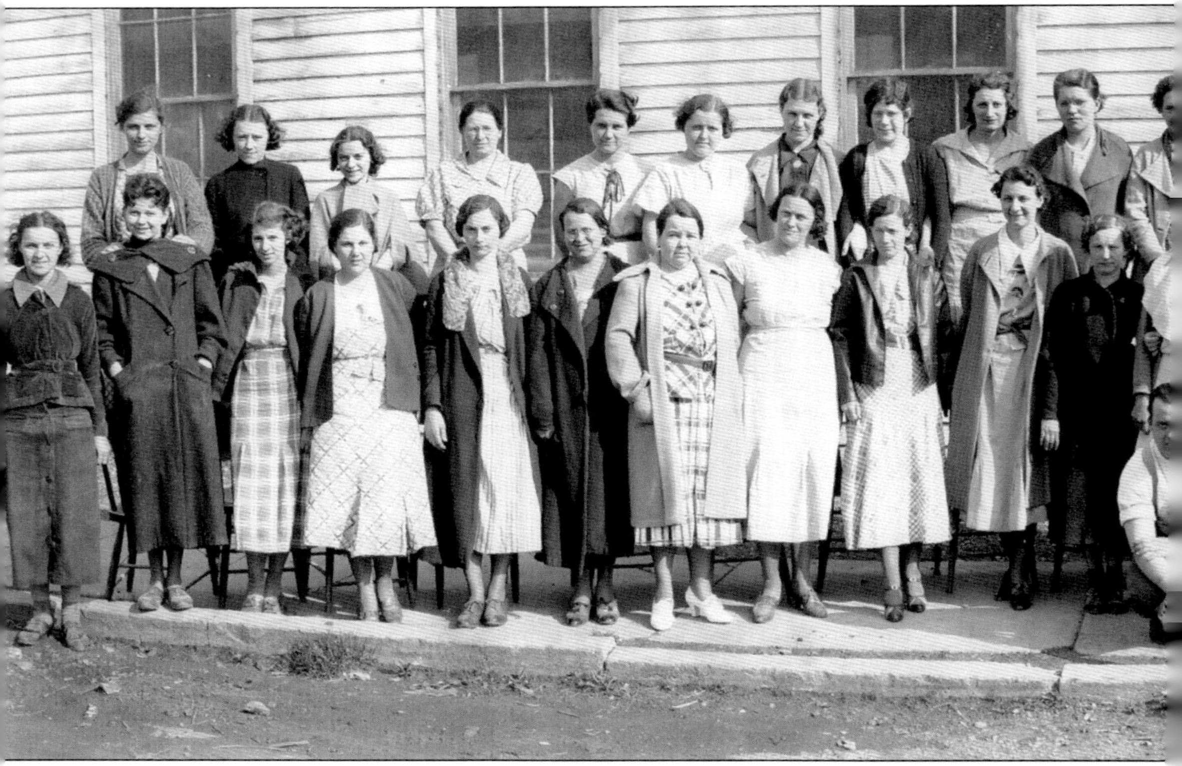

The headline for this image should be "H. D. Bob Company resumes operation." This November 23, 1938, photograph shows 55 employees the H. D. Bob Company located at the corner of South Morris and Railroad Streets. Not in operation since December 1937, this company was energized by a new lease drawn up by the Mary Lin Dress and Sports Wear Company. The finished product

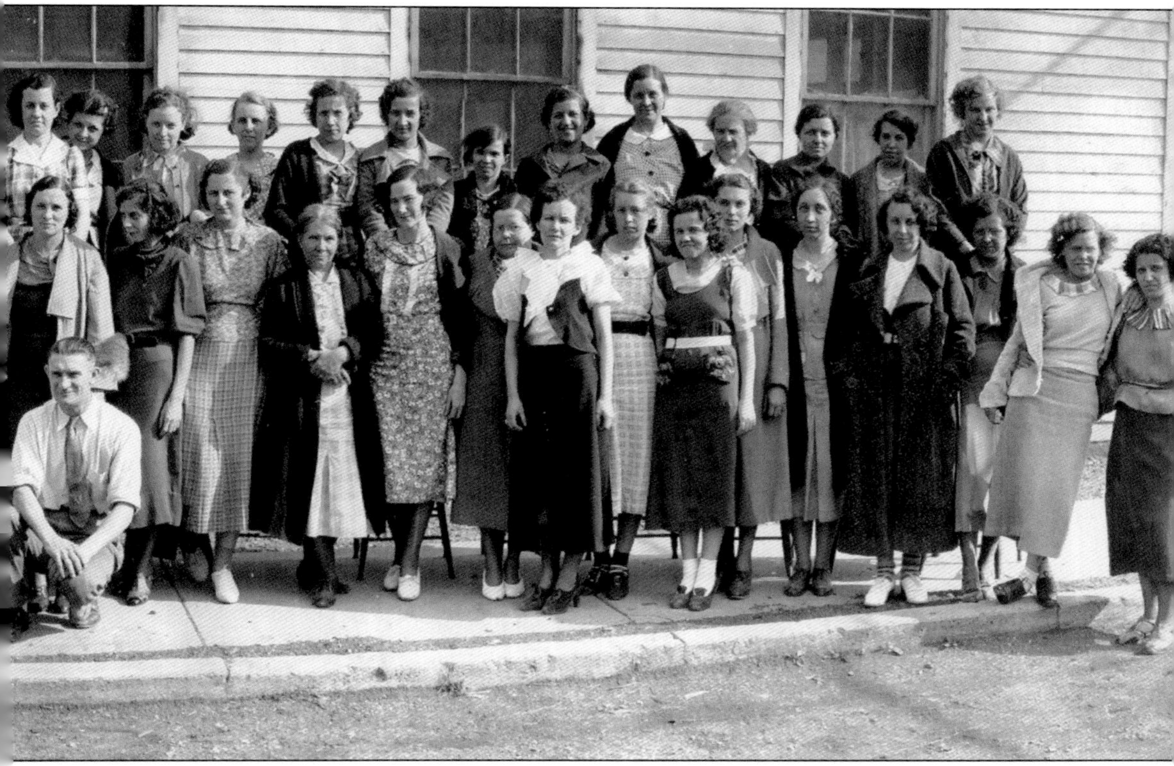

was transported to the New York area. In a few months, an increase to 125 employees was expected. Eventually this enterprise would be owned by Hank Podway and named the St. Clair Garment Factory; it continued in operation until the 1970s.

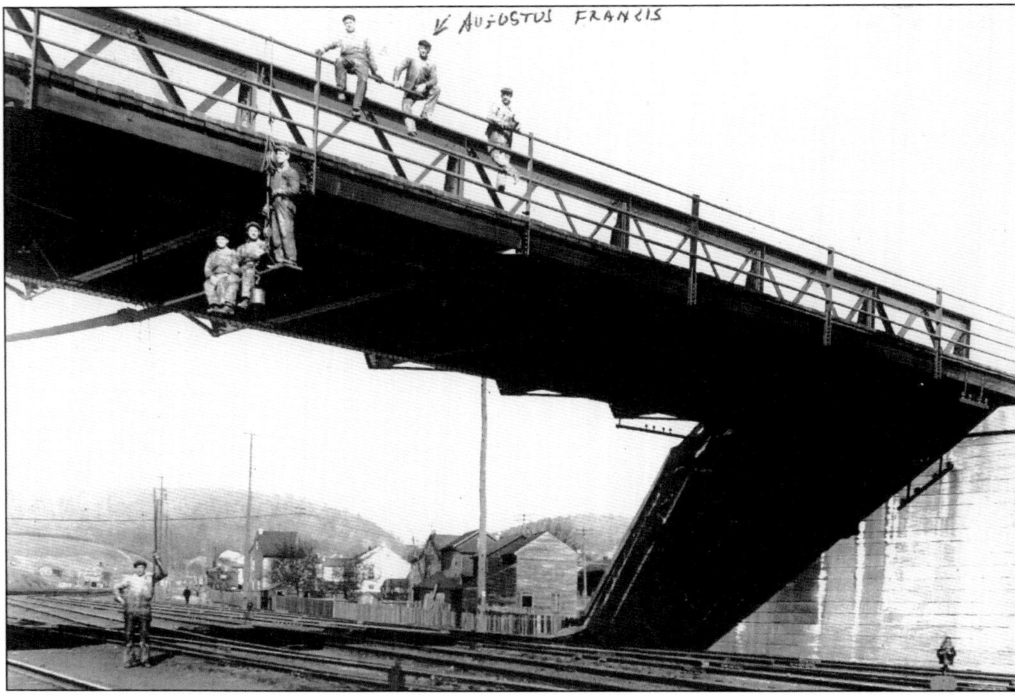

Looking north is the Russell Street Bridge leading into St. Clair just north of East Mines. In this 1909 picture, painters hang over the edge of the trestle held by simple rope harnesses. The photograph looks northward toward Fourth Street with tracks from the Reading Railroad and the Pennsylvania Railroad. The bridge was completed in early 1910, and with the completion of the rails in April, the new road between St. Clair and Pottsville was opened.

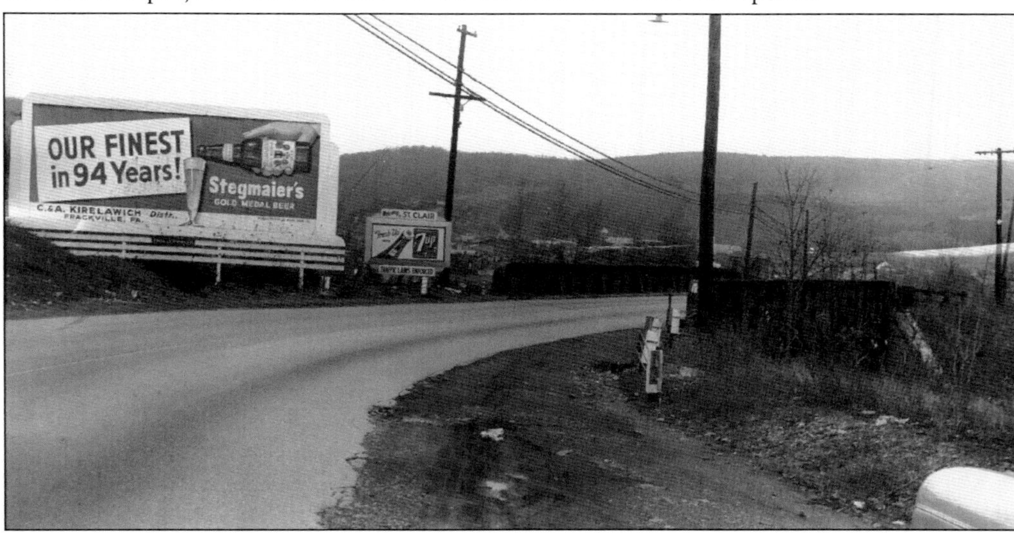

Heavy traffic passing through St. Clair on Route 61 caused traffic backups and many accidents. The town, and especially longtime mayor Joe Long, lobbied for a bypass of this route that connected Pottsville with the northern end of the county. This picture was taken shortly before the bypass became a reality, thanks to the hard work of the mayor. The bypass, when completed, was named the Joseph H. Long Boulevard.

National Air Mail Week was celebrated in St. Clair in 1938, with a special seal or cachet (seal with official approval) celebrating the new airmail service in the anthracite area. The airmail stamp was designed by a 13-year-old schoolboy, Michael Futchko. During the week of May 15–21, 1938, all airmail mailings carried this commemorative cachet. The cost of airmail postage was 6¢.

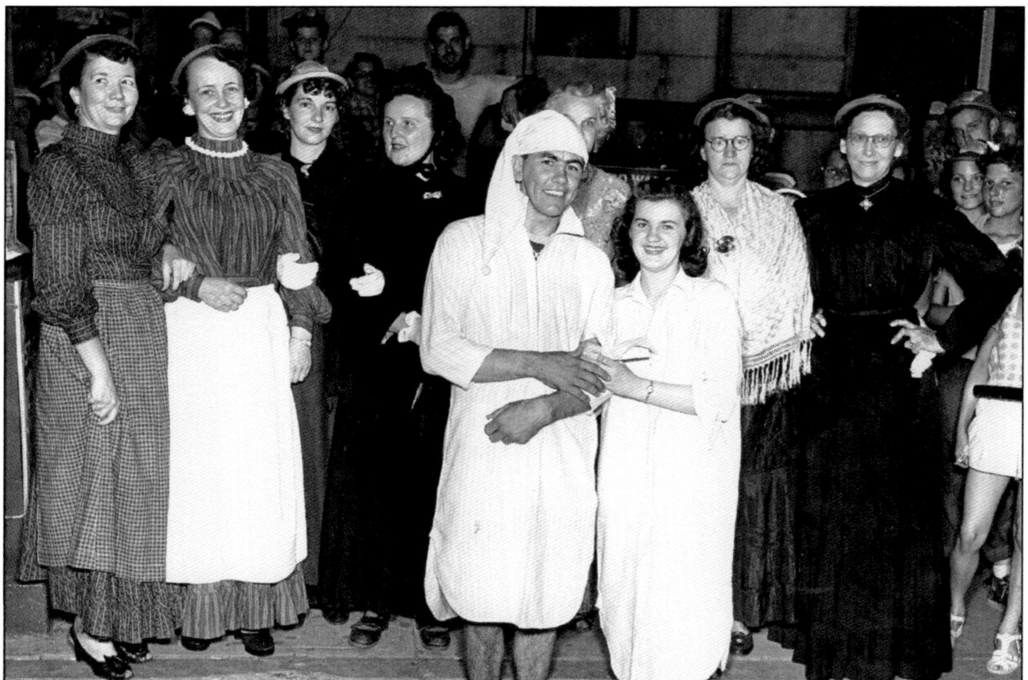

In 1950, St. Clair celebrated its 100th anniversary. Punishment was dealt out for those not wearing their centennial hats; this couple had to march up and down Second Street in their nightclothes. In the rear, members of the Sisters of the Swish wore dresses from the Gay Nineties during the centennial celebration. The ladies' organization came by its name from the "swishing" noise their skirts made when the women walked.

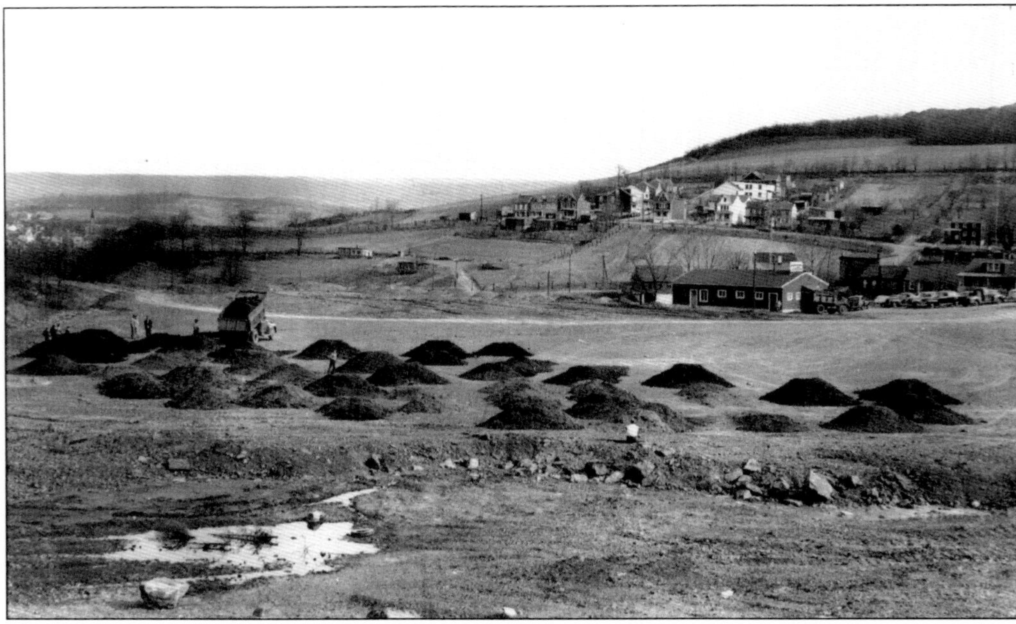

Construction is seen for the American Veterans (AMVETS) and baseball field in Arnots Addition early in the 1950s. The homes on Shaft Hill are seen in the background. Many a resident of Arnots Addition remembers when the circus would set up tents in this area.

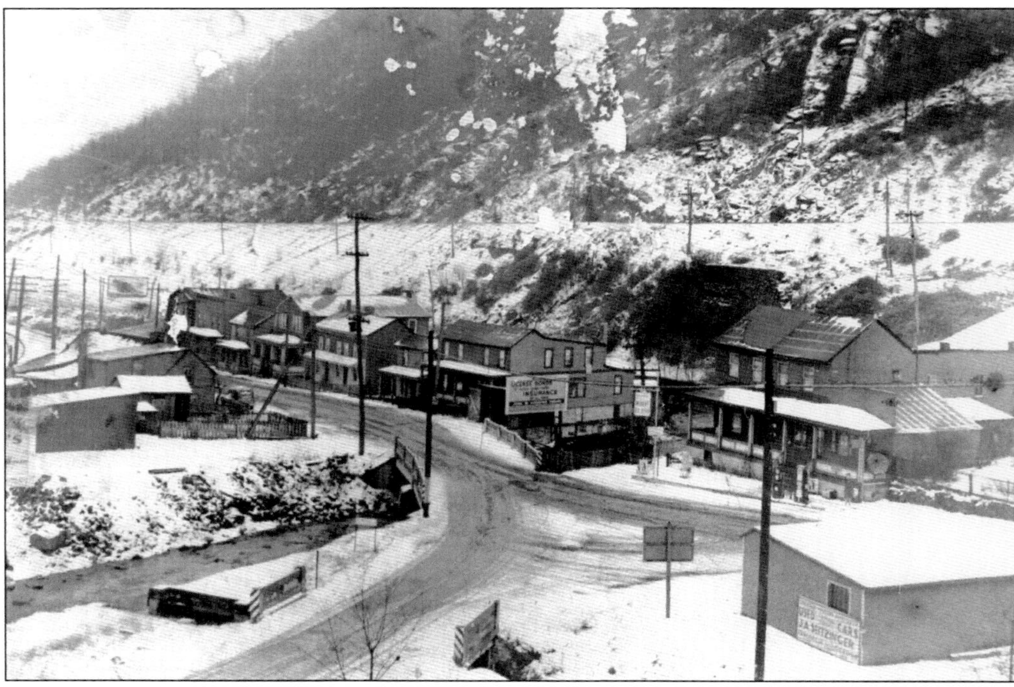

Darkwater was a patch town about one mile north of St. Clair. It was along the route from New Castle north to Frackville near the Repplier Colliery. To expand the highway, Route 61 between St. Clair and Frackville, most of the houses were torn down and the Mill Creek was rerouted. Today there are only a handful of homes remaining. (Courtesy of Rosemary McCoach.)

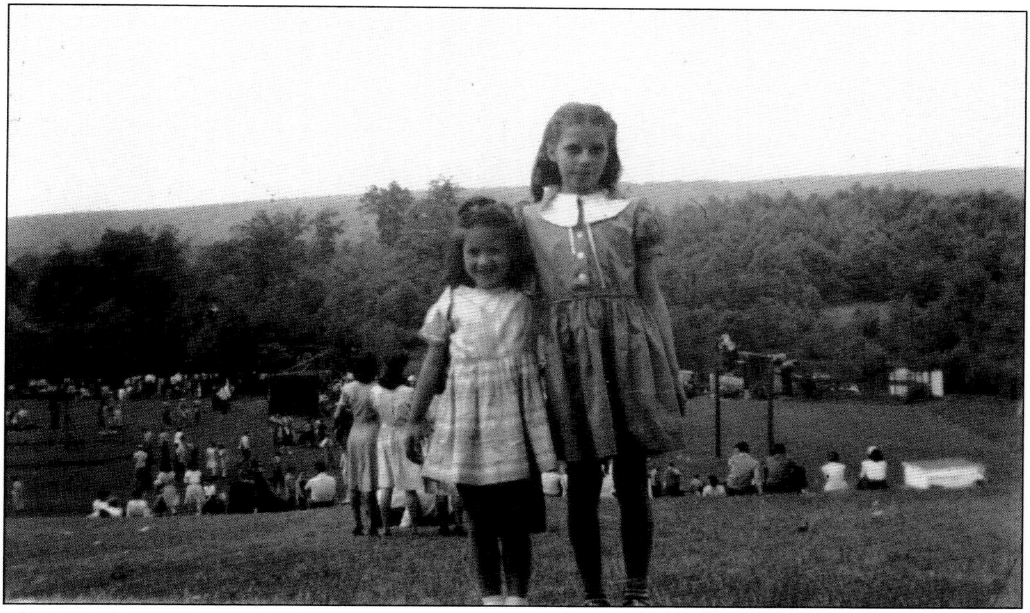

The St. Clair Fish and Game Club picnics for the Fourth of July were a highly attended annual event for just about everyone in town. During the day, families, friends, and neighbors gathered to eat, drink, and socialize. As dusk settled, everyone found a spot on the hillside, which was covered with people sitting on the ground or blankets in anticipation of the fireworks.

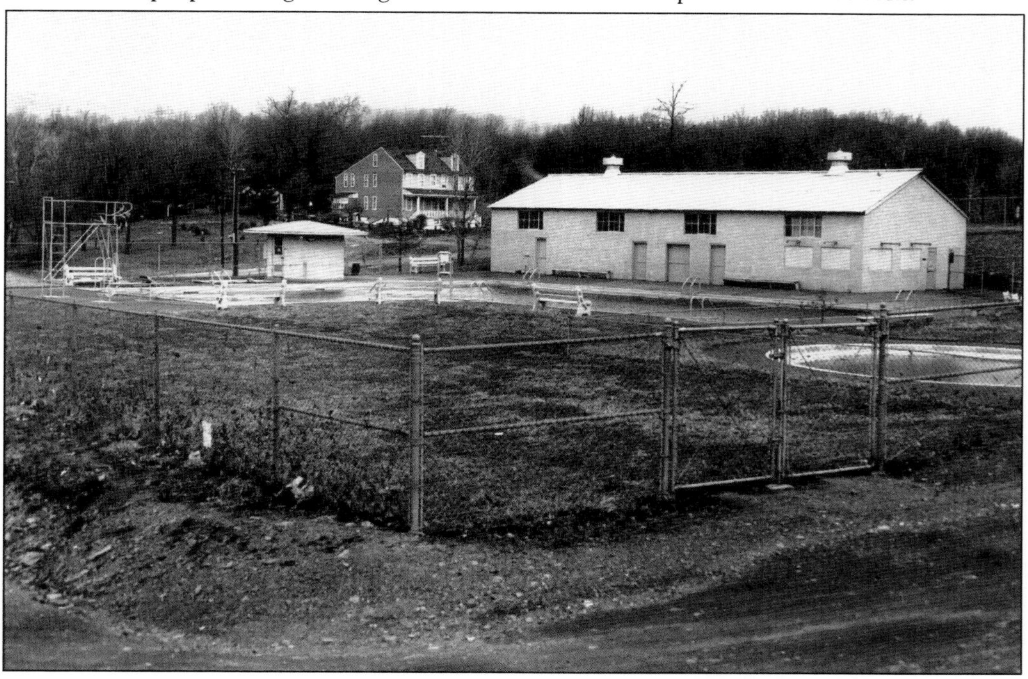

In the late 1950s, the St. Clair Swimming Pool Association was formed to raise funds to build a public swimming pool on top of Lawton Street next to the fish and game club. The association had a variety of fund-raisers, including a presentation of the play *The Vagabonds*. The pool opened in 1960 and continues to operate each summer.

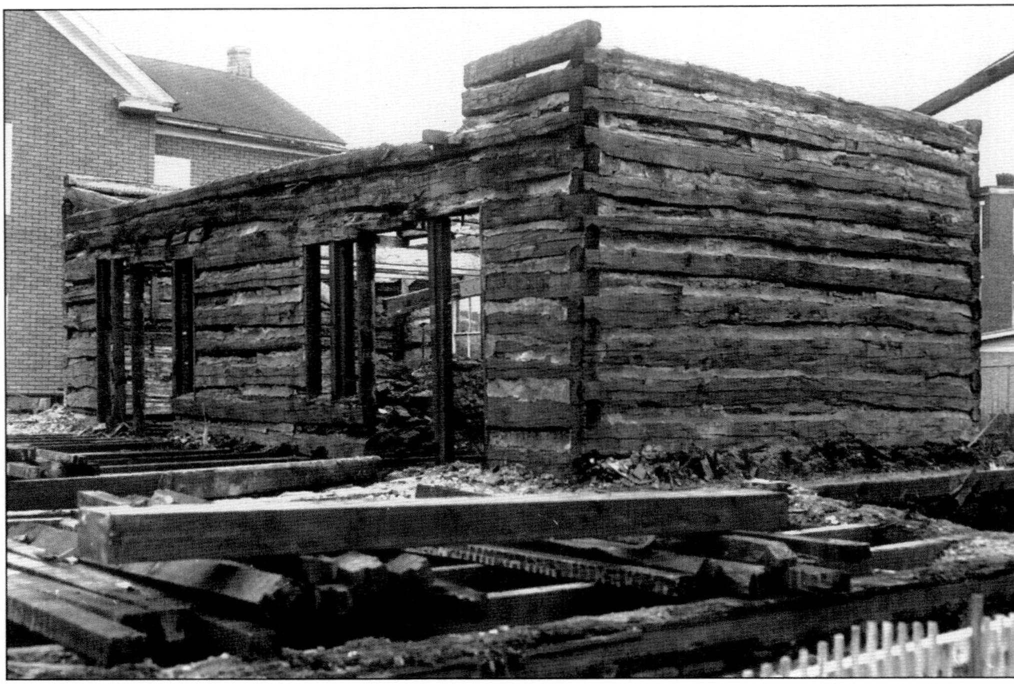

The first residents in St. Clair lived in log cabins. Most of them were covered by culm from area collieries, such as the Hickory Colliery. These cabins were mostly two-room structures built on one floor. This cabin home was found in 1966, when the property owners tore down the outer structure when clearing the lot to build a garage.

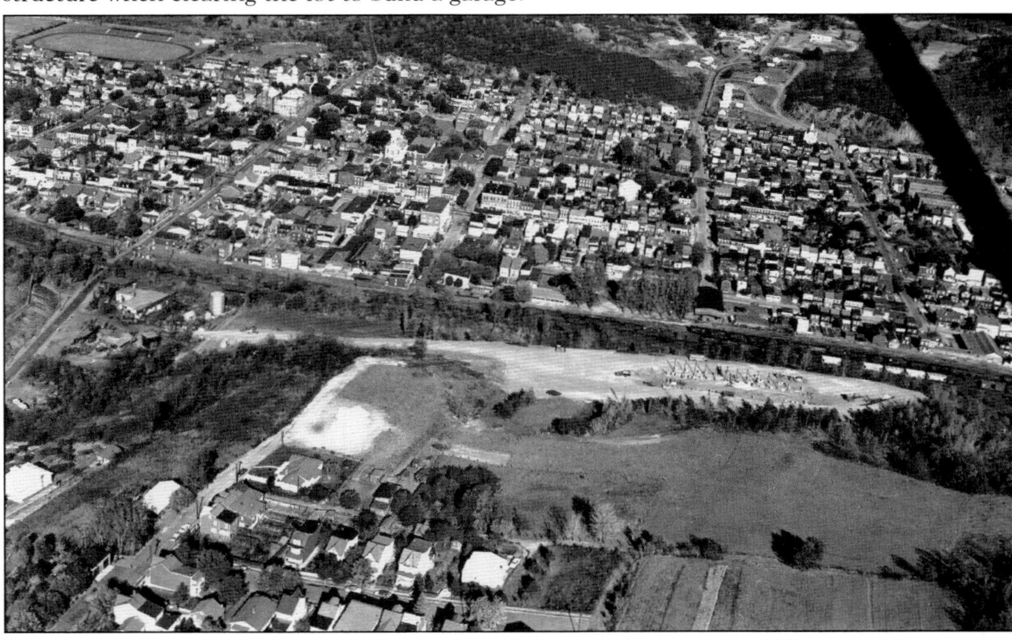

This aerial photograph was taken in the late 1960s and shows the middle to northern end of town. Along the top of the picture the farms along the Burma Road are visible and on the bottom right Quirin's Foundry is being built.

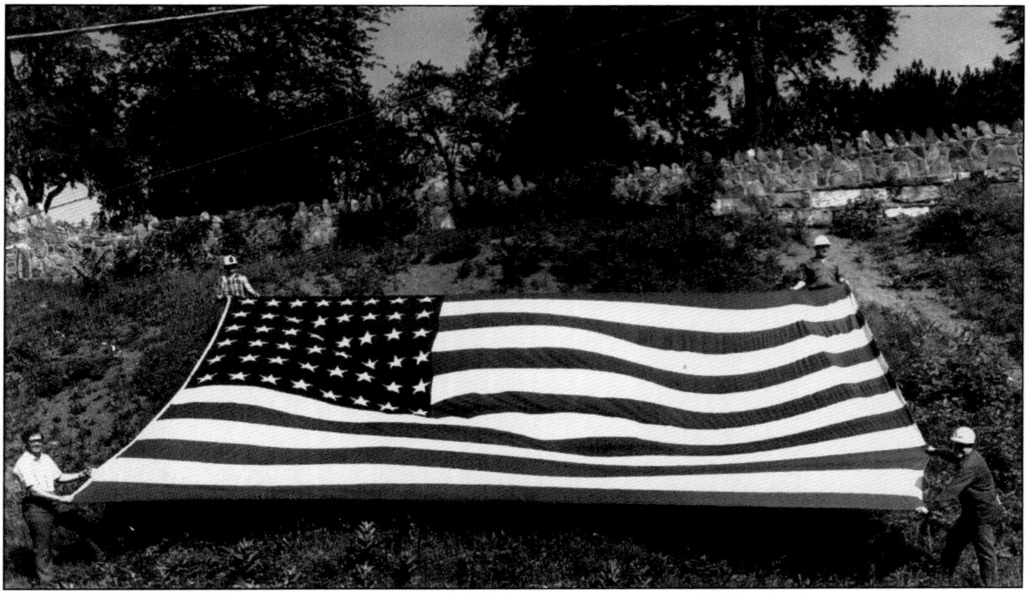

The flag from the St. Mary's Roman Catholic Church dedication parade in 1914 was lost for many years but was found shortly before the 1976 bicentennial celebrations in the rectory of the St. Boniface Church. The flag is being held by employees of the Quirin Foundry near the old borough cemetery. This flag is now carried each year by the St. Clair Community and Historical Society in the annual Halloween parade.

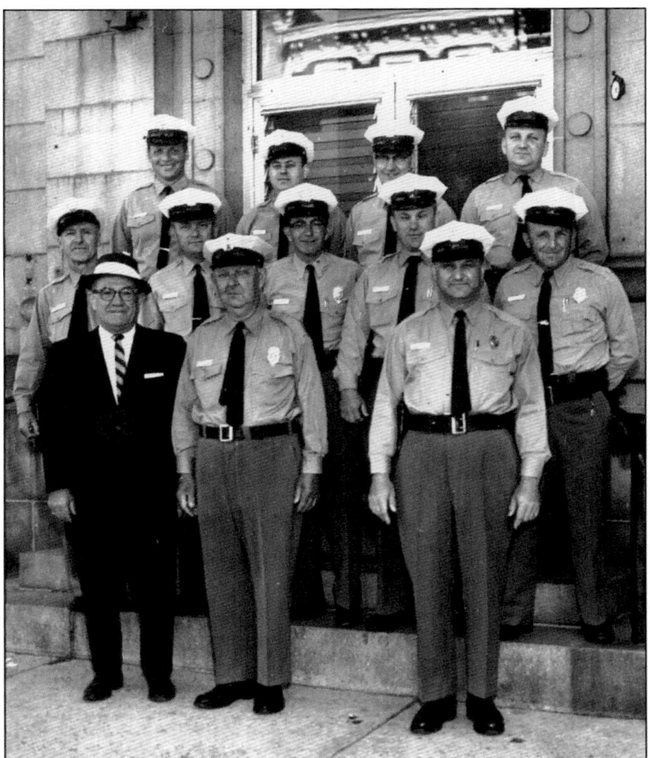

Shown here is a group photograph of the St. Clair police force from the 1960s. Members are, from left to right, (first row) Mayor Joseph Long, "Cap" Morrow, and Joseph Kaminsky; (second row) John Pretti, Wayne Rhoades, Philip Russell, Roland Price, and Tom Maley; (third row) Joe Peletsky, John Zamko, Charles Weber, and Walter Ughes.